The History of

ST EDMUND'S COLLEGE

The History of

ST EDMUND'S COLLEGE

NICHOLAS SCHOFIELD

[signature: N J Schofield]
31/iii/14

PREFACE
THE MOST REVEREND VINCENT NICHOLS
ARCHBISHOP OF WESTMINSTER

FOREWORD
PAULO DURÁN
HEADMASTER OF ST EDMUND'S COLLEGE

PICTURE EDITOR
DAVID J S KAY
PRESIDENT EMERITUS & ARCHIVIST OF
THE EDMUNDIAN ASSOCIATION

FIRST PUBLISHED IN 2013 BY THE EDMUNDIAN ASSOCIATION
COPYRIGHT © NICHOLAS SCHOFIELD, 2013

DEDICATED TO

FR MICHAEL PINOT DE MOIRA
THE LAST PRIEST-SCHOOLMASTER IN THE DOUAY TRADITION

FRONT COVER IMAGE
1829 PAINTING BY KENELM DIGBY

BOOK DESIGN
WWW.ORBITAL.CO.UK

CONTENTS

PREFACE

THE MOST REVEREND VINCENT NICHOLS, ARCHBISHOP OF WESTMINSTER.

The history of St Edmund's College goes back over nearly 450 years and as such it is the oldest Catholic school in England.

It was founded in France in 1568 to educate Catholic missionaries who were to risk death on return to their own country on account of their Faith. It is distinguished by having 20 canonised saints and 138 martyrs amongst its alumni.

The College later became a Catholic school for boys and during the French Revolution it transferred to England and found its present home on the beautiful site of Old Hall Green in 1793.

The College continued as a boys' school and seminary until 1975, and became fully co-educational in 1986.

Its Catholic heritage, combined with its location deep in the Hertfordshire countryside, provides its inspiration as it continues to deliver the objective to foster the spiritual, intellectual, physical and emotional development of each person in its community.

As St Edmund's College now looks forward to its next 450 years with confidence, I am delighted this book makes the College's history more accessible.

Vincent Nichols
25th President of St Edmund's College

FOREWORD

PAULO DURÁN, HEADMASTER OF ST EDMUND'S COLLEGE.

St Edmund's is a school unlike any other I have known – a place rich in history, tradition, architectural and environmental beauty; it wears its riches proudly but modestly, perhaps too modestly at times. This new history of the College tells our story with great learning, wit and passion and I am enormously proud to be associated with it.

When I first came here, some four years ago, I knew precious little about this unique institution, but from the first moment I stepped into the Ambulacrum and trod those well worn flagstones I was smitten. As the years have passed the people and the history of the College have never failed to inspire me and I hope that this fascinating new history, so wonderfully written and illustrated, will inspire others to learn more about 'England's College home'.

I thank Father Nicholas Schofield on behalf of the College for producing such a fine work and I also commend The Edmundian Association, most notably in the person of its President Emeritus, David Kay, for bringing this project to fruition. To all readers of this history: if this book inspires you to see St Edmund's for yourself be assured always of a warm welcome at the College, whether it be your first visit or your hundredth.

Avita Pro Fide.

Paulo Durán
10th Headmaster of St Edmund's College

INTRODUCTION

Situated in the rolling Hertfordshire countryside, the College of St Edmund, near Ware, is today a successful Catholic independent school for boys and girls. A closer look, however, reveals that this is a school with a difference. The chapel is unusually large for an educational establishment and within it there are tombs not only of past Presidents and pupils but bishops and even a Cardinal of the Holy Roman Church.

For much of its history, St Edmund's educated both ecclesiastical and lay students, training them for service in the Church as priests and in the world as laity. This twofold dimension is reflected in the College's twin ancestry, descending first from Cardinal Allen's College in Douay and secondly from several schools established in the Winchester area, going as far back as the reign of Charles II. There cannot be many schools in England with so rich and varied a history.

Any writer on this subject is indebted to the pioneering *History of St Edmund's College* (1893) of Mgr Bernard Ward, written to mark the first centenary. This encouraged subsequent study of the College's history, especially in the pages of The Edmundian, founded the same year, which not only presented well-researched historical articles but carefully preserved the events of each year for posterity. Added to this are the references to St Edmund's in the works of Mgr Ward, Canon Burton and others, Fr Garvey's informative guide to the College Chapel (re-issued in 2010), W. T. Gribbin's *Bicentenary Book* (1993) and David J. S. Kay's useful volumes on *The Buildings of St Edmund's College* (2000) and *The People of St Edmund's College* (2003).

In producing this book, I am fully aware that I stand on hallowed ground. I say this especially since I am not an Edmundian (as one person quipped 'through no fault of your own'), having been educated at another Catholic school in Hertfordshire and having trained for the Priesthood at Douay's sister College in Rome (the Venerable English College). However, I like to think of myself as an 'honorary Edmundian,' for all Westminster priests can surely claim that distinction.

I can claim a tenuous but quite personal connection with the College. On one of my first visits I commented, in jest, that the chantry jutting out at the side of the Chapel would make a rather pleasant family oratory. Imagine my amazement when I was told that this was the 'Scholefield Chantry' – a different spelling but essentially the same surname as mine. And I was even more astonished to discover that this was the resting place of one Edward Scholefield, for that was my father's name too. On a subsequent visit I had the privilege of celebrating Mass there for the repose of my father's soul – a moving occasion, in more ways than one, since I had to pray that none of the masonry would fall upon me or the small congregation!

In preparing this book, I was helped by many individuals. Shortly before his untimely death, that great lover of all things Edmundian and Archivist Emeritus of Westminster, Fr Ian Dickie, was able to read my draft and make some useful suggestions. I would like to also thank Paulo Durán, Fra' Duncan Gallie, Mike Jenner, David Kay, Mark Leslie, Chris Long and Fr Stephen Wang for their help and support; Fr Stewart Foster and Fr Mark Vickers for sharing their considerable expertise; and my colleagues at the Westminster Diocesan Archives, Claire Childs and Peter Kent, for helping me locate material and putting up with my Edmundian preoccupations. An appeal to my brother clergy for memories led to useful contributions from Canon Michael Brockie, Fr Anton Cowan, Mgr Canon Frederick A. Miles, Fr Brian O'Shea, Canon Robert Plourde and Canon Paschal Ryan, some of which are included in the text.

Above: Fr Nicholas Schofield offering Mass in the Scholefield Chantry.

Over the centuries many individuals, priests and laity alike, have dedicated their lives to the mission of the College: one immediately thinks of William Bower, Charlie Smith and Joan King, as well as countless others. Reading obituaries of past students in The Edmundian, it is edifying to see the genuine devotion they had to the spirit and traditions of the place, and how the College's story was carefully handed down through the generations. Of Fr 'Tim' Healy, for example, the College's first Headmaster, it was said that 'his whole life was bound up with things Edmundian, and of Old Edmundians, living and dead, he had a fund of stories'. It is hoped that this volume, though not claiming to be the definitive College history that will hopefully one day be written, will satisfy living Edmundians and pay tribute to those who have gone before us into eternity.

As the final proofs were being corrected, the sad news of Fr Michael Pinot de Moira's death was announced. This much-loved priest, once voted the most popular Edmundian, summed up in his person much of the recent history of the College, stretching from the time of Cardinal Griffin to that of Archbishop Nichols. It is with profound respect that this volume is dedicated to him.

Fr Nicholas Schofield
Uxbridge
16 June 2013

CHAPTER I

THE DOUAY INHERITANCE
1568–1795

The English College at Douay[2] was founded in 1568 as a sort of Catholic Oxbridge overseas. It was the brainchild of a Lancashire man, William Allen, who had been principal of St Mary's Hall, Oxford, but was dismissed in 1561 on account of his Faith. Many Catholic-minded academics fled overseas at this time; more than a hundred senior members left Oxford alone in the first decade of Elizabeth I's reign. Many settled at university towns such as Douay, Malines and Louvain, where two English houses of studies were briefly set up, appropriately nicknamed 'Oxford' and 'Cambridge'.

The members of this English Catholic diaspora were, at first, loosely organised and had little financial backing. William Allen, like many others, occupied himself with further studies and sought priestly ordination, which he received in 1567 despite a period of poor health and convalescence in Lancashire. His return home allowed him to see the gradual consolidation of the Church of England. The following year (1568), on the feast of Michaelmas, he put his vision of erecting a more permanent Catholic College overseas into action.

Douay seemed a good location for such an enterprise: situated near the English Channel, the town's university had received its charter in 1559 and, as already mentioned, was the home to many English Catholic exiles. The new College was founded with the help of John Vendeville, regius professor of canon law at Douay and a future bishop of Tournai. He had hoped to receive papal support for a mission amongst Muslims but, after he failed to secure an audience with the pope during a visit to Rome, he was persuaded to transfer his missionary energies from Barbary to Britain. The new English College would unite the exiled diaspora, provide a Catholic education that could no longer be found at Oxford and Cambridge and ensure a new generation of 'seminary priests' who could return to their homeland 'even at the peril of their lives'.

Thus the English College began in a rented house, receiving papal approval shortly afterwards. Initially conditions were basic and much of the financial pressure was placed on Allen's shoulders, though from 1570 he received an income for his work as regius professor of divinity at the university. Six years later his income increased further when he became a prebendary at Cambrai Cathedral. As time went on, donations and legacies were received and, crucially in 1575, a papal pension of 100 crowns a month (increased to 150 four years later), as well as support from Philip II of Spain (Douay was then part of the Spanish Netherlands).

Alongside constant worries concerning the running of the College was the fact that from 1568 the Dutch were at war with Spain. Life was periodically made unpleasant for the English and on 22 March 1578 the College was forced to move to Rheims, in French territory, where it remained until 1593.

Above left: Most of the Douay Martyrs had to face the gruesome punishment reserved for traitors: to be drawn to the place of execution on a hurdle, hanged by the neck (but not to the point of death) and then cut open, disembowelled, beheaded and quartered, as shown in a contemporary engraving.

Above right: St Edmund Campion (1540-81) was perhaps the most famous of the Elizabethan martyrs. A graduate of St John's, Oxford, he was reconciled to Catholicism at Douay in 1571 and entered the English College. He later became a Jesuit and during his brief ministry in England produced influential works such as the Challenge to the Privy Council, or, Campion's Brag (1580) and Ten Reasons (1581).

Thanks to the leadership of Allen, the support of the Holy See and Spain and the desperate need for an English College overseas, the institution managed not only to survive but flourish. It combined elements of a university, seminary and school – for while the College started with mature scholars studying either in house or at the university, it was soon providing younger students with an education that was not possible in England. As the historian A. C. F. Beales observed, it 'grew downwards' from the top: 'Douay College began with theology, but in time it learned to begin with "rudiments"'.[3]

Many of Allen's recruits were 'the best wittes out of England', such as the future martyrs St Edmund Campion and St Cuthbert Mayne, both formerly of St John's, Oxford. In September 1576 there were some 120 students and by 1580 about 100 priests had been sent on the English mission. The growing numbers led to the foundation of a daughter house in Rome, the Venerable English College (1579). The large student body created problems of security, for it proved easy enough for the English authorities to plant spies within the College and during the 1570s several attempts were even made to assassinate Allen.

What was life like at the nascent English College? As might be expected, there was daily Mass, weekly reception of Holy Communion, prayer using the method of St Ignatius Loyola (the founder of the Jesuits) and twice weekly fasting for 'the conversion of England'. The academic syllabus was partly influenced by the Jesuits and included a comprehensive grounding in scholastic theology (particularly that of St Thomas Aquinas), although the course was adapted to suit future missionaries in Protestant England. Much attention was paid to preaching, disputation and the study of Sacred Scripture, the chief 'weapon' used by Anglican controversialists. With this in mind, the College sponsored a translation of the New Testament in 1582. The timetable included daily Scriptural lectures, classes in the Biblical languages, readings from the holy book at meal times and regular debates on disputed points. There were also lectures on English church history and Allen's own university lectures were prepared with 'the heretics of our time' firmly in mind.

The result was a new type of missionary: the 'seminary priest', highly trained in theology and controversy, and eager to return to his homeland, despite the obvious dangers. In 1577 St Cuthbert Mayne became the first 'seminary priest' to be hanged, drawn and quartered. Nearly two-thirds of Douay priests were imprisoned at some point and a total of 116 were executed during Elizabeth's reign. The College in Douay began to be seen as the headquarters of the English Mission and Allen as its leader. Indeed, in 1572 Gregory XIII gave him faculties to delegate missionary powers to priests making the journey across the Channel.

There is no space here to look at the subsequent history of the College in detail. Allen lived on until 1594 but became less involved at Douay. A sister College was founded in Rome in 1579, using the buildings of the English Hospice. From 1581 Allen acted as 'Prefect of the English Mission', the effective superior of the secular clergy, and as well as providing their spiritual and material well-being, involved himself in various schemes to restore a Catholic government to the country. He was named a Cardinal in 1587, at the recommendation of Philip II, who mounted his Armada the following year and, in the event of its successful outcome, hoped to install Allen as Archbishop of Canterbury. After its failure, Allen was named Archbishop of Malines (though he never took possession) and spent his final years in Rome, living at the English College and enjoying the title of Prefect of the Vatican Library.

At Douay, Allen's shoes were hard to fill. His two immediate successors, Richard Barrett (President, 1588-99) and Thomas Worthington (President, 1599-1613), are generally seen as disappointments during whose Presidencies the College faced insufficient funding, falling numbers (caused partly by the competition of the new Jesuit-run College at St Omer, founded by Fr Robert Persons) and demoralising infighting (a key issue being the appointment of a Jesuit confessor, much resented by the secular clergy). During this period, however, the College managed to move to new buildings on the Rue des Morts (later re-named Rue St Jacques). A print from 1627 shows an attractive quadrangular structure, with turrets at each of the inner corners.

Fortunes began to improve under Dr Matthew Kellison (President, 1613-41), who stabilised the financing of the College and limited the Jesuit influence within the house. Not only had there been a Jesuit confessor but many of the older students studied humanities at the nearby Collège d'Anchin, run by the Society. The outbreak of the plague in 1617 and the subsequent 'confinement' of the students within the College gave the President a perfect excuse to expand the in-house studies and appoint masters for the schools of Rhetoric, Poetry and Syntax.

Life at the College continued to be disturbed by outbreaks of plague and warfare. During the War of the Spanish Succession, for example, the College had to be evacuated to Lille (1710)

GUILIELMUS ALANUS, S.R.E. CARDINALIS S.T.D.
Duac Archiepus Mechlin designatus obiit Romæ
A° MDXCIV

Above: Cardinal William Allen.

William Allen (1532-94), originally from Rossall in Lancashire, was Principal of St Mary's Hall, Oxford during the reign of Mary I. Shortly after Elizabeth's accession he went into exile overseas and founded English Colleges at Douay and Rome. He was named a cardinal in 1587 and, four years later, Prefect of the English Mission.

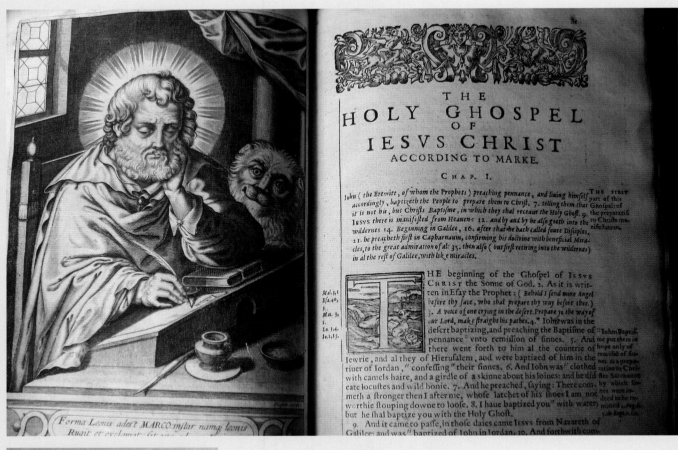

Above: An extract from the Douay-Rheims Bible.

Left: Douay-Rheims Bibles bound in vellum, still preserved at the College.

THE DOUAY-RHEIMS BIBLE

The English College at Douay (and Rheims) sponsored a translation of the New Testament in 1582, made by Gregory Martin, Thomas Worthington, Richard Bristow, John Reynolds and, of course, William Allen himself (all of them Oxford men). The volume included extensive notes and, although it was described as a translation from the Vulgate, use was clearly made of the existing English Bibles of John Wycliffe and Miles Coverdale. The Old Testament followed in 1609-10, which meant the complete 'Douay-Rheims Bible' was already available by the time the King James Bible was produced in 1611. Indeed, the New Testament of 1582 was one of the sources used by the translators of the King James. The text was later revised (essentially retranslated) by Bishop Challoner (1749-52) and others, and the Douay-Rheims remained standard among English-speaking Catholics up until the second half of the twentieth century. Indeed, at his presidential inauguration in January 1961, John F. Kennedy used his family's copy of the Douay-Rheims.

and Arras (1712). One boy, William Roe (alias Roberts), escaped from the College in August 1706 with the hope of reaching the Duke of Marlborough's army, which was stationed nearby. Unfortunately he was captured by the French and only released thanks to the College's connections with the exiled Stuart court. With the ending of hostilities in 1713 and the Treaty of Utrecht, Douay passed securely into French hands and Louis XIV soon granted the College a royal charter and pension. Around this time, a villa was purchased at Coutiches, to which the students could retire in the summer – after all, most of the College was not able to return to their families for the whole duration of studies.

Ecclesiastical politics could be just as troublesome. Dr Edward Paston (President, 1688-1714) was not only criticised for introducing 'modern' elements into the seminary regime (borrowed from the those used at the seminary of Saint Sulpice, Paris) but also fought accusations of Jansenism. This was initially a theological movement, based on an austere reading of the works of St Augustine of Hippo, especially with regard to the relationship between God's grace and man's free will. Those with Jansenist leanings included British Catholics who were living in exile in France and Flanders. Even James II, then based at Saint Germain, was given permission by the Archbishop of Paris to read Jansenist authors and appointed Dr John Betham, a pro-Jansenist priest, as tutor to his son and heir.

Jansenism would have probably remained an internal ecclesiastical matter had it not been for its alliance to Gallicanism, which criticised the 'absolutism' of King and Pope and stressed the power of the regional parlements and 'local' Church. It came to be seen not only as a deviant theology but a threat to established authority. Jansenist propositions were condemned by several popes and the movement became the focus of Louis XIV's aggression. It is little surprise that there were frequent 'witch-hunts' for those with Jansenist tendencies, a fact that could be easily manipulated by the various warring factions within the Church.

At the English College accusations of Jansenism were chiefly aimed at the Vice-President, Dr Edward Hawarden. He had been successful in gaining the prestigious chair of Divinity at the university, which caused jealous opposition and provided a fertile ground for charges of heresy. Added to this, were the continuing tensions between the secular clergy (who ran the College) and the Jesuits (the great opponents of Jansenism). Hawarden eventually departed for England in 1707, a move interpreted by some as an admission of his guilt, but the attacks soon widened to include the whole College. Despite the professors being 'so careful not to say or write anything that even our greatest adversaries could interpret in a bad sense', Cardinal Paolucci wrote in threatening tones to the English bishops in 1710:

'It having been known to His Holiness that in the Colledge of Douay, there are found many readers and schollars, who publickly teach and learn respectively the false doctrine of Jansenius, His Holiness has commanded me to signify to your Honor, that you procure to remove them with what care you possibly can, for to substitute in their places other persons remarkable for their piety, and particularly professors of Catholick doctrine, to the end that the Holy See be not necessitated to provide otherwise by suspending those Ecclesiastical Rents, which every year it has caused to be subministred to the same Colledge, and to turn them to other uses'.[4]

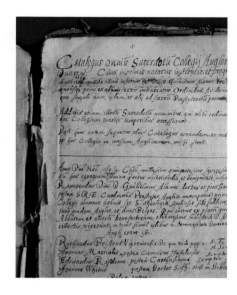

Above: The opening page of the first 'Douay Diary', beginning in 1568 and listing the students at the College and important events. This volume is kept in the College museum.

THE MARTYRS

St Edmund's College, through its descent from the English College at Douay, claims 158 of the English and Welsh Martyrs. These priests suffered for the Catholic Faith between 1577 and 1680. Many others, who were not in the end executed, had to endure trial, imprisonment, even torture, as well as years of exercising the priestly ministry in secrecy. Persecution was not constant in its intensity and tended to increase at times of national crisis – many suffered in the aftermath of the Spanish Armada (1588), for example, while there were only a small number of martyrdoms during the early years of James I's reign, as he tried to arrange alliances with the Catholic powers.

A complete list of the Douay Martyrs is given in Appendix 1.

Left: St Edmund Campion was hanged, drawn and quartered at Tyburn in 1581.

Above near right: Blessed John Sherte was executed in 1582.

Below near right: St John Payne was hanged in Chelmsford in 1582.

Above far right: St Cuthbert Mayne, the first seminary priest, was hanged, drawn and quartered in 1577.

Below far right: Blessed Thomas Sherwood was executed at Tyburn in 1579.

B · LUKE · KIRKBY · M

B · JOHN · SHERTE · M

B · EDMUND · CAMPION · M

B · JOHN · PAYNE · M

B · CUTHBERT · MAYNE · M

B · THOMAS · SHERWOOD · M

Dr Paston noted that 'the removal of any [professors] from hence upon pretence of Jansenism would cause a great scandal to our Mission (of which this Colledge is the fountain), occasion division amongst Catholics and other evils'.[5] The King agreed to write a letter to Rome, along with an Attestation signed by Dukes of Berwick and Perth and other Jacobite notables. Fortunately, the College was cleared of all charges of heresy and praised for its teaching. Unsurprisingly, the College made a point of welcoming the Apostolic Constitution *Unigenitus* (1713), which condemned 101 Jansenist propositions, but the suspicions continued and, as a result of the controversy, professors were prevented from applying for vacancies at the university.

Paston also encountered student discontent, which prefigured the 'Great Affair' at St Edmund's in 1809. In October 1689 complaints were left in the professors' common room and the following day, after requests for a play day were turned down, the students decided to ring the bell (indicating a day free of study) and go forth into the town. That night they noisily ran about the corridors and huddled around a makeshift fire. A fortnight later, when a similar disturbance seemed likely, five of the ringleaders were called to the President's room and expelled from the town by soldiers. Several were eventually allowed to return.

Then in 1692, on the advice of Bishop James Smith of the Northern District, the President decided to abolish the 'frivolous liberties' of Christmastide, in solidarity with the deprivations faced by Catholics across the Channel. The measure proved deeply unpopular, especially Paston's warning that 'if any person whatsoever, of what rank, state or condition soever, shall move anything in favour of them [the Christmas liberties], I further declare that person factious, seditious and rebellious: to be immediately expelled with infamy'. Added to this were complaints that the Prefect of Studies was too severe in flogging boys with a 'rod of iron'. The result was another period of unrest.

Above: The 'Howard Goblet' is an example of the treasure made by the silversmiths at Douay. It was saved from the ravages of the French Revolution and is now preserved in the College museum.

Paston's successor, Robert Witham (President 1715-38), had the task of re-building the College, made necessary by the wear and tear of the years and the damage inflicted during two recent sieges of the town. Indeed, parts of the building were deemed highly unsafe. There were also financial worries, especially when Louis XV reduced interest on the public loan from 6% to 2% in 1719, thus affecting the value of the College investment in these stocks. Nevertheless Witham decided boldly to pull down the old structure, which dated back to the era of the martyrs, and managed to raise enough money to build the main block (at the cost of £4,000) and chapel (opened in October 1724).

Witham was never entirely happy in his role and hoped to be succeeded by Richard Challoner, who had served ably as a Professor, Prefect of Studies and Vice-President (1720-30). While working at the College, Challoner had published his first two books. His bibliography would eventually amount to over sixty titles, including collections of prayers (the highly influential *Garden of the Soul*), catechesis (*An Abridgement of Christian Doctrine,* which later formed the basis of the popular *Penny Catechism*) and hagiography (such as *Memoirs of the Missionary Priests*, which traced the lives of many of the Douay Martyrs). It was appropriate that, in his early days at the College, Challoner's nickname was 'Book'. Witham had tried to gain permission for Challoner to enter the competition for the university chair of catechetics; since the Hawarden dispute College professors were prohibited from doing so. Challoner won the right to enter the *concursus* but eventually lost to the stiff competition.

Left: Bishop Challoner's silver mitre is preserved in the College museum. It was made no later than 1758.

Above: A portrait of Bishop Richard Challoner which hangs in the College museum.

Challoner probably would have been appointed President had Bishop Benjamin Petre not asked for him to become his coadjutor bishop in the London District, with right of succession. One of Challoner's former students, William Thornburgh (President, 1739-50), was appointed in his place at Douay, even though he had just left the College to work in the Northern District. Indeed, he professed to have been happy 'amongst the poor people, who seemed very willing to profit by what instructions I endeavoured to give them, and never thought of quitting them to engage in as difficult a task as the government of so important a College, whether considered as a nursery of ecclesiastics or laics'. At Douay, one of his first tasks was to respond to a series of questions sent round the seminaries by the Holy See. Thornburgh spoke of the many achievements of the College despite difficult conditions and stressed that the presence of lay students 'brings patrons to the missionaries in England, and benefactors to the College' and that no difference was made between the alumni (students paid for by bursaries) and convictors (students who paid for themselves). He included a revealing description of daily life at the College during the mid-eighteenth century:

…those who sleep in separate rooms rise at five in the morning. At half-past five they proceed to Church, and devote themselves to Mental Prayer till six. At six, those who sleep in the Common dormitory come to Church, the Litanies of the Saints are said, and Mass is celebrated for the conversion of England and Scotland. At the end of Mass, studies are carried on for a little over an hour; then they go to the Refectory for breakfast. When this is over, Schools begin and continue till ten o'clock. From ten to twelve they study, and at midday dine. Recreation in the grounds

THE DOUAY COLLEGE WAS ACTUALLY EMBARRASSED BY THE SITUATION IN WHICH IT HAD BEEN PLACED UNDER PRESSURE BY THE FRENCH AUTHORITIES.

follows dinner till two. From two till four they have Schools again, and from four to six Study. At six the Litanies of the Saints and some prayers for the conversion of England and Scotland are said, after which a quarter of an hour is spent in Spiritual Reading. Then they proceed to Supper and after Supper are free till half-past eight, when Night Prayers are said, the Examination of Conscience made and points of meditation for the next day read. When this is finished they retire to their rooms and bed.[6]

During the first half of the eighteenth century the English College was solidly 'Jacobite' in its sympathies, showing allegiance to the *de jure* King (the deposed James II and his Catholic heirs) rather than the *de facto* monarch (the Protestant Hanoverian actually sitting on the throne). Masses were regularly offered for the Stuart cause and the Te Deum was sung when there were victories. In his diary Edward Dicconson, at the time College Procurator and later Vicar Apostolic of the Northern District, recorded meeting Dr Paston in June 1705 as he made 'his journey to Paris and St Germain, there to wait on the King and Queen'.[7] In September 1745 the College Diary records that High Mass was celebrated for 'the happy success of the Prince of Wales [Charles Edward Stuart] in the expedition he had undertaken against George, the Elector of Hanover [George II]'. Further Masses and periods of Exposition of the Blessed Sacrament followed for this intention. In June 1746 the students were allowed to kiss the hand of Henry, Duke of York (soon to become a Cardinal) during a visit to Douay. However, after the failure of 'the 45' the College gradually became more Hanoverian in its sympathies, a process helped by the presence of British troops in northern France and growing feelings of patriotism during the various wars of the period.

In 1753 a preparatory school was opened at Esquerchin, a few miles west of Douay, with Robert Johnson as its first master. The house was purchased by James Talbot, the future bishop and founder of Old Hall Green Academy, and was used as a school until 1772. Numbers were never large – in June 1757, for example, there were fourteen boys there – but it provided an education to those too young to enter Rudiments at Douay (below the ages of thirteen or fourteen).

THE ENGLISH COLLEGE AT ST OMER

In 1762 the Jesuits were expelled from France, due mainly to political factors, and the Society's successful College at St Omer, founded by Fr Robert Persons in 1593, was handed over to the secular clergy by the French authorities. Given the long-standing disagreements between the Jesuits and the seculars, this was the last blow to the Society, who suspected a plot. Matters worsened in 1767 when the Jesuit-run Royal English College at Valladolid, Spain, was amalgamated with the secular-run institutions at Seville and Madrid and several Douay professors and students, including John Douglass, were sent there as an advance guard.

The Douay College was actually embarrassed by the situation in which it had been placed under pressure by the French authorities. The transition was fraught with ill-feeling and most of the original St Omer community moved to Bruges and later Liège. Thomas Talbot was appointed the first secular President and, since he was initially detained with business in England, oversight of St Omer was placed in the hands of Henry Tichborne Blount, the master at Esquerchin. By 1766 there were fifty students and numbers eventually grew, especially under the Presidency of Alban Butler (1766-73), who was well-regarded as a scholar and produced the famous *Lives of the Saints*.

St Edmund's claims, in a sense, to be a successor to the secular College at St Omer since its last President, Gregory Stapleton, became the first President at Old Hall. Following the French Revolution, two professors also went to Old Hall together with several students.

Englishmen in the Reign of Terror

In 1783, no one would have thought that the English College at Douay only had a decade left on French soil. William Gibson had been President for two years and was pushing forward an ambitious plan of modernisation and rebuilding. Soon there would be a new infirmary and study place and alterations to the dormitory. New subjects were added to the curriculum, including English literature, elementary mathematics and a new focus on learning French. Gibson's efforts seemed to meet with success, with numbers of students rising to 164 in 1784, although some complained that his reforms carried an imprudent financial risk and brought the College close to bankruptcy. Gregory Stapleton, the long-suffering Procurator, was Gibson's chief critique and the latter must have been relieved when he was appointed President of St Omer in 1787.

Above: Esquerchin is a commune about four miles west of Douay. The preparatory school was located here from 1753.

Opposite top: James II (1633-1701) lost his throne partly due to his staunch Catholic Faith. Those who supported his claims and those of his descendents were known as 'Jacobites'.

Opposite middle: James II chalice veil of 1659. The embroidery is late Elizabethan and may have been removed from a dress of that period. It is still in the College's possession.

Opposite bottom: Dr Gregory Stapleton was President of St Omer between 1787 and 1793 and President of St Edmund's College between 1795 and 1801.

Adeste fideles læti triumphantes,
Venite, venite in Bethlehem.
Natum videte
Regem angelorum:
Venite adoremus (ter)
Dominum.

O come, all ye faithful,
Joyful and triumphant!
O come ye, O come ye to Bethlehem;
Come and behold him
Born the King of Angels:

Chorus:
O come, let us adore Him,
O come, let us adore Him,
O come, let us adore Him,
Christ the Lord.

Deum de Deo, lumen de lumine
Gestant puellæ viscera.
Deum verum, genitum non factum.
Venite adoremus (ter)
Dominum.

God of God,
Light of Light,
Lo, he abhors not the Virgin's womb;
Very God,

Chorus

Cantet nunc 'Io', chorus angelorum;
Cantet nunc aula cælestium,
Gloria! Soli Deo Gloria!
Venite adoremus (ter)
Dominum.

Sing, choirs of angels,
Sing in exultation,
Sing, all ye citizens of Heaven above!
Glory to God
In the highest:

Chorus

Ergo qui natus die hodierna.
Jesu, tibi sit gloria,
Patris aeterni Verbum caro factum.
Venite adoremus (ter)
Dominum.

Yea, Lord, we greet thee,
Born this happy morning;
Jesus, to thee be glory given!
Word of the Father,
Now in flesh appearing!

Chorus

Above: One of three manuscripts of Adeste Fideles in the College museum.

ADESTE FIDELES AND JOHN FRANCIS WADE

O Come All Ye Faithful, one of the most popular and widely sung of our Christmas carols, is a Victorian translation of the Latin hymn, *Adeste Fideles*. Variously attributed over the years to the likes of St Bonaventure, King John IV of Portugal and the English musician John Reading, the writer and composer was almost certainly John Francis Wade (1711-86), who spent much of his adult life in Douay and had close associations with the English College. He taught music and Latin and produced books of plainchant both in printed and manuscript form. Harking back to the days of the medieval monks and their illuminated manuscripts, Wade delighted in the arts of calligraphy, copying and illustration. His books were widely used by English Catholics and he has been called the 'Father of the English plainchant revival'.

Like many Catholics of the period, he was an ardent Jacobite and many of his manuscripts were 'coded' with suggestive political imagery, instantly recognisable to other supporters of the Stuarts. It has been suggested that *Adeste Fideles*, written in the 1740s, either originated as a birth ode to 'Bonnie Prince Charlie' or came to have these connotations. Centuries earlier, in the late sixth century, St Gregory the Great had declared that the English slave boys he had seen in Rome were not Angles but Angels. A similar play on words was used in *Adeste Fideles*, where 'Regem Angelorum' (King of Angels) really referred to 'Regem Anglorum' (King of the English). Moreover, 'Bethlehem' was a common Jacobite code name for England and the 'faithful' were those loyal to the true King and the true Faith. There are three 'Wade manuscripts' of *Adeste Fideles* kept at St Edmund's, one of which is on display in the museum. It seems that the hymn was originally sung at Benediction of the Blessed Sacrament 'infra benedictionem', giving added meaning to the 'Venite adoremus', 'Come let us adore Him'.

Adeste Fideles quickly became famous and was widely used in England, France and elsewhere, partly because the text was in the international language of Latin. In England it was initially known as the 'Portuguese Hymn', probably because it was used at the Portuguese Embassy Chapel in London, though this led some to assume its origins were Iberian. Soon, verses were being added and many English translations were being made. The most famous of these is by Canon Frederick Oakeley, the prominent convert and Old Edmundian.

The College authorities kept an eye on wider developments in France. They stressed that the institution was British rather than French property and claimed exemptions from revolutionary legislation, such as the taking of the oath accepting the Civil Constitution of the Clergy. In the meantime, the day-to-day life of the College was more affected by changes closer at hand – the quick succession of three Presidents. Gibson left in 1790, upon his appointment as Vicar Apostolic of the Northern District (in succession to his brother). His successor as President, Edward Kitchen (or Kitchin), arrived the following July and, due to poor health, lasted only three months. His place was eventually taken by the Vice-President and Professor of Theology, John Daniel. He would be the last of the Douay Presidents and although he kept the title until his death in 1823, his effective government lasted three short years.

Collegians first experienced the storm clouds of revolution in 1791, when some of them witnessed a large demonstration in the town's main square. Two locals were lynched by the mob, hanged from the lamp post and then dragged through the streets; 'one of whom, Derbaix, was the printer employed by the College, and had become obnoxious to the orators by the loyal tone of the press; and the other was an extensive baker, whom they charged with starving the people for the gratification of his avarice'.[8]

Above: One of the treasures of Douay, this relic is part of the hair shirt of St Thomas of Canterbury.

Shortly afterwards some angry knocks were heard at the College door, which was opened by William Poynter, the Prefect of Studies. According to Thomas Gillow:

Immediately four or five of the soldiers in a state of intoxication entered, and pushed forward through the porch and inner door into the corridor. They called out for the young men to be led out into the streets to go along with them. Dr Poynter attempted to remonstrate, saying that the students were many of them in bed, and the rest were now retiring, and begged that they would not disturb them. "Where are your prisons? Open your prisons," they exclaimed. "We have no prisons," replied Dr Poynter, and would have added that the young men were free and happy, but the soldiers grew furious. One drew his sword, and the consequences threatened to become serious, when, in an instant, Messrs Gillow, Silvertop, Riddell, and one or two more, as if moved by a common influence, rushed forward, and taking each of the soldiers by the arm, cried out Vive la nation! And so drew them out into the streets. The doors were closed, and the crowd moved away to the cry of Vive la nation! Vive la liberté! The students were carried in a sort of triumphal procession through the streets of Douay; and were out most of the night; and in this manner the College was temporarily saved.[9]

Another account, by Lewis Clifford, suggests that the students took less of an initiative and merely showed republican sympathy to escape harm.

In January 1793 the situation was irrevocably altered by the declaration of war between France and Britain, following the guillotining of Louis XVI. Trickles of students began to return home. Of the 89 registered at the College in October 1792 around 25 left before hostilities broke out. In February 1793 armed guards arrived at the College and the other British institutions in the town; rooms were sealed and the contents listed in inventories. 'The pretended motive of these proceedings', reported one student, 'was to put our property in security, as a storm, they said, seemed to be gathering against us from people of inferior conditions, among whom several rumours, unfavourable to us, had been spread'.[10]

Right: An image of the English College, Douay, in the Douay Window in the choir of the current College chapel.

Below right: The English College possibly by Thomas Haydock, as it appeared in the years leading up to the French Revolution. Sadly none of the building remains.

COLL: ANGLO - ROM: DUACI

Despite the attentions of the 'spiders', as the guards were soon nicknamed, some of the more daring students decided to enter the sealed parts of the College and save some of the treasures. One clambered down a rope to save the more precious instruments kept in the Physical Science Room; another climbed up a chimney to enter the President's Room. Various valuables, including some of the College plate, were thus carried off by four philosophers (including the future bishop, Thomas Penswick) and buried in a safe place. Relics, including the body of St John Southworth, the hair shirt of St Thomas Becket and the biretta of St Charles Borromeo, were hidden on the property itself and only rediscovered in 1927 during town redevelopment.

The Douatians were first removed in August to the relative peace of their country house at Equerchin; the allies had recently captured nearby Valenciennes and an attack on Douay was thought imminent. Finally, on 12 October 1793, the Collegians were told to move to the Scots College in Douay, where sleeping accommodation was hurriedly provided in the refectory – space was at a premium since several suspected French aristocrats were being held there. Poynter wrote that, in the meantime, 'the doors [of the English College] were thrown open for three days, during which part of the furniture was sold, and the rest of the goods that could easily be moved and carried off was plundered by the mob'.[11]

On 16 October the College community was moved to the Citadelle at Doullens in Picardy. In the course of the two-day journey several students managed to escape. At Doullens, the Collegians were joined by six English Benedictines from St Gregory's, Douay (a community that in due course relocated to Downside). The stories later told by the 'Confessors of Doullens' quickly passed into College lore. There were, for instance, heroic escapes. Since Doullens lay in a different diocese to Douay, the priests lacked faculties to hear Confessions. In November 1793 a party of four students climbed down a rope fixed at the top of the castle wall and disappeared into the night to apply for the appropriate documentation from the bishop of Amiens. This arrived in time for the Christmas celebrations.

Conditions were harsh. Richard Thompson compared the first night, without mattresses, to 'a black hole' but added that 'never, I am persuaded, did either our superiors or the boys pass a more merry and sportful night at Esquerchin'. The following day they were moved to a larger, wind-exposed garret, although conditions were still cramped and the food insufficient. Communication was soon established with Stapleton, who was then imprisoned at St Omer, and messages were sent to England asking for money. A window was unhinged and placed horizontally, so that Mass could be discreetly celebrated.[12]

In May 1794 a large group of new prisoners arrived at Doullens, including 65 members of the English College, St Omer, much to the Douay collegians' delight, and the French guards were reportedly astonished by the daily games of leapfrog and (appropriately enough) Prisoners' Base. All this time, petitions were sent to the authorities in the hope that the prisoners would be allowed to return home. Eventually the permission was given; the St Omerians were released in October 1794 and left the prison singing the psalm 'In exitu Israel de Ægypto'. Shortly afterwards, on 24 November, it was the turn of the remaining 'Trente-deux', as they came to be called – the six Benedictines and twenty-six from the English College (others had managed to escape). Amazingly, although they had watched fellow French prisoners be led to Madame Guillotine, the only English casualty of the imprisonment had been Richard Brettargh, a professor from St Omer, who was in poor health and died at Doullens on 24 July 1794.

On their release, the Douatians stayed a night at Arras and then were kept for several months at the Irish College, Douay. The regime was comparatively relaxed and in December the students were even given permission to go skating. Several of them tried to visit their old College, now a military hospital. They must have been shocked to find the sacristy being used as latrines and the church and refectory as storage space for bedding and linens. Much of the archive and library had sadly disappeared, some of the paper being pulped to make cartridge cases.

Stapleton went to Paris to negotiate the prisoners' release and the issuing of passports so that they could return home. On 13 February 1795 he arrived triumphantly at Douay and uttered the long-remembered words: 'Good news, my boys. Thank God, we are going to England.' One of those present later recalled, 'I believe we never in the whole course of our lives experienced such lively emotions of joy; many of the collegians gave loud cheers of applause.'[13] The staff and students left Douay for the last time on 26 February and on 2 March crossed from Calais to Dover on an American ship.

THE REFECTORY AT DOUAY COLLEGE.

Above: The Refectory at the English College.

Below: The English College, St Omer. From an engraving at the Bibliothèque Nationale, Paris.

A NEW CHAPTER IN THE COLLEGE'S LONG HISTORY WAS ABOUT TO BEGIN.

STANDON-LORDSHIP

To the Right Hon.ble
and truly Noble
WALTER Lord ASTON
Baron of FORFARE in the
Kingdom of SCOTLAND.
This Draught Shewing
the Front and Side Prospect of
STANDON Lord SHIP.
Is most humbly Prsented and Dedicated

CHAPTER II

FROM SILKSTEAD TO OLD HALL
1660–1769

Catholic education was not only provided overseas. Despite the penal laws, there were a number of clandestine schools in England and Wales during 'penal times'. Indeed, numbered among the English Martyrs are twenty-three teachers who worked either as school-masters or private tutors.

The origins of St Edmund's as a lay academy can be traced back to a group of schools in the Winchester area, originating in the seventeenth century. In his College history, Bernard Ward spoke of a school at Silkstead (or Silksteed) dating back to around 1686, under the direction of Fr Augustine Taylor. In 1692 he was succeeded by Fr William Husband, whose departure four years later coincided with the school's removal to Twyford in Hampshire. Subsequent research has shown that the Silkstead school was even older than was first thought. Founded before 1660, the boys cheered Charles II on his way from Southampton to Winchester at the Restoration. For a time it was probably located in the manor house of Philip Taylor and his wife, who were childless. Despite the small size of their household, an inventory attached to his will lists as many as twenty-six bedsteads.[14] Moreover, rather than Silkstead moving to Twyford it appears that the two institutions co-existed for a time and the latter served as a sort of preparatory school. Many of its students would have gone overseas to Colleges such as Douay.[15]

The most famous alumnus of Twyford was undoubtedly the poet, Alexander Pope, who benefited in particular from the tuition of Fr Edward Taverner (alias Banister). Samuel Johnson later noted that under Taverner's guidance 'his proficiency was considerable'; before leaving the school the young Pope managed to translate a quarter of the *Metamorphoses* and much of the poet Statius. However, the penning of a witty satire on one of the masters led to a savage thrashing which impelled his parents to move him to another Catholic school kept by Mr Deane in London.

From 1726 the school was directed by Fr Francis Fleetwood, who had grown up at the court of the exiled Stuarts at St Germain-en-Laye. As 'chief master', the school flourished and produced two future bishops (the brothers Talbot) and two future earls (Shrewsbury and Fingall). Around 1732 Fleetwood left the school and went to join the Society of Jesus. His departure led to a period of decline. Bishop Stonor, Vicar Apostolic of the Midland District, complained that that the loyalties of many parents went with Fleetwood, Jesuit schools benefiting from Twyford's loss.

Financial difficulties plagued the school and it finally closed after the Jacobite Rebellion of 1745. However, it was soon revived at Standon Lordship, not far from Old Hall Green. It was an ideal location, conveniently near London but discreetly hidden from the main road to Cambridge by a low range of hills. The school made use of the manor house that had been built by Sir Ralph Sadleir, secretary to Thomas Cromwell, and later passed into the hands of the Catholic Aston family.

Above: Silkstead. This is the site of Silkstead Manor, demolished in 1830.

TIMETABLE AT STANDON LORDSHIP			
Weekdays		**Sundays / Holidays**	
6.00am	Rise	7.00am	Rise
6.15am	Washing and combing	7.30am	Washing, combing and powdering
6.30am	Morning prayers, mass	7.45am	Morning prayers
7.15am	Breakfast	8.00am	Breakfast
8.00am	Study (Catechism at first; then Latin or Greek)	9.00am	Spiritual reading
10.00am	Recreation	10.00am	Mass
10.15am	Study	11.00am	Study
12noon	Dinner, recreation	12noon	Dinner, recreation
2.00pm	Study (writing/geography or the like)	2.30pm	Vespers and compline, recreation
4.00pm	*(in Summer, 'small beer')*	*4.00pm*	*(in Summer, 'small beer')*
6.00pm	Evening prayers	6.00pm	Supper, recreation
6.30pm	Supper, recreation		
8.00pm	Bed time	8.00pm	Bed time
(in Summer 'small beer' at 8.00pm and bed at 8.30pm)			

Sir Walter Aston was received into the Church in Madrid in 1620 while (unsuccessfully) negotiating the 'Spanish Match' between the future Charles I and the Spanish Infanta. Secret Masses were celebrated at the manor as often as possible and its priestly visitors included the Jesuit martyr, Blessed William Ireland. The new site for the school thus offered plentiful accommodation and an existing Catholic chapel.

The school was established in the summer of 1749 by Fr Richard Kendall, with the help of the newly-ordained Fr James Postlethwaite and the enthusiastic support of Bishop Richard Challoner, then coadjutor to the Vicar Apostolic of the London District. It is clear that it was considered a continuation of Twyford; not only do Bishops Talbot and Stonor say as much in their correspondence, but the rules at Standon Lordship were adapted from those at Twyford.

There were vacations at Christmas, Shrovetide, Easter and Whitsuntide and the regime was relaxed not only on Sundays but also on Tuesdays and Thursdays, which were half play-days. For recreation students played nine-pins, drew each other about in 'ye cart' and, when allowed, walked in the country or bathed in the river Rib. Sunday, however, was a day devoted to rest and devotion 'for which reason, nine pins and drawing ye cart about are forbid, as also whistling or singing'. On the first Sunday of the month there was, in addition, Benediction, followed by an explanation of the Douay Catechism. Boys were punished by forfeiting a half-penny to the poor, having their pocket money stopped, being served last in the refectory or, in extremis, receiving 'ye rod'.

School dinners consisted of an appetising selection of boiled milk and milk pottage for breakfast, meat, bread and beer for dinner and, in the evening, bread and butter or cheese, with milk. In the summer 'small beers' were provided twice a day and mince pies were sometimes produced around Christmas, together with the traditional plum cake on Twelfth Night.

Bernard Ward argued that 'in its purely English foundation, at Twyford, or even dating from Standon, it [St Edmund's] is older than any other Catholic school by many years, and is the only one that can be said to have had a long and trying experience of the Penal Laws'.

Above: Alexander Pope is the most famous alumnus of Twyford.

Alexander Pope (1688-1744) is generally regarded as the greatest English poet of the eighteenth century, he is best known for his satirical verse and for his translation of Homer. He is the third most frequently quoted writer in *The Oxford Dictionary of Quotations*. This famous painting of him hangs in the National Portrait Gallery in London.

Below left: Segar's Buildings, Twyford, near Winchester, which were believed to house Twyford School. The buildings were demolished in 1962.

Above: The Old Hall was in front of a large old-fashioned garden and orchard covering about eight acres of land.

OLD HALL GREEN ACADEMY

The school was not to stay for long at Standon Lordship, for the manor was sold by the Astons in 1767 and over subsequent years became derelict. The school subsequently made use of a house, no longer standing, at Hare Street belonging to Mrs Dorothy Brand, who was listed as a Catholic nonjuror. The little hamlet of Hare Street, outside Buntingford, later became famous as the residence of the convert priest Mgr Robert Hugh Benson, who died in 1914 and left his house for the private use of the Archbishop of Westminster.

Little is known of the school's brief sojourn at Hare Street, though numbers were low and space limited. Alternative accommodation was urgently needed. It is at this stage that Bishop James Talbot, an old boy of Twyford and now coadjutor bishop to Challoner, came onto the scene. He was aware of the school's vicissitudes and looked out for suitable properties in the area. One option was Hammel's (or Hamels) Park, near Puckeridge; the other was Old Hall Green, sometimes known as 'Odey Green'. This estate included the 'Old Hall' dating back to around 1640, a large garden and orchard and a cottage known as 'The Hermitage'. It was deemed most suitable and the bishop, using his own funds, began to rent the property in 1769 and finally bought it on 12 July 1771. Given the nature of the establishment, the purchase had to be made discreetly. A friend, John Hollingworth of Puckeridge (a surveyor), acted as an intermediary, buying the property himself the previous day and then selling it on to Talbot for £800.

Fr Kendall stayed behind at Hare Street to minister to his small flock and his place in the new Academy was taken by a relative, Fr James Willacy – after whom Willacy's (the north wing of Old Hall) is named. At its opening, the school probably had no more than fifteen pupils but numbers soon grew and included names from the prominent Catholic families: Arundell, Bedingfield, Blount, Clifford, Dormer, Giffard, Heneage, Howard, Jerningham, Riddell, Petre, Stonor, Talbot and so on.

Although conditions were gradually improving for English Catholics, caution still had to be exercised, as was revealed by an anonymous letter to Bishop Talbot received in March 1775:

My Lord Bishop, A Friend to the roman Catholicks begs leave to inform your Lordship that the number of Roman Catholick schools which of late have been set up in this nation, have given cause of complaint, and there are several informations lodged which are supposed to take place soon, among the rest your Lordship and two or three Chaplains at Odey Green, near Puckeridge, in Hertfordshire. Your Lordship is left to make what use you please of this friendly admonition, but its great pity you could not be satisfied with one or two Schools which have always been winked at, without drawing on yourselves the just odium of all, by establishing Popish seminaries all over the kingdom. Real Charity has induced me to give you this intelligence, begging you would take care of yourself not only in this Country, but also in London where diligent search will soon be made for you.

In reality there was only a handful of Catholic schools up and down the country with small student numbers but this never prevented the spectre of 'Popery' from rearing its frightful head and cause Englishmen to panic. Bishop Talbot, who was the last English priest to be tried for celebrating Mass, was forced on several occasions to temporarily close the Academy and send the students home to safety.

The period saw a number of Relief Acts that improved conditions for Catholics, allowing the registration of churches as places of worship and the existence of schools. The Academy could thus be openly advertised:

Old Hall Green Academy, Puckeridge, Herts
1. For a yearly pension of twenty-five guineas young gentlemen will be furnished with board, lodging, washing and taught reading, writing, arithmetic, book-keeping, geography and the use of globes, English, Latin, Greek, and French, which last they will be obliged to speak in their familiar conversation on certain days. A strict attention will be given to cleanliness, civility, and, above all, to their morals and religion.
2. The young gentlemen will contend for precedency several times in the year, and before the vacation, which begins on the 24th June and continues to the end of July, when all are expected to be at home or pay according to the time. The most advanced will give public exhibitions of their improvement, and all undergo a public examination, when the first in each class will be rewarded with a suitable premium.
3. At dinner, two good dishes besides vegetables. Breakfast: milk, milk pottage, or tea and bread and butter, if parents desire it. Supper: milk, bread and butter and cheese, or sometimes tarts, besides a piece of bread at eleven and four o'clock. None admitted after the age of twelve, but may continue after that age as long as parents choose.
N.B. The situation is one of the most pleasant and healthy in all England.

Around this time, Rev. John Potier became chief master at Old Hall Green, having worked on the staff for seven years. He witnessed the first exiles from Douay reach the Academy — individuals at first, such as Edward and James Tichborne. Events moved quickly. Their number increased dramatically and the Academy transformed into St Edmund's College, a successor to the great English College, Douay.

THE SITUATION IS ONE OF THE MOST PLEASANT AND HEALTHY IN ALL ENGLAND.

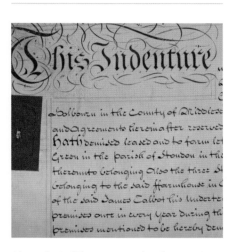

Above: Part of the conveyancing document relating to Bishop Talbot's purchase of Old Hall, now preserved in the Westminster Diocesan Archives.

CHAPTER III

ENGLAND'S COLLEGE HOME
1793 – 1795

T he news of the closure of the English College, Douay necessitated an emergency plan, so that its work could continue, if only temporarily, in England. Over the summer of 1793 a trickle of Douatians arrived home; even after the imprisonment of the remaining students at Doullens, some managed to escape and reach London.

The Vicars Apostolic considered various options for a 'New Douay'. Already in May Bishop Gibson of the Northern District, a former College President, looked into renting Flass Hall, near Ushaw Moor in County Durham. This would be a joint project with the London District but it fell through. Gibson thought the north was the best location given its relative seclusion and lower living costs. On the other hand, Bishop Walmesley of the Western District opposed the idea of a new College in England on the grounds of expense and the lack of teaching facilities. Some suggested that, just as Douay moved to Rheims during political troubles in the sixteenth century, so the Collegians should now move to the security of the Austrian Netherlands.

Bishop Douglass suggested that the refugees could be housed, at least temporarily, at Old Hall Green. With an operating school and a recently opened chapel, it had the essential facilities for a Catholic College and the juniors could easily fit into the existing classes. As time went on, he came to believe that a more permanent College could be grafted on to the Academy.

New premises were needed urgently and Gibson reluctantly agreed to accept Douglass' offer of housing northern students at Old Hall Green — even though, as President of Douay, he had had a low opinion of the Academy, thinking its alumni too worldly.

Bishop Douglass subsequently wrote in his Diary:

1793. On the 12th of November I took Messrs William Beauchamp and John Law to Old Hall, and on the 16th, the feast of St Edmund, Archbishop of Canterbury, we commenced studies or established the new College there, a substitute for Douay. Mr Thomas Cook, who had been at Old Hall Green half a year, employed in teaching the children and Mr Devereux, joined the other two. These four communicated at my hands. I said Mass, and after Mass exposed the Blessed Sacrament, and these four, with Mr Potier, sang the O Salutaris, Pange Lingua, Deus misereatur nostri, and Laudate Dominum omnes gentes ad finem. Thus was the new College instituted under the patronage of St Edmund, Archbishop of Canterbury, the aforementioned students recommencing their studies in divinity. Felix faustumque sit![20].

*Left: A painting of Old Hall of 1892 by F Swain
showing how it was believed to have looked in 1793.*

By the end of February 1794 there was a community of fifty at Old Hall Green, including twenty-one Douay men (six of them northerners) and one each from the English Colleges at Rome and Lisbon.

Above right: Bishop John Douglass was Vicar Apostolic of the London District from 1790 until 1812. This portrait is the College Museum.

Top left: Bishop Douglass and the inaugural students depicted in a stained glass window in the current College chapel.

Above left: The tomb of Bishop Douglass in the crypt below the College chapel. The top slab was originally in Old St Pancras Churchyard, London, from where the bishop's body was

Two members of the Douay staff were present: Fr William Coombes, late Professor of Rhetoric, and Deacon John Lee, late Professor of Syntax. A letter of George Haydock dating from December 1793 gives a picture of life at the nascent College:

We rise at 6 o'clock, go to church at ye half hour, and meditate out of Bp Challoner in ye same, manner as during ye retreat at Douay. At 7 study divinity till 8 when we all repair to hear prayers or mass 2 with the boys, who do not bear us company in ye aforesaid meditation. At a quarter to 9 breakfast of milk and bread (tea on fasting days), study till 1, when a dinner equal to what we had at Douay saltim is served up…After dinner we play till 3, go to school at 5 till 6, common prayers for half an hour, supper at 8, music for half an hour to prepare for ye church, where we have sung ye offices and masses since our arrival here, to ye great satisfaction of ye auditors. At 10 we go to bed in ye dormitory, for we have no better accommodations, and indeed we may think well to have so good, when we consider ye sufferings our friends undergo at Doullens, where they have only a little straw to sleep on, and are forced to cover themselves with their old tattered coats, which now scarce defend them from ye injuries of ye weather.[21]

Indeed, the brethren at Doullens were not forgotten and periodic votive Masses were offered for their intentions.

There were, of course, inevitable tensions between the boys of Old Hall Academy and the refugee seminarians, and between northerners and southerners. Accusations of bullying were raised on both sides. To counter this, the boys were separated from the Divines during 1794, the latter being lodged in a building north of Old Hall known as 'The Hermitage'. This was perhaps appropriate for a small seminary since its picturesque name is thought to have originated in a medieval hermitage founded on the site. The wooden outhouses and stables were also adapted - including 'The Ship', so-called because its timbers reminded the Divines of the ship on which they sailed from France. The small cells inside were nicknamed 'coffins'. Another building on the property was soon being used for classes and known as 'The School in the Garden'. Sadly, these relics of the early years of St Edmund's are no longer extant; 'The Ship' was demolished around 1952 and 'The School in the Garden' finally fell down in 1982.

Tensions continued to exist and matters came to a head over an incident involving a student and an unfortunate cat. A northern Divine, Charles Saul, claimed one evening at the fireside that cats had a strength superior to that of men. A southern student, Thomas Pitchford, said he could prove the opposite if a cat was provided. The following day the boys went to a nearby pond and stretched a rope across the water, tying a terrified cat to one end and Mr Pitchford to the other. The latter was asked to turn his back on the cat, in case he frightened the animal any further. As soon as he turned, he found himself pulled into the water — not, it seems, because the cat was 'the Samson of his race' but because of its human supporters energetically tugging the rope. When Douglass heard of this, he was angry at such rough behaviour and thought the boys 'low, vulgar fellows, and was pleased to call them a parcel of Lancashire blackguards'.[22]

Soon afterwards, the northern students petitioned Bishop Gibson that they be removed from Old Hall. By the end of 1794 they had been released; four of them (Charles Saul, Richard Thompson, Edward Monk and Thomas Penswick) left after Mass on All Saints Day and are said to have walked off with their luggage in a wheelbarrow. They eventually arrived at Crook Hall, where the other northern students had gathered after brief sojourns at Tudhoe and Pontop. In 1808 they moved to Ushaw, where St Edmund's sister seminary and co-heir to the Douay tradition remained until its formal closure in 2011.

It should be noted that there were several students for the Midland District at Old Hall during the early 1790s, until the foundation of a College at Oscott, near Birmingham, in 1794 under the Presidency of John Bew. With Colleges now at Old Hall, Crook Hall and Oscott, there was still some confusion in the minds of the Vicars Apostolic about the future of Catholic education on English soil: should there be a single 'new Douay' or several Colleges in the different Districts? Many still advised that Old Hall Green should revert to being a purely lay school and that a single College should be founded, probably in the north. The arrival of those who had been imprisoned at Doullens, on 2 March 1795, made the matter even more prescient. Unsurprisingly most of the 'Trente-Deux' returned to their families to recover from a traumatic eighteen months and to await further instruction from their bishops. Three arrived at Old Hall in April: John Bulbeck, Richard Broderick and Lewis Havard.

Above: An extract from a letter from Bishop Douglass concerning the College's finances.

Below: The Ship housed some twenty students. It derived its name from the fact that its internal timbers resembled the boat on which the students sailed from France to England.

FOUR OF THEM... LEFT AFTER MASS ON ALL SAINTS DAY... WITH THEIR LUGGAGE IN A WHEELBARROW.

Top and right: The Hermitage. Its estate included much of the land on which the main College buildings now stand. Its history is believed to date back to the 10th century. The building was used to accommodate the early students and later served as a convent until 1902.

Above: The sundial in the garden of The Hermitage is carved with the Sadleir family crest and coat of arms. This was originally at Standon Lordship. The last member of the Sadleir family died in 1660, so the sundial must pre-date that time.

A decisive moment came when Bishop Douglass and Dr Stapleton, formerly President of the College at St Omer, visited William Pitt the Younger, the Prime Minister, and William Cavendish-Bentinck, Duke of Portland and a friend of Stapleton's. Before embarking on an ambitious scheme to open a new Catholic College, it was thought best to get the advice of the Government. It is hard to think of this meeting being possible just a few years previously and is testament to the growing sympathy towards English Catholics, especially in the aftermath of the French Revolution. However, caution still had to be exercised and Pitt recommended that Old Hall Green would be the most sensible location for the new institution. The erection of new buildings would be seen as the extension of the existing school rather than a brand new venture; popular outcry would therefore be limited. The future of Old Hall Green seemed thus to be decided and Douglass received additional support from Mgr Erskine, a protégé of the Cardinal Duke of York, who was sent to England by Pius VI to thank the British Government for 'having taken the ecclesiastical state under protection' as well as 'secretly to inquire into the state of the English mission and report the same to Rome'.[23]

*Left: The School in the Garden. This was where
some of the original classes took place. The
building was used for a variety of purposes until
it suddenly fell down on 22 October 1982.*

Around the same time a Catholic who thought he was close to death, John Sone, offered a large amount of money to the new College. He was a wealthy miller from Brockhampton, Hampshire, who had been familiar with the school at Twyford. It seems that he was with Dr Poynter one day and heard him lament the downfall of Douay. He said quietly to the priest, 'Sir, would ten thousand pounds help you to meet the difficulty? If so, you shall have it.' In July 1795 he made over £2,000 to Bishop Douglass; the rest would follow after his death, which occurred several months later. In addition to this gift, up until the French invasion of Rome in 1798, the Pope continued to provide an annual pension originally intended for Douay and now divided between Old Hall and Crook Hall.

With the help of this funding, St Edmund's was thus reconstituted as the 'New Douay', with the agreement of Bishop Berington of the Midland District and Bishop Walmesley of the Western District. Bishop Gibson continued to support his own foundation at Crook Hall, although Douglass hoped that his mind would change once things were running at Old Hall Green. Indeed, Dr Stapleton was appointed first President of St Edmund's on the condition that he would resign 'when all the secular clergy Bishops shall unite to form a general College at Old Hall Green'. In the meantime, he would have 'the same powers for the internal government thereof as the President had in Doway in College'.[24]

Above: The original crucifix was presented by The Edmundian Association in 1876 in memory of John Sone who left £10,000 to build the College in 1795. It was blown down in a gale in 1903 and the bronze corpus was destroyed. A temporary terra cotta corpus was erected, and this was replaced eight years later with a new bronze figure. The terra cotta figure is now in the graveyard next to the College chapel.

Left: John Sone, from a portrait which hangs in the College.

The out-going President of the school, Fr Potier, continued to reside at St Edmund's 'as Pastor of the country congregation and convictor at the President's table'.[25]. He effectively became the first 'parish priest' of Old Hall Green and Ward notes that 'he was greatly beloved by the people, and much respected in the neighbourhood' though on handing over the institution to Stapleton also passed on a deficit that mounted up to over £500.

According to the earliest surviving copy of the Rules:

The College of St Edmund is instituted for the purpose of promoting the good of religion and society by forming Catholic youth, particularly of the London District, to the duties of the sacred ministry, or of civil life, according to each one's respective vocation. The exercises of piety, the course of studies, and the rules of discipline to be followed for the attainment of these ends, shall be the same as were established for the College at Douay, with such alterations and improvements, as the change of circumstances requires.[26]

The College remained under the patronage of St Edmund of Abingdon, together with St Gregory the Great, St Augustine of Canterbury, St Thomas of Canterbury and St Charles Borromeo (on whose feasts a High Mass was sung) as well as St Bede and St Erconwald (a Saxon bishop of London).

The daily timetable changed little until the 'New Rules' of 1852. Students rose at 6am and went to the chapel for Meditation and Mass, although the younger students (or, from 1818, the lay boys) were exempt from the former. Before breakfast (at 8.30am) there was a study period and then lessons for the rest of the morning until 12.45pm. Dr Poynter introduced a quarter of an hour's recreation at 11.30am around 1801. Dinner was served at 1pm, followed by recreation, before lessons resumed at 3pm. There were further fifteen-minute recreations at 5.15pm and 6.45pm. At 7pm the students went to the refectory for supper, followed by recreation and, at 8.30pm, Night Prayers. The 'children' then went to bed, while the older students undertook spiritual reading for fifteen minutes. All lights had to be out by 10pm. On half play-days – Tuesday, Thursday and Saturday – there was a longer morning recreation (9am-10am) and a free afternoon up until 5.45pm.

The course of studies closely followed the venerable Douay tradition, although the philosophy course was reduced to one year. Thus the whole course, from Third Rudiments to the end of Theology, lasted eleven and a half years. The philosophers and theologians had monthly disputations and repetitions and a Divine was asked to preach a 'sermon' each Sunday after Vespers. Church students had an hour's worth of tuition in plain chant each week and there were regular exhibitions in elocution.

Above: The citation on the Crucifix reads:

TO THE GOOD MEMORY
OF JOHN SONE
OUTSTANDING BENEFACTOR
OF THIS COLLEGE
THIS MEMORIAL WAS DEDICATED
BY THE EDMUNDIAN ASSOCIATION
IN THE YEAR OF OUR LORD 1876

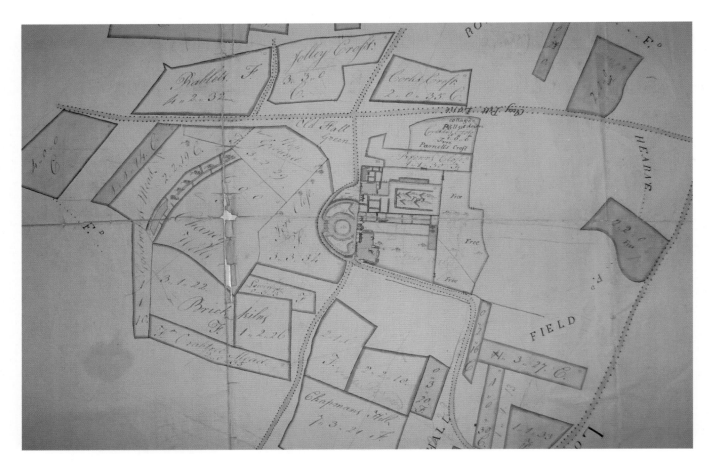

Above: The oldest existing estate plan of between 1769 and 1795.

Below: A close-up reveals sketches of the facades of individual buildings

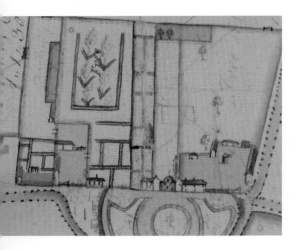

The original chapel was initially in the loft of the Old Hall. Following the 1791 Relief Act, which allowed the building of Catholic churches under certain conditions, a more appropriate chapel was built both for students and local Catholics. This was opened by Douglass on 9 December 1792. By modern standards this 'Parish Chapel' was tiny, 35 feet long, but just about large enough for the 25 or so boys. With the coming of the Douatians there must have been a distinct lack of space, although it was here that Douglass 'instituted' the new College of St Edmund in November 1793.

While making Old Hall Green 'England's College Home', the ecclesiastical authorities kept an anxious eye on the original English Catholic property in France. A brief period of peace in 1797 allowed for Francis Tuite (Procurator at St Edmund's) and Thomas Cleghorn to spend three months at St Omer, where they managed to reclaim a few valuables. A similar visit to Douay was prevented by the resumption of hostilities. Dr Stapleton seemed to expect one day to return to St Omer, where he had been President, and in 1797 there was even talk he would leave Old Hall to become Rector of the English College, Rome. As Ward points out, 'his loss to St Edmund's at that time, however, would have been very serious, and it was a matter of thankfulness, so far as Old Hall was concerned, that the disturbed state of Rome in the following spring brought these negotiations to a sudden termination'.[27]

Cat.

THINGS are indeed changed from the time of which Mr. Bower gives some reminiscences in the "History of the College." After relating how Lord Grimston in vain petitioned the President (Dr. Griffiths) to allow three of the leading cricketers of the College to play for the county in some important match, he goes on to say, "but our great game was Cat, and there was always in those days more enthusiasm exhibited at the latter game that even at the best House Cricket Matches." Cat being a traditional game, will probably never die out here, but it is safe to predict that it will never regain its former popularity. Still the Cat season was very successful this year.

———

There were more games played than there have been for the last five or six years, and much more spirit and interest manifested in them.

———

The play too is decidedly improving. There are quite a number of good hitters, and some smart fielders ; but the feeding is extremely bad : there is hardly a single good feeder.

CAT

This game is thought to have originated at Douay; it certainly was brought to St Edmund's from France and is similar to the 'cat' once played at Ushaw. 'Cat' involved a ring in which nine or seven holes were placed at equidistant spaces, one of which was the 'Feeding Hole' where the Striker (of the innings side) was stationed. There were two teams of nine players and the game operated in a similar way to rounders.

According to William Bower, 'in "Cat" out and in players are always employed, whilst in cricket nine out of eleven are merely watching the play. Almost all the Professors joined in the game of "Cat". I remember Fr Albery striking a ball from the feedhole close to the College wall, into the oak tree now in the cricket field but then outside the Bounds wall. No other College had such cat-balls as ours made of worsted wound whilst wet. Every week the Public Keeper came round with a lottery in which the Blanks were real prizes, for if you drew not a blank it was "make a cat-ball or pay 6d." A jar of water with the worsted in it was handed to you. When made the balls were securely wrapped in many folds of paper and sent to the oven. These balls would rebound 20 feet'.[29]

'Cat' was regularly played by Edmundians until the early twentieth century. Indeed, one of the highlights of the 1893 centenary was a match between 'Past' and 'Present'. The younger team won. However, it was clear that the game was no longer as popular as it had once been. The first edition of *The Edmundian* complained that 'the art of covering cat-balls is rapidly dying out; all the balls last year had to be covered by the same two or three good Samaritans. Will some of the rising generation come to the rescue, and prevent the art from being lost?'[30] By the end of 1894 it was reported that 'many of the present Edmundians have a positive dislike to this game, and that at times it is very difficult to get up a big game of Cat'.[31]

Above left: Extracts from the Edmundian, July 1893.

Above right: An illustration showing a game of 'Cat' circa 1846.

Below: Two 'Cat' sticks preserved at the College.

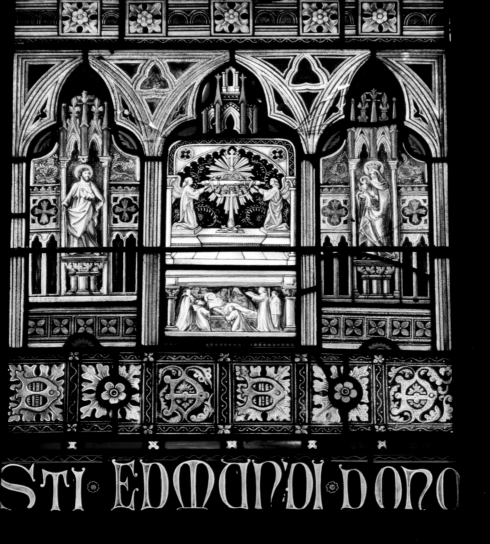

STI · EDMUNDI · DONO

'THE WISDOM OF OUR FIRST FOUNDERS, THOSE SAINTLY
MEN WHO PASSED THE GREAT PORTION OF THEIR LIVES IN
EXILE BECAUSE OF PERSECUTION, CHOSE OUT OF THE MANY
SUITABLE SAINTS – ST EDMUND OF CANTERBURY TO BE THE
PATRON OF THIS COLLEGE.

It seems to me that gentleness is distinctly the characteristic quality of his life. Though I know
not their reason for choosing him, their early action in setting the form and giving a character to
this College seems to me to have shown their appreciation of his gentleness; and therefore that
their desire was that gentleness should be the character of the training to be given in this place.'[28]

(Bishop Cahill of Portsmouth, from a sermon preached at St Edmund's on 24 May 1905)

ST EDMUND

This 'gentle' saint, St Edmund, was born in Abingdon around 1175. His father, Reginald was given the epithet 'Rich' on account of his success as a tradesman, though tradition claims that he later turned his back on the world and joined the monastery of Eynsham. The saint's mother Mabel lived an austere life of penance and was a strong influence on her children. St Edmund studied at Oxford and Paris. As a young man, he made a vow of chastity and exchanged rings with a statue of Our Lady. He was one of the first to teach Aristotle at Oxford. He is also the first known Master of Arts at that University and the house that he used became St Edmund's Hall ('Teddy Hall').

He soon shifted his attention to theology – apparently after a dream in which his dead mother questioned him reproachfully about the geometric diagrams he was studying and, taking his hand, drew three circles in which she wrote 'Father, Son, Holy Spirit'. 'My dear son', she said, 'henceforth apply yourself to no figures other than these'. St Edmund was ordained a priest, continuing to teach at Oxford and show great pastoral care for his students. He produced various written works, including his influential *Speculum ecclesie*, a treatise on the spiritual life. In 1222 he became Treasurer at Salisbury – at the time the splendid new cathedral was being built – and also looked after the rural parish of Calne. In 1227 he was chosen to preach the Sixth Crusade throughout England.

Finally, in 1233, St Edmund was reluctantly appointed Archbishop of Canterbury. With the help of a strong team, including his Chancellor St Richard of Chichester, he did much to promote peace, reform ecclesiastical discipline and defend the rights of the Church. If he was 'gentle', he was not afraid to make bold decisions. His episcopate was overshadowed by conflicts over ecclesiastical jurisdiction, most notably with the monks of his own Cathedral. He died on 16 November 1240 at Soisy (France) while on his way to Rome to meet with the Pope and was buried at the Cistercian Abbey at nearby Pontigny, where he had been staying (though he never went into 'voluntary exile' there, as some writers suggest, perhaps to make comparisons with St Thomas).

St Edmund was canonised in 1246 by Innocent IV. A chapel was soon built in his honour at Dover – unusually this was dedicated by his friend, St Richard, shortly before his own death in 1253. The Society of St Edmund ('Edmundites') was founded at Pontigny in 1843 by Fr Jean Baptiste Muard to organise missions and spread the Gospel in France. After the separation of Church and State, the Edmundites established themselves around the world and for a time ran the parish and school at Hitchin.

Left: Details from the widow in the sanctuary of the College chapel depicting the death of St Edmund. The panel is a representation of the altar and shrine of the saint as it existed in 1884. This window was destroyed by a bomb blast in 1940 and replaced in 1952.

Above right: St Edmund depicted in the centre of the lower row in the East Window of the College chapel. He is bearing his archiepiscopal cross.

CHAPTER IV

THE NEW COLLEGE: DOUGLASS AND POYNTER
1795–1817

A reconstituted College demanded new buildings and the designs were entrusted to James Taylor of Islington, who would later also be responsible for Ushaw College. His son, James Molyneux Taylor, had been educated at Old Hall. Although later dismissed by Pugin as the 'Priest Factory', the 'New College' was an impressive statement by the Catholic community. Indeed Sir Nikolaus Pevsner, the great architectural historian, wrote that the new buildings were 'an enterprise comparable in scale only with College work at Oxford and Cambridge, but far exceeding what English public schools did at that time'.[32]

The foundation stone was laid on 15 August 1795 and work was commenced by a team of six bricklayers and eight carpenters, under the direction of Taylor. Bricks were made in a huge brickfield in front of the College. However, it took four years for the work to be completed. This was caused by a number of factors. Most seriously, work was delayed by a long Chancery suit, when Mr Sone's brother-in-law disputed the money left to St Edmund's. For over a year the new buildings were unroofed and the old College had to be mortgaged to the banker in order to raise necessary funds. Further complexities arose with the 'Triple Assessment Act' of 1797, a special war levy which increased the taxation of the College considerably. The workmen, also, had no formal contract and during hay and harvest times they could often be found working on local farms, where the pay was better. Moreover, the original plans had to be adapted when news reached Old Hall of the purchase of Ushaw by Bishop Gibson in December 1799. Although there had long been a separation between north and south, Douglass never gave up hope that a national 'general College' might be established in Hertfordshire.

By 1799 building work had resumed and continued at a brisk pace. In the meantime, a notable incident occurred that Maundy Thursday (21 March) in the old chapel. The students had assembled there early in the morning. It did not take them long to realise that the Tabernacle had disappeared and that the plate had gone from the sacristy. Thieves had obviously visited the College during the night. Two Irishmen who had behaved strangely in the chapel during Mass on Palm Sunday were immediately suspected and it was noted that two French servants had only recently left the College. The President suggested that, being so heavy, the thieves had probably left the tabernacle nearby after removing what they thought was valuable. A search was quickly made and the Blessed Sacrament, along with the Tabernacle, was found dumped in a pond, near what later became the entrance to Allen Hall. Various traditions were passed down embellishing the story, involving trees bowing their branches, nearby sheep gathered around the pond on their knees and a mysterious light seen on the water. The profanation undoubtedly caused a great sensation and over subsequent years a service of reparation was held each year on Maundy Thursday. In 1875 The Edmundian Association built a small memorial chapel at the end of the 'New Wing', close to the pond, with a mosaic of Christ walking on the waters. This was incorporated into the Divine's Oratory, opened in 1905, now the Staff Parlour, while the mosaic can be found beside the entrance to the Refectory.

Above: The mosaic of Christ walking on the waters.

Left: The ceiling of the entrance, or 'Introitum', to the Ambulacrum

Above: The Bibliotheca Tyronica in the Ambulacrum was renamed from the Museum in 1908. In 1970 it was refitted as the 'Southworth Room' as a reading room for Rhetoric. In 1993 it became the study of the Priest-in-Residence.

ORIGINAL NAMES OF THE ROOMS OFF THE AMBULACRUM (FROM NORTH TO SOUTH)

Studium	Study	
Museum	Museum	Before 1908
Bibliotheca Tyronica	Boys' Library	After 1908
Schola Musices	Music School	Before 1908
Lusorium	Playroom	After 1908
Introitum	Entrance	
Hospitium	Hospitality	
Exedrium	Sitting Room	
Bibliotheca	Library	

By the autumn of 1799 the new building was nearing completion. Bishop Douglass wrote in his Diary:

1799. On this day (September 29th), sacred to St Michael, we entered the new College. I blessed the College by going to each gallery, praying in each according to the Ritual (Benedictio domus novae), sprinkling each with Holy Water, and sang Mass in Pontificalibus in the new Chapel; and at Dinner treated the Professors and the Students with wine. [33]

However, the students did not move in until the beginning of 1800. There was accommodation for sixty-five students, with a dormitory on the top floor and new meeting rooms, playrooms and libraries (including the Bibliotheca Tyronica). In recognition of the architect's work, it was decided 'to educate *gratis* in this College his sons and all the sons he may have by Mrs Taylor his present or any future wife'.[34]

THE COLLEGE UNDER DR POYNTER

Dr Stapleton moved over to the new 'President's Room' in 1800 but his days at Old Hall were numbered. That autumn he was sent to Rome on 'a deputation of equal secrecy and importance,' concerning the validity of the secret marriage, confected fifteen years previously, between the Prince Regent and Mrs Fitzherbert, a Catholic. On returning home, Stapleton was appointed to succeed Bishop Berington as Vicar Apostolic of the Midland District and consecrated bishop at St Edmund's on 8 March 1801 by Bishop Douglass, assisted by Bishops Sharrock (of the Western District) and Moylan (of Cork). Ward surmised that 'this seems to have been the first occasion that the full number of three Bishops took part in a consecration ceremony. Hitherto it had been customary to use the privilege conceded to England for two priests to assist the consecrating Bishop'.[35] The new Bishop, however, was declining in health. He died the following year while visiting his beloved St Omer and thus the first President of St Edmund's was buried in the cemetery of St Martin-au-Laërt.

Stapleton's successor at St Edmund's was his trusty deputy, William Poynter. Soon after taking office, he had to make an unpopular decision caused by poor harvests:

The Administrators of St Edmund's College beg leave to represent to those Parents and Guardians who have honoured them with their confidence, that the extraordinary pressure of the present time and the unexampled dearness of every article of life, particularly of wheat, have reduced them to the painful alternative, either of raising their terms for a limited period, or of considerably diminishing the conveniences and comforts which the students enjoy. This latter plan, they are convinced, would meet with the general disapprobation of their friends. They have, therefore, adopted a resolution which is fully justified by the necessity of the case, of making an addition of £6 6s. 0d. to the annual pension of each student. This temporary demand, which is to commence on the 15th day of April, 1801, and to continue till wheat has fallen to the price of 4 per quarter, must be approved by all who take into consideration the peculiar hardship of the present calamitous period. However painful it may be to resort to this expedient, the Administrators have the fullest assurance that the necessity of the measure will not admit of a doubt, and under this impression they venture to appeal to the good sense and candour of their numerous and respectable friends.[36]

On 29 May 1803 St Edmund's saw another episcopal consecration: this time of the President himself, who had been appointed coadjutor to Bishop Douglass. The previous week John Milner was consecrated as Vicar Apostolic of the Midland District and the two ceremonies allowed a much-needed 'synod' of the English bishops, together with invited clergy, part of which took place at Old Hall.

Despite his onerous new duties, Bishop Poynter remained President of the College for a further ten years. He added to Taylor's buildings (despite the architect's disapproval) and provided the 'New Chapel and Refectory,' completed in 1805 at the cost of £1,550. These are now the Religious Education classrooms and Library. When Bernard Ward wrote the first College history, the appearance of the 'new' chapel was still within living memory:

The altar stood at the north end, the sanctuary being still discernible by the raised floor and vaulted roof. Behind the altar stood a picture, generally understood to represent St Edmund, but in reality a copy of the celebrated picture of St Andrew Corsini, in the Palazzo Corsini at Rome. The chapel was entered by the double doors underneath the organ gallery, which are now fastened up. The entrance in use at the present day then led to the sacristy, which was in the place now occupied by the passage at the end of the Ambulacrum. Over one of these doors stood the picture of St Charles Borromeo, which is now over the door of the "New Chapel."

The boys all knelt facing the altar, but there were stalls for the Divines and priests, and the old black "eagle" – now at St Thomas's Seminary – stood in the middle of the choir. In front of the stalls on each side stood a large iron bookstand, on which the plain chant books were placed. These stands, the work of a Puckeridge blacksmith, rough as they were, served their purpose, and prevented the necessity of the singers continually coming out to a central lectern. Some of the old boys used to tell how they went down in a party to Puckeridge in the year 1805, while the chapel was building, and carried the lecterns home upon their shoulders.[37]

BEHIND THE ALTAR STOOD A PICTURE, GENERALLY THOUGHT TO REPRESENT ST EDMUND.

Above: The copy of a portrait of St Andrew Corsini now hangs in the Sacristy.

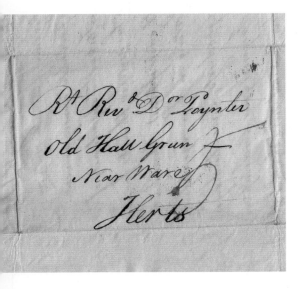

A student of the 1820s recalled the intense cold of the chapel, so much so that 'the water in the cruet for Mass froze in the very short time since it had come from the Sacristy'.[38]

The chapel was opened on the Feast of the Assumption 1805. The same year College Medals were struck for the first time, with a representation of the new buildings and, on the reverse, the allegorical figures of Science and Religion, and the motto *Religioni ac Bonis Artibus* ('For Religion and Culture'). 'Three medals of this description are to be annually presented,' the Prefect of Studies explained, 'one to the greatest proficient in the art of speaking, the second to that student in Rhetoric who, on an average calculation, shall have gained the superiority over his school-fellows in his exercises in the Latin, Greek, English, and French languages. The third is to be presented to the student in Poetry who shall have gained the same superiority'. The aim was 'to excite a spirit of emulation and to promote the cause of learning'.[39]

The horrors of the Revolution were still fresh in people's minds and the progress of the war with France was carefully followed. In 1804 the College successfully appealed against an order that the older students should serve time in the Hertford Militia. In the event of Napoleon's invasion, a contingency plan was devised whereby the College community would seek refuge in either Cambridgeshire or Huntingdonshire, a safe distance away from London. News of Nelson's victory at Trafalgar in November 1805 was greeted enthusiastically and the professors were allowed wine.

Above: A letter addressed to Dr Poynter in connection with the 'Great Affair' of 1809.

Below: John Talbot, 16th Earl of Shrewsbury, the great-nephew of Bishop James Talbot, was one of the ringleaders of the 'Great Affair'.

THE 'GREAT AFFAIR' OF 1809

As Vicar Apostolic Bishop Poynter had less time to devote to College affairs and, especially as Bishop Douglass' health declined, he was frequently away for meetings and visitations. This led to a breakdown in management and discipline at St Edmund's and a period of financial anxiety.

Old Edmundians wrote years later of the poor 'ecclesiastical' spirit at the time. One recalled that 'things were not well regulated for students destined for the Church. We were all mixed with future Lords, Earls, and Dukes, and other lay students, who, at the end of each vacation, used to return full of London news and London pleasures, and I got more harm than good from such conversation'. Poynter himself referred to church students being 'often discouraged and sometimes laughed out of their vocation by the young gentlemen of the world'.[40] The situation was not helped by the comparatively small number of Church Boys, especially after the Northern and Midland students were lost to Ushaw and Oscott respectively. Between 1800 and 1815 only seventeen men were ordained from St Edmund's and in the year of Waterloo Poynter reported there were only 88 priests serving an estimated 69,000 Catholics in the London District. The shortage of priests also meant a shortage of available teaching staff that would be able adequately to continue the Douay tradition.

Rumours spread of the President's absenteeism, the lack of order and state of material and moral neglect. Poynter himself wrote that during the two winters prior to 1809 some students 'were in the habit of going out from the College in the evening principally for the purpose of procuring Spirituous liquours' and that 'in summer moreover they went out with a view to bathe,' which was considered highly dangerous.[41]

The underlying discontent among the students led to 'the Great Affair' of October 1809. The President was away administering the sacrament of Confirmation in his native Hampshire and his deputy, the unpopular Fr Tuite (who many feared would soon take over as President), refused a play-day since one had already been granted that week. In fact, he had promised Poynter that only one extra play day would be given during his absence. A Poet also received a summons for a thrashing, a punishment normally reserved for younger boys, because he had missed the morning Meditation due to his feeling indisposed. The result was open rebellion from many of the students, as Fr Tuite reported:

They proceeded to Haddam [sic] and there rioted in an Inn the whole Evening. They Drank, Smoked, broke every bowl and glass served up, and returned through Standon, alarming every inhabitant in the place. They reached the College at Nine armed with thick sticks and proceeded to their respective apartments.[42]

The following day, 7 October, about thirty students walked as far as Waltham Cross and stayed at an inn, where they wrote to Fr Tuite:

Sir, From the discontent so generally prevalent amongst the students, we have been under the disagreeable necessity of having recourse to these measures; and to obtain a promise of a total remission of punishment of any kind, and better treatment, is the motive which actuates us to address these few lines to you. Should this be complied with, we will immediately return to the College and to our duty. But if not, it is our firm resolution not to return to the College, and to persevere in the measures we have adopted. Think not this the impulse of a moment, nor the idle boast of inexperienced youth. Our means are equal to our perseverance and more than may be imagined, and our perseverance is such as will ensure success. We rely upon your honour for no equivocation concerning punishment, and that your answer will include that of Dr Poynter. It will be needless to except any individual in the remission of punishment, as there is not one who has taken a more active part in it than another. We solicit a clear and unequivocal answer to every article contained in the above. If we receive an answer suitable to our expectations, we shall comply with your desires. In case you should think it necessary to have a personal interview, we shall receive you with respect; but should your intentions be to enforce our return, they will be totally useless, as in that case we shall oppose force to force. Our words of honour are given not to deviate from any particular of the above.
Waltham Cross, 5¼ of the clock.
October 7th, 1809.[43]

The horrified Fr Tuite sent for the President and also informed the Chief Constable at Ware and the College agent in London, Fr John Jones. The 'fugitives' meanwhile had dispersed in order to avoid the Hertfordshire police; one group had headed north, hoping eventually to reach Scotland, while the other travelled to London. This latter group were soon apprehended and agreed to return to Old Hall, providing they should not be punished until they had presented their grievances to Bishop Poynter. The more adventurous party was eventually found at an inn in Stilton, then in Huntingdonshire.

THEY DRANK, SMOKED, BROKE EVERY BOWL AND GLASS SERVED UP, AND RETURNED THROUGH STANDON, ALARMING EVERY INHABITANT IN THE PLACE.

AN EDMUNDIAN AT WATERLOO

Michael Browne (1793-1825) was son of the Earl of Kenmare and a student at St Edmund's between 1801 and 1809. Around 1812 he became Ensign in the 40th Regiment of Foot (2nd Somersetshire Regiment) and fought with Wellington in the Peninsula War. He was seriously injured at Waterloo on 18 June 1815, although tradition states that his life was saved by an officer in the French Cuirassiers, who recognised him as a fellow Edmundian. Captain Browne (as he became) never fully recovered and died ten years later, aged 31.[48]

Above: The entrance to the old 1818 parish church in Old Hall Green.

Above right: The altar in the old parish church.

Below: A floor plan of 1799 showing side wings which were never built.

THE PARISH OF OLD HALL GREEN

Although the present church of St Edmund and the English Martyrs only dates back to 1911, Old Hall Green is actually the oldest Catholic parish in Hertfordshire – and for many years was the only public chapel in the county. The first parishioners had to share the small chapel in the attic of Old Hall's south wing with the students of the Academy. In 1793 a separate chapel was built alongside Old Hall, replaced in 1818 by a larger structure which today houses the squash courts.

Of all the parishes in the Archdiocese of Westminster, Old Hall Green boasts the greatest number of priests, who, due to the speedy change-over in College staff, typically served for a few years. The first was Fr James Willacy (1769-92).

It is important to note that Edmundian priests made an important contribution in the revival of Catholicism in the area and for many years celebrated Mass in the chapels at St Albans, Hertford, Ware, Buntingford, Hare Street, Puckeridge, Much Hadham, Furneaux Pelham and Walkern, as well as over the county border in Essex. St Edmund's is truly the cradle of the Catholic Revival in Hertfordshire.

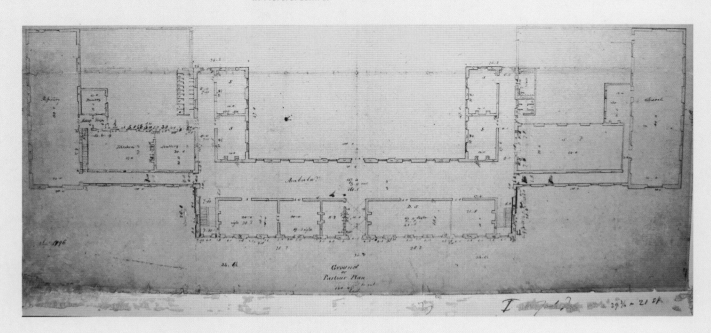

Above: An architect's elevation of the new College in 1795. This was one of three alternative designs considered.

According to Fr Tuite, one of the 'Grand Leaders' was John Talbot, who 'has not only Expended all his own Cash but has borrowed more to support his infamous cause and I hear they have Cash to a very large amount amongst them'. This, of course, was the John Talbot who boasted Bishop Talbot as his great-uncle and who would later become sixteenth Earl of Shrewsbury. In the end, the three ringleaders were expelled and eight others left of their own accord. Tuite resigned shortly afterwards, returning to the mission where he eventually acted as Vicar General to the London District, and Robert Varley was soon relieved of his duties as Prefect. Bernard Ward noted that 'the people who profited most by the whole affair were the inn-keepers and chaise proprietors. They evidently took in the situation and saw what class of people they had to deal with. They gave unlimited credit, but when the bills came in the charges were exorbitant'.[44]

Old Hall Green, meanwhile, had lost the confidence of many parents and benefactors and its student numbers, finances and morale continued to decline. It is significant that the following year the school's former President, Fr Potier, left to found a new school at Puckeridge, which then moved to Shefford, Bedfordshire in 1813. It is likely that Fr Potier was disillusioned with the regime at St Edmund's and that his institution acted as an alternative and a refuge for disaffected families, including some distinguished names. An advertisement in the Laity's Directory of 1814 stated that the school accommodated 'those parents who are unwilling to expose their children, at so tender an age, to the inconveniences necessarily attendant on more extensive establishments' and that 'the young gentlemen will be treated on every occasion with all the kindness and attention which the most affectionate parent can desire'.[45]

A Period of Transition

Above: Bishop William Poynter was President of St Edmund's between 1801 and 1813. This portrait hangs at the College.

On 8 May 1812 Bishop Douglass died after a long illness and was buried at Old St Pancras cemetery. His Requiem was graced by the presence of six French bishops, all refugees from the Napoleonic regime, and the preacher, Fr Lewis Havard, stated that Douglass 'considered St Edmund's College as claiming his first, his fostering concern, because it is the only remaining nursery from which the faithful of this district can expect an adequate supply of spiritual instructors'.[46]

The death of the founder of St Edmund's had an immediate impact on the College. Now Vicar Apostolic in his own right, Bishop Poynter reluctantly resigned from the Presidency at Midsummer 1813. He was succeeded by Fr Joseph Kimbell, who tried to keep a 'tight hand' on the boys but failed to improve the prospects of the College. He soon became disillusioned and offered his resignation in 1816, which was turned down by Bishop Poynter. To help his cause, some promising changes were made to the teaching staff: Fr Mark Tierney, who later became a well-respected historian, arrived as Professor of Mathematics, while the new Vice-President was Fr Thomas Griffiths, who since his ordination two years previously had worked at the preparatory school and Old Hall mission. Indeed, under his guidance the building of a new 'parish church' was commenced, though it was not completed until 1818. This still stands and is used as squash courts. Another material change dating from Fr Kimbell's Presidency was the purchase of 'Riggory's Farm' in 1813, expanding the College estate and income.

Fr Kimbell, however, seemed not to be at ease managing the College and his resignation was accepted the second time round on 11 February 1817. It was not until June that his successor was announced and it caused great surprise: Dr John Bew, the founder of Oscott, who since 1808 had been serving the Catholics of Brighton. Bishop Poynter wrote in a circular that 'the talents and estimable qualities of Dr Bew, as likewise his experience acquired by having long respectably filled a similar situation, are so well known and so highly appreciated, that to dwell on them must be wholly superfluous'.[47] Dr Bew set to work, beginning repairs and minor improvements to the building and fostering the ecclesiastical spirit that had been in decline. He made an important change in separating the church and lay students and designating the old house as the 'Ecclesiastical Seminary' for the younger Church Boys in the classes of Grammar and Second and Third Rudiments. The 'seminarians' were placed under the guidance of Fr Thomas Griffiths, who introduced monthly half-day retreats and the wearing of cassocks, with removable skirts and without the Roman collar (a later development). This was quite an innovation, for hitherto cassocks had only been used in choir. Poynter, who himself liked to wear a brown suit, represented the established view when he remarked: 'Church dress for Church use, Sir.'

The other boys remained in the new College. Student numbers increased but the new President soon became weighed down by worries about the debt he had inherited and failing health. In December 1817 he resigned and returned to Brighton, before taking up a chaplaincy at Brockhampton.

SEEKING FRENCH COMPENSATION

Above: An engraving of the College from the 'Catholic Gentleman's Magazine' in 1818.

The buildings of the English College, Douay continued to be used as a military hospital, a cotton factory and (from 1834) a barracks. Though in poor condition, they were only demolished in 1926. Though it seemed unlikely that the English would ever return, a key concern was the recovery of the debt owed after the confiscation of the Colleges in France. The 1814 Treaty of Paris offered compensation to all British subjects who had suffered from French confiscatory decrees since 1793. Bishop Poynter crossed the Channel four times to appeal to the French government and even secured the support of Louis XVIII and the Duke of Wellington.

It was eventually settled that £120,000 should be paid in compensation and Poynter hoped to use this money for the education of priests in England. However, in November 1825 the British government decided to prevent the money from reaching the Catholic community since it would be used for 'superstitious purposes'. Different theories abound as to the eventual fate of the confiscated money: variously spent on furnishing Windsor Castle, the building of Marble Arch or the construction of the Royal Pavilion at Brighton. Meanwhile, an arrangement was made with the French Government for the administration of the *fondations anglaises*. By 1826 it seems that three English students were using surviving bursaries from the old English Colleges to study at the Paris seminary of St-Nicolas-du-Chardonnet. The bishops continued to be preoccupied by the issue into the twentieth century; a 1907 Memorandum declared that 'the claims of the English Bishops at the present day are the same as those of their predecessors at the beginning of the last century'.

CHAPTER V

GRIFFITHS AND THE COLLEGE
1817–1850

Thomas Griffiths has a special relationship with St Edmund's. Entering as a student on 5 January 1805, he became the first English bishop since the Reformation to receive all his priestly formation on home soil. Moreover, Bernard Ward wrote that the College owed more to Griffiths 'than to any other man, living or dead'.

After his ordination in 1814, Griffiths began teaching in the Preparatory School and, from 1815, took charge of the mission at Old Hall Green. The Catholics of the surrounding area used to attend Mass in the little chapel of the Preparatory School and, as already mentioned, it was Griffiths who raised the money to build a larger chapel. According to Ward, 'the interior decorations were plain, and the whole was devoid of beauty, but it answered its purpose'.[49]

In 1816 Griffiths was named Vice-President and two years later was appointed Dr Bew's successor as President, despite the fact he had only been ordained four years and was aged 27. It was decided that henceforth St Edmund's would be a solely ecclesiastical College and up to thirty lay boys were dismissed, though the Preparatory School continued as a lay establishment. Dr Bew's separate 'Ecclesiastical Seminary' was therefore no longer necessary and the students now lived once again under one roof. By 1818 there were forty students, including ten philosophers. Then in 1819 things changed again. Lay boys were once more admitted to the College but had separate dormitories, playrooms and 'bounds'. It was a necessary reconstitution which restored confidence in the College and led to increasing student numbers. Alumni from this period included Charles Baggs (later Rector of the English College, Rome and Vicar Apostolic of the Western District), Edward Cox (a future President) and the twelfth Lord Petre.

Griffiths was an able administrator and kept a careful eye on College finances. He made several economies: the window tax was lessened, for example, by replacing the glass windows in the Divines' rooms with wooden shutters. A recollection of Griffiths was recorded in the Edmundian of 1903 by William Bower, who entered the College in September 1827. Bower later returned to end his days there, the much-loved 'Old Man' who died aged ninety in 1905:

Though it is 76 years ago, I remember all as if it had only been yesterday. The President, Dr Griffiths, a small figure beside my father's stalwart form, was dressed in a University gown, and his hair, trimmed pied de cheval as it was called, was very closely cut and well powdered. He gave us a very kind greeting and taking me by the hand when my father was leaving me said "you must now consider me as your father," and during all the years I was here he ever held that kind position.[50]

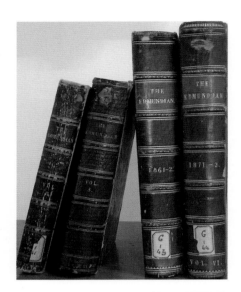

St Edmund's became a well-known centre of Catholicism and the only Mass centre for miles around. Two regular visitors in the late 1820s were the Cambridge converts, Ambrose Phillipps de Lisle (father of the future Edmundian VC) and Kenelm Digby. On Sunday they would often be seen riding the twenty-six miles from Cambridge to Old Hall, while still keeping their Eucharistic fast. A twentieth century biographer of Phillipps wrote that 'much as the attendance at Mass at St Edmund's must have meant to the two Cambridge men, the lack of harmony and beauty and the kind of antiquity that both admired so much in their surroundings, was surely a source of pain. So much so that the extreme care which Ambrose was later to devote to furnishings and decoration in his chapel at Grace Dieu [Leicestershire] would seem to have its origin in the experience of these earlier days'.[51]

Their visits to Old Hall were important, however, in nurturing their Faith and exciting their imagination. William Bower recalled that Kenelm Digby's 'well known *Mores Catholici* was written at St Edmund's, and the opening of that book is in fact a description of one of the College services'.[52] If that was the case, then Digby's pen transformed the humble Ambulacrum into a monastic cloister:

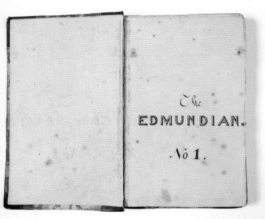

The hour was day's decline; and already had Placebo Domino been sung in solemn tones, to usher in the hours of special charity for those who are of the suffering church. A harsh sound from the simultaneous closing of as many books, cased in oak and iron, as there were voices in that full choir, like a sudden thunder-clash, announced the end of that ghostly vesper. The saintly men one by one slowly walked forth, each proceeding to his special exercise. Door then shutting after door gave long echoes, till all was mute stillness, and I was left alone under cloistered arches, to meditate on the felicity of blessed spirits, and on the desire that presses both the living and the inmates of that region in which the soul is purged from sinful stain, to join their happy company.[53]

Above: Some manuscript copies of
The Edmundian going back to 1841 still
exist in the College archives.

Bower himself was strongly affected by the College's ecclesiastical spirit. He remembered that the 'constantly recurring ordinations gave a tone to the whole house' and that 'many times during the year the Deacons used to preach in the Refectory on Sunday evenings, a custom brought from Douay, the President at the conclusion of the sermon giving his opinion not only of the matter but also of the delivery of the discourse'.[54]

On 26 November 1827 Bishop Poynter died, aged 66, and was buried at the newly constructed vault at St Mary Moorfields. This became one of the main burial sites for Catholics in the London area and its famous interments included the composer, Carl von Weber, though his body was later taken back to Germany. Poynter's heart was brought to the chapel of St Edmund's and placed 'in front of the high altar, under the spot where the priest used to stand to begin Mass'. There could be found 'a small square in the floor was movable, and if taken up, there could be seen underneath a case covered with purple velvet, with a metal plate on which was an inscription'.

The new Vicar Apostolic of the London District was the jovial James Yorke Bramston, unusual among the Vicars Apostolic for having been a convert and trained in the legal profession. He liked to jest that, being a Popish priest grafted on to a Protestant lawyer, he ought to be a match for any devil. Despite not having been trained in the Douay tradition, he became a great friend to St Edmund's. William Bower recalled that 'he had a kind and genial presence, a boy's heart, though burdened with many years. No visit passed without an hour or so in the play-room amongst us, whom he called his dear, very dear children'.[56] Aged sixty-four at the time of his succession to the London District, he soon acquired a Coadjutor Bishop in the person of Robert Gradwell, who had entered Douay in 1791 and served as Rector of the English College, Rome.

Above: A painting of the College from Foxhunters Lane, near Standon Lordship, by Kenelm Digby in 1829.

However Gradwell's health was fragile and he died in March 1833. Shortly afterwards, Dr Griffiths was appointed Coadjutor in his place. He was consecrated Titular Bishop of Olena at a five hour ceremony in the College chapel on 28 October. His association with St Edmund's meant that he was highly respected by many of the clergy, but it was feared that he lacked experience in the ways of the world since he had spent his entire adult life at the College. Like Poynter, he initially remained President despite his episcopal duties but finally resigned in April 1834. He continued to be a regular visitor, often spending Sunday at St Edmund's, where he could be refreshed by the country air and assist at High Mass.

THE PRESIDENCIES OF NEWELL AND ROLFE

Griffiths was replaced by perhaps the most enigmatic of Edmundian Presidents, Dr Richard Newell. A former Prefect of Studies, he served as President between 1834 and 1837, when he seems to have literally disappeared, deserting the post and leaving little trace behind him. At some stage he travelled across the Atlantic and formally left the Priesthood in 1854. Newell is said to have closely resembled Pope Pius VI, who died in French captivity two years after Newell's birth (1799). When a portrait was required of the President for the series hanging in the Ambulacrum, an image was used of the pontiff but with a different hairstyle.

Dr Newell was replaced by Fr John Rolfe, formerly Rector of St Mary Moorfields in the City of London. His Presidency, even briefer than that of Dr Newell, saw some important work to the College estate. The park in front of the main buildings was opened up, while Chestnut Drive was added and trees and shrubs were planted in the land recently purchased under the Standon Enclosure Act.

Below: An estate plan of 1839 from the College archives.

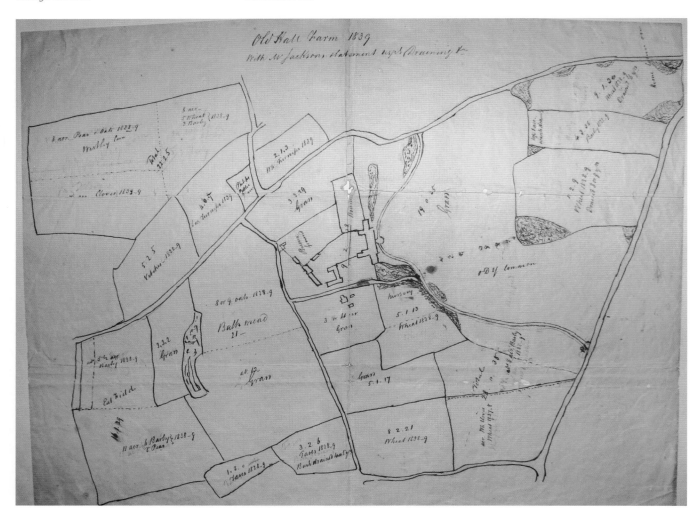

One of the students at the time, Frederick Rymer, recalled that 'the President, though an excellent priest and universally respected had had no experience of the management of youth, and proved in his own person that the administration of a parish and the administration of a College are two very distinct things'. His brother, George, had also arrived in the College as Procurator but this was not a happy appointment: 'in a subordinate position, full of life and spirit and energy he had been known to be somewhat reckless of rule, or to put it in its mildest form, and without insinuating the slightest harm in his character, he did not bear the reputation of being a model and earnest student. Such a one,' continued Rymer, 'on being taken suddenly from the midst of his companions and placed in a position of authority is, as is well known, apt to shew himself somewhat of a martinet and to provoke opposition'.[57] The result was a period of discontent and even rebellion, resulting in the expulsion of four students, including one Divine, in the Spring of 1840.

An important development occurred at the end of Rolfe's Presidency. On 8 June 1840 St Edmund's was affiliated to the newly-founded University of London. Among the first students to matriculate was James Danell, later bishop of Southwark. The College enjoyed some academic success: George Pringle took the first place in Classics in 1847 and Frederick Rymer, the future President, secured the fifth place in Mathematics in 1841. Unfortunately this was no reflection on teaching standards at the College, for he only discovered a few weeks before the exam, thanks to the visit of some Oxford men, that he had done no work on Analytical treatment. As a result, changes were made to the mathematical syllabus. Moreover, resources were extremely limited. Fr Alfred Dolman, who entered the College in 1839, 'used to tell of how a whole class had to work through their Greek translation with one Lexicon between them, and a boy possessing a Euclid for his exclusive use was a rare specimen'.[58]

Studying for London degrees was seen as a return to the Douay tradition, since one of the disadvantages of leaving France was the severance of links with the local University. For the next sixty years, until the College's affiliation with Cambridge, the older students could thus be prepared for the London degree in Arts – especially important since Catholics were not able to attend Oxford or Cambridge.

PRESIDENCY OF DR COX (1840-51)

In 1840 Fr Rolfe returned to Moorfields and was succeeded by his Vice-President, Dr Edward Cox, who had himself been a student at the College in the 1820s. Deeply conservative, Dr Cox sought to make no radical changes but nevertheless his Presidency proved to be momentous.

There were, firstly, several memorable events. Much excitement was caused on 25 October 1843 when Queen Victoria and Prince Albert passed the College on their way from Windsor to Cambridge. A triumphal arch was quickly erected and the College community assembled by the roadside, the professors and Divines in their gowns. So much energy was put into the cheering and waving of hats, that the College band forgot to strike up 'God save the Queen' as the cortege went by. This they managed to do on the royal party's return journey a few days later. Although a request to present the Queen with an Address was turned down, the Lord Chamberlain noted that the enthusiastic greeting had been 'duly observed and much admired'. Then, two years later, modest celebrations were held for the golden jubilee of the College's foundation under Douglass.

The Queen and Prince Albert on their return from Cambridge passing under the Triumphal Arch erected by their loyal subjects, the students of St Edmund's on 28 October 1843 (reproduced from The Edmundian of 12 November 1843).

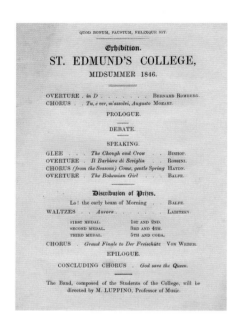

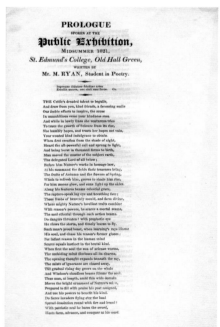

The 1840s also saw two student tragedies which were long remembered. The first concerned a young pupil, Charles Lynch, who had entered the school in 1840. On the afternoon of 7 January 1841 he went skating on the frozen River Rib, near Braughing, and fell in after the ice broke beneath him. 'I pulled the body to me with a hooked stick', the prefect in charge of the party, Henry Telford, later recounted, 'but when we got him out he was quite dead, having been apparently frozen to death by the cold. He was about fourteen years of age and was considered a good boy. He had been to the Sacraments very shortly before his death'.[59]

The other drowning gave rise to the famous 'Weld ghost story'. Philip Weld belonged to a well-known recusant family and was the nephew of Cardinal Thomas Weld. He entered the College in 1841. On Easter Thursday 1846 he went with some friends to Rye House, without the knowledge of the superiors, and began a happy afternoon on the River Lea. At about three o'clock, a certain movement threw Philip into the river. At first all seemed well, for the water only came up to his waist and he shouted, 'row the boat over to me'. These were his last words for he was suddenly sucked under the water and his body was only recovered after the Master of Enfield Lock had lowered the river. According to the boy's sister, when Dr Cox arrived with the sad news, Mr Weld said:

"You need not say one word, for I know that Philip is dead. Yesterday afternoon I was walking with my daughter Katherine and we suddenly saw him. He was standing on the path at the opposite side of the turnpike road, between two persons, one of whom was a youth dressed in a black robe. My daughter was the first to perceive them, and exclaimed, 'Oh, papa, did you ever see anything so like Philip as that is?' 'Like him!' I answered, 'why it is he!' Strange to say, my daughter thought nothing of the circumstance beyond that we had seen an extraordinary likeness of her brother. We walked on towards the three figures. Philip was looking with a smiling, happy expression of countenance at the young man in a black robe, who was shorter than himself. Suddenly they all seemed to me to have vanished; I saw nothing but the countryman whom I had before seen. I, however, said nothing to any one, as I was fearful of alarming my wife, I looked out anxiously for the post the following morning; to my delight no letter came (I forgot that letters from Ware came in the afternoon), and my fears were quieted. I thought no more of the extraordinary circumstance until I saw you in the carriage outside my gate. Then everything returned to my mind and I could not feel a doubt but that you came to tell me of the death of my dear boy."

A few months later the family was visiting relations at Leagram Hall, Lancashire, and Mr Weld suddenly stopped in front of a picture, exclaiming 'that is the person whom I saw with Philip. I do not know whose likeness it is supposed to be, but I am certain that that is the person whom I saw with Philip'. It turned out to be St Stanislaus Kostka, a Polish novice in the Society of Jesus who died in 1568 aged seventeen. The Weld boy, who was the same age, had had a devotion to the saint and, as it happened, he was also a patron of drowned men. Philip was buried at St Edmund's and later placed in the vaults under the sanctuary.[60]

A future President and Bishop, Fr William Weathers, became Prefect of Discipline in 1840. According to tradition,

On one occasion before the introduction of gas, a clandestine meeting had been arranged (with, no doubt, a second supper) to take place after night prayers in one of the student's rooms, the guests being met at the Post-box and transported on the shoulders of some hefty but bootless Christopher so as to avoid risk of discovery through the creaking floor-boards, and that Mr Weathers placed himself at the point of up-take and was borne triumphantly into the midst of the revellers to the consternation and immediate disruption of the party.[61]

Top: A drawing of the College from "Catholic Miscellany" in 1826.

Below: An image of St Stanilaus Kostka, a polish novice of the Society of Jesus. His untimely death was the month before the foundation of the English College in Douay. The representations of him are very varied – this is a statue of him in Houston, Texas.

Above: Pugin's original drawing of the Chapel, now in the College museum.

Below: Augustus Welby Pugin

'A Dream in Stone'[62]

Bishop Griffiths' great desire was the building of a new chapel at St Edmund's. From 1844, with the support of Dr Cox, he began putting his energies into the project. The existing chapel had been built by Poynter and witnessed a number of episcopal consecrations, but a larger and more dignified sanctuary was desperately needed. The Oxford convert, Frederick Oakeley, attended an ordination in the old chapel in 1846 and wrote that 'neither its construction nor its appendages were such as to enhance the dignity of the sacred offices celebrated within its walls', although he added that the 'truly paternal manner of administering the Ordination rite' of Bishop Griffiths was 'more than ample compensation for the want of external accessories to its celebration'.[63]

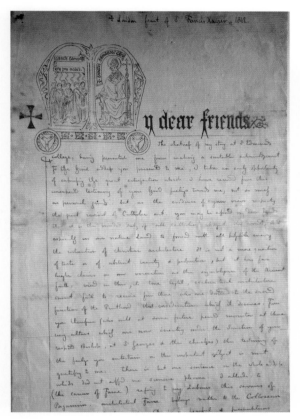

Above: An example of a letter from Pugin.

In 1845 Griffiths commissioned Augustus Welby Pugin, the great champion of the 'gothic revival,' to produce plans. He had already visited the College in 1842 and acknowledged an address presented to him by the students in an interesting letter, where he summarised his approach to architecture, which involved a moral and religious crusade:

It is not a mere question of taste, or of abstract beauty and proportion, but it has far higher claims on our veneration as the symbolism of the antient faith. Viewed in this, its true light, ecclesiastical architecture cannot fail to receive from those who are destined to the sacred function of the priesthood that consideration which it deserves.

He was, however, reluctant to be viewed as a celebrity architect:

It would be a fearful and presumptuous attempt in any man to exalt himself by means of the temples of God. It is a privilege and a blessing to work in the sanctuary. The majesty of the vast churches of antiquity is owing to the sublime mysteries of the Christian faith and the solemnity of its rites. The ancient builders felt this. They knew the small share they could claim in the glories they produced, and their humility exceeded their skill. How unbecoming then would it be for any man at the present time to exult where works are after all but faint copies of antient excellence. God has certainly permitted me to become an instrument in drawing attention to long-forgotten principles, but the merit of these belongs to older and better days. I still enter even the humblest erections of Catholic antiquity as a disciple to the school of his master, and for all that is produced, we must cry in most bounden duty, Non nobis, Domine, non nobis, sed nomini tuo da gloriam [Not to us, not to us, o Lord, But to your name give glory].

Griffiths followed the new chapel's progress with great interest and was successful in raising funds; roughly £6,500 was needed for the main building, with additional costs for the interior decoration – a modest £1,350 for the rood screen, for example, and £725 for the High Altar and reredos. All in all, the church by the time of its opening had cost less than £11,000.

The foundation stone was laid on 28 October 1845 and building work began under the direction of George Myers, Pugin's trustworthy co-worker, whose two sons were Edmundians. Soon the exterior was complete, the roof was on and the great east window put in place. However, Griffiths died unexpectedly on 12 August 1847, and his successor, Thomas Walsh, was in poor health and, despite having been a great supporter of Pugin over the years, did not have the same interest in St Edmund's as his predecessor. There were delays in finishing the chapel and it was left to Dr Cox to raise the necessary money, part of which came from Old Edmundians. Pugin grew restless and even agreed that student volunteers could paint the transepts and sanctuary roof, under his careful direction. These amateur artists included John Vertue, a future bishop of Portsmouth.

Top: Design for the proposed Griffiths Chantry dated 1848.

Above: Great Rood (detail).

Above: The Rood Screen showing the Great Rood. This is almost precisely as carried out. The only apparent difference is that the Rood is drawn hanging from the roof by two chains, but it is exactly the same position as now. The high altar, shown in the distance, is also like the existing one.

WE SHALL HAVE HALF
THE COUNTRY COMING
TO SEE IT.

Additions were slowly made to the chapel. Six months after Griffiths' death the east window was completed, a personal gift of the late bishop, and Cox was so impressed that he commented 'we shall have half the country coming to see it'.[64] It was decided also to build a Griffiths Chantry. The subscribers included the elderly father of the bishop, whom he had had the joy of receiving into the Church shortly before his own death. It was ready by June 1849 and the heart of Bishop Poynter, originally buried in the old chapel, was placed in the vault alongside the body of Griffiths.

Above left: A design for the chancel ceiling.

Above right: A panel design.

COLLEGE MUSIC

The 1840s saw a trio of talented musicians on the student body: John Crookall, James Danell (future bishop of Southwark) and William Dolan. A College Orchestra was set up and music of the more 'florid' school was sung in the Chapel, much to Bishop Griffiths' distaste. Crookall, who duly returned to St Edmund's as a member of staff, was an accomplished composer, despite his unceremonious appearance and manner, and his pieces formed a staple of the College repertoire. The story was told of how 'the night before the funeral of Cardinal Wiseman [1865], it was found that there was no music ready for the Absolutions, and how Dr Crookall being consulted, undertook to supply the deficiency; how he stayed up late at night writing his now well-known *Subvenite* and the others; and before the hour of the Requiem had collected a choir of priests and others who prepared them and practised them under his direction, and sang them as though they were quite familiar with the music'.[65]

Above: Dr William Ward depicted in the Ward Window in the College chapel. The window was installed in 1883. He is shown kneeling, in academic robes. The portrait is said to be a very good likeness, and recalls the fact that Dr Ward, as a professor, used to kneel at a prie-dieu in the choir just beneath this window.

St Edmund's and the Oxford Movement

Dr Cox's presidency coincided with the coming of the first converts resulting from the Oxford Movement, which had been concerned with rediscovering the Catholic roots of the Church of England as well as protecting its independence from state interference. Perhaps the most famous convert, Blessed John Henry Newman, stayed the night at St Edmund's on 21 November 1845, shortly after his reception into the Church. An address of welcome was read by the Vice-President, to which the future cardinal gave a brief reply. Shortly afterwards Newman wrote in a letter, 'Mr Whitty I liked extremely, though an Irishman. He is a very simple, natural, warm-hearted reflecting person – apparently not thirty – very expectant of great accession of information, instruction etc from converts. Dr Cox is not more than 39, but looks 50. He is mild and taking in his deportment. I liked him too very much'. However Newman thought 'there is apparently little learning or cultivation there – they are behindhand – and have not the worldly set out (I am using the words in a bad sense) of Prior Park'.

It is worth noting that the Passionist priest who famously received Newman into the Church, Blessed Dominic Barberi, came to St Edmund's twice in 1847 to preach retreats. One of those present, Canon Doyle, later recalled that 'it was a refreshing novelty when Father Dominic preached the retreat and superseded the old practice of reading the meditations of Bourdaloue or some similar stiff spiritualist [i.e. spiritual writer]'. Indeed, the previous year the fiery Rosminian missionary, Luigi Gentili, had preached the clergy retreat at the College and 'great was the alarm when the sacristans were seen darkening the windows of the Chapel and preparing it for the instructions on the Four Last Things'.[66] Continental practices were thus beginning to reach the College.

After Oxford and Littlemore, institutions like St Edmund's must have constituted a culture shock for Newman. The faith and piety to be found there, though deep and sincere, was of the 'old English Catholic' variety: reserved, unostentatious, with no 'foreign' devotions and little interest in theology beyond what was necessary for priestly formation.

To make up for the 'little learning or cultivation' that Newman complained of, some hoped that the new generation of converts could fill the gap. Newman himself was not to make a personal contribution – he came to the College once again on 26 December 1845, since he was in the area, but does not seem to have returned, though he wrote to congratulate St Edmund's on its centenary in 1869. However, two prominent converts were to be particularly associated with the College: Frederick Oakeley and William George Ward.

The first of these, Frederick Oakeley, had been a tutor at Balliol, preacher for the University of Oxford at the Chapel Royal, Whitehall and minister at the Margaret Chapel, later to become All Saints, Margaret Street, one of the great London Anglo-Catholic centres, where the congregation included William Ewart Gladstone. Oakeley is perhaps most famous for translating the carol *Adeste Fideles* into *O Come, All Ye Faithful*. In his final weeks as an Anglican, Oakeley had joined Newman's community at Littlemore and was received into the Catholic Church on 29 October 1845. He arrived at St Edmund's in January 1846 and quickly became 'a leading spirit in the house', admired for his 'unassuming' manner. One of his fellow students, William Dolan, recalled how Oakeley was at first 'bewildered' by the Edmundian regime; not surprising given his background and his limited exposure, up until then, to English Catholics. 'For example', wrote Dolan, 'the first time he saw a High Mass, when the Priest, Deacon and Subdeacon said the Confiteor [I confess] in turns, he thought they were disputing with each other as to what should be done next, and as to the proper rubrics'.

Oakeley soon settled in and became a prominent member of the Society of St Vincent de Paul (SVP), begun in 1845 though not formally established for another nine years since there was debate about whether clerical students were permitted to join. The St Edmund's Conference did much good work, even in those early years, visiting the poor and preaching in a small chapel created in a barn at Nasty. The charitable work of the SVP effectively continued in later times through the work of the College's 'Community Service Group'. Oakeley stayed at the College until 1848 and went on to become a Canon of Westminster (1852) and Rector of St John the Evangelist, Islington (1850-80).

William George Ward was also an Oxford man and (like Cardinal Manning) an early President of the Union, the undergraduate debating society. A close friend of Oakeley, he was a Fellow of Balliol and claimed to have 'the intellect of an archangel, and the habits of an eating, walking and sleeping rhinoceros'. He became a leading figure in the Oxford Movement, defending Newman's controversial *Tract 90* and writing *The Ideal of a Christian Church Considered in Comparison with Existing Practice* (1844). He subsequently became known as 'Ideal' Ward, especially after University Convocation voted to condemn the book and degrade the author of his MA in February 1845. That year would prove momentous for Ward; he married Frances Wingfield on 31 March and, along with her, was received into the Catholic Church at Farm Street on 5 September. When he met with Bishop Griffiths shortly afterwards, the prelate said: 'We are glad to welcome you, Mr Ward. Of course we have no work for you'. Nevertheless, Ward settled near St Edmund's and commissioned Pugin to build him a house, which later became the nucleus of St Hugh's.

Mention should also be made briefly of Henry Nutcombe Oxenham, another Balliol man, who had been ordained in the Church of England in 1854 and was received into the Catholic Church by Manning three years later. He taught for a while at St Edmund's but, despite having received minor orders, never progressed to the Priesthood. He upheld the validity of his Anglican Orders and continued to wear clerical dress. His theological views were considered 'liberal' for the time and he was much involved in the Association for the Promotion of the Unity of Christendom, which prayed for Corporate Reunion but was eventually condemned by Rome.

Above: William George Ward came to St Edmund's in 1847, in 1851 was appointed lecturer in moral philosophy, and the following year dogmatic theology.

THE CHAPEL

The building of the Chapel was commissioned by Bishop Thomas Griffiths. It was designed by Augustus Welby Pugin and construction began in 1845. The main structure was completed in 1853, when it was consecrated by Cardinal Wiseman. The choir was some 90 feet long, and the whole building 120 feet in length. The Chapel cannot be said to have been totally completed until the last two stained glass windows were installed in 1893.

Above: The ceiling above the sanctuary was painted to Pugin's design and under his direction. It is notable that most of the work was done by students. Alfred White, with some assistance from John Vertue, painted most of the panels in 1848 and 1849. They completed fifty seven of the sixty panels; the other three were painted professionally and are said to have cost as much as the amateur fifty seven. The panels includes the monograms of Our Lord, Our Lady, St Edmund, the Cross and St Peter's Keys.

Top right: The High Altar is carved in white stone. The stone Tabernacle, with brass doors ornamented with crystal bosses, is crowned with a pinnacled throne for the Blessed Sacrament.

Below left and right: Pugin designed every detail of the Chapel.

THE ROOD

Left and top below: The Rood Screen may justly be regarded as the principal feature of the Chapel. Thought to be the most beautiful work of its kind and time when it was built, it still stands as a monument to all that was best in the Gothic revival of the nineteenth century.

Below left: The great Rood is of carved Riga oak with painted pinewood figures of Our Lord, Our Lady and St John.

Below right: Bishop Thomas Griffiths' tomb is in the Griffiths Chantry. He died in 1847 while the church he had founded was still being built

CHAPTER VI

CARDINAL WISEMAN AND ST EDMUND'S
1850-1865

I n 1850 the Hierarchy was restored in England and Wales, and the system of dioceses with ordinary bishops replaced the tired system of apostolic vicariates. Nicholas Wiseman was created Archbishop of Westminster and Cardinal. Bright opportunities existed alongside the inevitable practical problems; the division of the old vicariates into dioceses led to much discussion about the distribution of finances and jurisdiction. Many bishops hoped that each diocese would eventually have its own seminary, as the Council of Trent envisaged, and that the old Douay system of educating laics alongside clerics would soon come to an end. Moreover, while large Colleges such as St Edmund's continued to train priests for several dioceses, the question arose of which bishop was in charge. It was a vexed question and in 1863 Rome eventually decided that the bishop in whose diocese the College was situated had spiritual jurisdiction and responsibility for the students' care. Temporal matters, on the other hand, were the remit of the local bishops, which in St Edmund's case meant Westminster and Southwark.

Cardinal Wiseman had spent much of his life in Rome first as a student and then Rector of the Venerable English College. He had little sympathy with the conservatism of many 'old' English Catholics and wanted to introduce 'Roman' principles into his new diocese. In 1851 William Weathers was appointed President at St Edmund's. The Cardinal wrote to Mgr Talbot, the English-born confidante of Pius IX, that with Cox's departure St Edmund's had been 'cleared of its terrible obstruction'; now, 'the whole system will be reformed, and a sound, high-toned ecclesiastical spirit will be introduced'.[67] Weathers seemed to be of sounder sympathies and knew the College well, having been there since 1828.

As part of Wiseman's strategy, W. G. Ward was appointed lecturer in moral philosophy in 1851 and, the following year, dogmatic theology. The fact that a married lay convert had such a prominent position, effectively in charge of the intellectual formation for the next generation of southern priests, caused much opposition. Moreover, he was zealous in his Ultramontanism and later became editor of its chief organ, *The Dublin Review*. One priest refused to have a 'Wardite' as his assistant; even the President seems to have fallen out with him over a theological point. Archbishop Errington, who became Wiseman's coadjutor in 1855, was also staunch in his opposition; he was generally suspicious of converts and more 'English' than 'Roman' in his outlook. When he made a visitation of the College shortly after he moved to Westminster, he tried to limit Ward's teaching. Ward promptly resigned; Wiseman reinstated him; and Errington retired temporarily to the diocese of Clifton as administrator. The matter even reached the ears of the pope, who made the famous statement that 'it is a novel objection to any one engaged in the work of God that he has received one Sacrament of Holy Church which neither you [the English prelate to whom he was speaking] nor I could possibly receive'. Ward had been tactful enough to refuse the title of 'professor' but his cause was helped when the pope awarded him an honorary doctorate of philosophy in 1854.

Above: Cardinal Wiseman, a portrait which hangs in the Staff Parlour at the College.

Far left: Detail from a window in the Shrine Chapel depicting Cardinal Wiseman receiving the Relic of St Edmund from the Archbishop of Sens in 1853.

A MINOR CHANGE
OCCURRED UNDER WEATHERS
WHICH SAW PUDDINGS
INTRODUCED AT THE END
OF DINNER IN PLACE OF THE
CURRANT PUDDING.

*Top: William Weathers was President of
St Edmund's between 1851 and 1868.*

*Above: Detailing in the Weathers Window in
the Ante-Chapel.*

Away from such controversy, there were many changes within the College under Weathers. Most obvious to the beholder was the 1858 extension, known for many years as the 'New Wing', which included a large refectory (taking up most of the ground floor) and above rooms for professors and (on the top floor) a dormitory. Meanwhile, changes in the internal life of the College became collectively known as 'the new Rules': new forms of prayers in the morning and evening based on Roman models, new arrangements for play days and a revival of the old Douay 'pedagogue' system, which had fallen into disuse thirty years previously. As Ward explained, 'the boys used to be with their "Pedagogues" during the "hours" – i.e. six till half-past-seven – at which time the professors had their dinner; but the arrangement was not successful, and a few years later the "Pedagogues" were once more abolished and the professors dined again in the middle of the day'.[68]

Talking of food, a minor change occurred under Weathers which saw puddings introduced at the end of dinner in place of the currant pudding, colloquially known as a 'Cart-wheel', which used to be served as a sort of starter. Another sign that times were changing was when Weathers discontinued the practice of singing Mass in powdered hair. This policy change, we are told, created 'a painful impression'.[69]

THE OPENING OF THE NEW CHAPEL

Weathers inherited the task of completing Pugin's chapel, though he was reluctant, as Cox had been, to put the College into debt. In his *Treatise on Rood Screens* (1851) Pugin lamented the on-going delays with the 'great Chapel,' which though 'very nearly complete, yet lingers on in an unfinished state, when a little effort might render it available for divine service, and, in the meantime, many students must quit the College without that true love of ecclesiastical art that is only imparted to the soul by a devout assistance at the functions of religion in these solemn edifices'.[70]

A final fundraising effort in 1852, helped by the convenient appearance of several legacies, meant that the chapel was ready to be opened the following year. Sadly, it was too late for the architect, who died at Ramsgate on 14 September 1852. The work at St Edmund's continued under his son, Edward.

The magnificent new chapel was consecrated by Cardinal Wiseman on Whit Monday, 15 May 1853 – quite an achievement since churches could only be consecrated when they were free from debt and, in the case of parish churches, this often took years if not decades. The ceremony was highly complex and took five hours. The Cardinal consecrated the High Altar, while Bishop Grant took care of the two screen altars. That evening, once everyone had recovered, Benediction of the Blessed Sacrament was held, using the new Pugin monstrance.

The following Thursday (19 May) the chapel was formally opened. Bishop Grant celebrated Pontifical Mass and the Cardinal preached. The choir, which was directed by the Vice-President, sang Haydn's 'Nelson' (or 'Imperial') Mass. After lunch the community gathered again in the chapel for Pontifical Benediction, given by Bishop Wareing of Northampton, and the singing of Crookall's new *Te Deum*. Bernard Ward later noted that:

Those who remember that day speak of the moving effect of the ceremonial amid surroundings so different from those to which they were accustomed, and the force with which this was brought before their imagination when the long procession wended its way from the sacristy and antechapel up the choir to the sanctuary. Many visitors came down to assist at the ceremonies, and possibly the day was all the more joyful because it had been so long deferred. Conspicuous among them was the familiar figure of Dr Cox, who while he was still at the College had longed to see that day, and now rejoiced to see his hope at last fulfilled, and the church he had taken so great a share in building at length ready for use.[71]

The same year Wiseman obtained from Bishop Bernadou of Sens a major relic of St Edmund: his left fibula. Brought to the College for veneration soon afterwards, it took time for Edward Welby Pugin to design and construct an appropriate reliquary and so it was not until St Edmund's Day 1861 that the relic returned to the College to be solemnly enshrined. To mark the occasion, Wiseman wrote the hymn *O Beate mi Edmunde*, familiar to all Edmundians. There it remained, except for its presence in the Roman Court at the Great Exhibition and its occasional visits to the sick and dying. Before the construction of the Shrine Chapel in 1905, it was kept in the Lady Chapel.

Above: The Lady Chapel altar.

Below: Early musical notation of 'O Beate mi Edmunde.

Course of Studies

The course of studies was essentially that passed down from Douay and similar to the widely-used Jesuit Ratio Studiorum (1599). The teaching was based on 'schools', with separate classroom and master, rather than 'forms', which in many institutions implied just one bench in a large room of other 'forms'. The course of studies traditionally involved:

Rudiments I-III – study of first principles of Greek and Latin, together with passages from Scripture and secular authors (eg Cicero) and the Catechism (this was studiously read in all classes up to Rhetoric).

Grammar – emphasis on Cicero, Aesop, Lucian, Cornelius Nepos, Quintus Curtius and Justin

Syntax – work on Greek New Testament, Caesar, Sallust, Florus and more Cicero

Poetry – Virgil as well as Ovid, Claudian, Statius and various Greek authors. History and geography was also studied.

Rhetoric – work on Cicero, Horace, Seneca, Terence, Juvenal, Herodian, Isocrates, Demosthenes and Xenophon.

Between 1869 and the introduction of the House System, St Edmund's was organised into two separate Divisions, each with differing status, bounds and rules. First Division students had more liberty, often acted as Prefects and used the Poets' playroom and front field. In later years they had private rooms. Church Boys lived alongside Lay Boys up until 1922, their main distinction being they rose half an hour earlier for Meditation and had additional Conferences and Retreats. The 'Second Division' (often referred to as 'Bounds') comprised the lower classes of Rudiments, Grammar and Syntax. They used the old 'church bounds'

First Division
(older students undertaking a College course)
Philosophy
Rhetoric
Poetry

Second Division
(or 'Bounds', school course)
Syntax
Grammar
Rudiments I-III

The traditional titles are still used, with the additional class name of 'Elements' having been subsequently added.

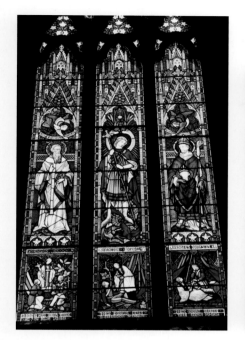

A further addition was made in 1857 in the form of the Crimea Window, erected in honour of three priests connected to the College who had lost their lives as chaplains during the conflict. Two of these, Fr John Wheble and Fr Michael Canty, had died at Balaclava and had both been present at the opening of the chapel – indeed, Fr Wheble had been the Master of Ceremonies, while Fr Canty had been on the teaching staff. The third was Fr Denis Sheahan, who died of fever and was anointed by Fr John Butt (future Bishop of Southwark). Fr Sheahan had only recently given the Last Rites to Fr Butt, whose life was despaired of, and so the latter had to be carried across the snow-swept landscape by eight men. Bernard Ward recounts that 'Father Sheehan was still conscious, but had evidently not much longer to live. The two priests were laid side by side, and one heard the other's confession and gave absolution. The sacrament of Extreme Unction presented greater difficulties, on account of Father Butt's extreme weakness. A Catholic soldier was therefore called to assist him, and taking his hand, he lifted it to the Holy Oil and thence to Father Sheehan's forehead, where he had just strength enough to make the sign of the cross, and pronounce the words'.[72]

W. G. Ward immersed himself in the liturgical life of the College and paid for the new organ in the Chapel. His daughter, who became the Abbess of Oulton, later recalled:

When the new Chapel was built, my father presented the organ, and in return the college superiors promised that his family should have a sitting in the organ gallery over the Rood screen. It was said that Mr Pugin did not like this idea, and declared he would build a staircase such as no lady would mount. But he was outwitted, for a second staircase was built, having an outside door of which we kept the key, and so we became quite independent. In that organ gallery we children faithfully attended the college services, and our interest in them grew with our years. Occasionally there would be an adventure. One of my sisters once dropped a prayer book which slipped through the balustrade into the choir. It was full of pious pictures which flew out and scattered in all directions. When the procession came down the choir at the end of Mass, the students all picked their way in and out, not liking to tread on what were evidently religious pictures. The spectators above looked on with interest.[73]

Above left: The Crimea Window in the College chapel. It was installed in 1857 to commemorate three chaplains who gave their lives in the Crimean War. Two of the priests were Edmundians – Fr Denis Sheahan and Fr Michael Canty – and the third, Fr John Wheble, was a benefactor of the College. After being destroyed by a bomb blast in 1940, the window was replaced in 1951.

Above right: The three lower panels commemorate scenes in the Crimea: a priest attending a dying soldier, Fr Wheble, preaching to soldiers before battle, and Fr Sheahan's deathbed.

Opposite top: The front of the College in 1876.

The Ward children, including Bernard, future President, soaked up the ecclesiastical atmosphere at St Edmund's and imitated the Sacred Liturgy in their games. Wilfrid Ward later wrote, 'I still know by heart the Gregorian music and words of St Augustine's beautiful hymn, the "*Exultet*," which, as deacon, aged eight years, I was taught to sing for the blessing of our toy Paschal candle. My brother Bernard, as sub-deacon, learnt the short Epistle for Easter Day, when he could hardly read at all'.[74] Dr Ward, however, disapproved of the plainchant, saying 'I always stop my ears from hearing it, it reminds me of original sin'.

HERBERT VAUGHAN AND THE OBLATES

In 1855 Wiseman appointed an energetic young priest as Vice-President: Herbert Vaughan. Aged only 22, he had just been ordained but was already a protégé of both the Cardinal and Fr Henry Edward Manning, a distinguished convert who was fast attaining great prominence in the diocese. It was indeed a risk to appoint such a young man, still below the canonical age for ordination, as Vice-President but he had energy and vision and soon became popular with the younger pupils. Looking back to those days, Bishop Fenton wrote that 'the boys were proud of him as their Vice-President when they saw him galloping over the park on a fine charger his father, the Colonel, had given him'. He also showed them great kindness, counselling them in times of difficulty and 'in the winter, when boys were suffering with coughs and colds, he would go round at night with a large jug of black currant tea to give them'.[75]

Vaughan was less popular with the other members of staff and many of the Divines, some of whom were nearly the same age. There was, moreover, a further complication. Manning, with Wiseman's encouragement, had set up the Oblates of St Charles. This was inspired by the diocesan congregation established by St Charles Borromeo in the sixteenth century, as well as similar communities across Catholic Europe. Wiseman had stayed at La Délivrande in Normandy, a

WE SHOULD TAKE THE HIGHEST AND LARGEST MOUNTAINS IN THE ALPS AND PUT IT OVER ALL PAST QUESTIONS AND DISSENSIONS.

house of the Missionnaires Diocésains, who gave retreats and missions, undertook pastoral work and directed the seminary. Not only did the Cardinal believe 'that steady, continuous, and persevering work among the dense sinful masses [in the cities] could be carried on only by religious communities,'[76] but he was dissatisfied with many of the existing religious orders whose members were subject to their own superiors and did not necessarily share Wiseman's priorities. The beauty of the Oblates was that they were secular priests directly subject and available to the bishop. The congregation was officially approved by the Holy See in 1857 and based at St Mary of the Angels, Bayswater.

Vaughan was an early recruit to the Oblates but there seemed to be a real conflict of interest between his role as Vice-President at St Edmund's, under Weathers, and his membership of the Oblates, under Manning. The same year as the Oblates were formally approved, Manning (still a relatively fresh convert) became Provost of the Westminster Chapter, furthering his power within the diocese. When other members of staff at St Edmund's also joined the Oblates, it seemed as if the College would soon lose its independence. The Westminster Chapter rose against their Provost, with the support of Archbishop Errington, who had recently returned from Clifton, and Bishop Grant, who also saw the presences of the Oblates in a seminary used by his students as an unlawful intrusion. The Canons of Westminster asked Manning to produce the Oblates' Rule for examination and the case was sent to Rome in 1858.

Similar battles had occurred in the past in the Colleges at Douay and Rome, when the secular clergy feared that the presence of Jesuits on the staff would affect the College's identity and lead many of the best students to join the English Province. Added to these historic tensions between secular clergy and religious orders, were disagreements between the 'old' Catholics and the 'new' converts, differing jurisdictions and, of course, the ever-present clash of personalities. As might be expected, these 'wars of Westminster' affected life on all levels in the College. A petition was sent by the Southwark Divines to their bishop in June 1859, stating that 'the oblates have completely failed in gaining the confidence or affection of the students' and that they viewed 'with the greatest alarm and dissatisfaction the displacement of our present beloved Rector in whom we feel not only an undiminished but an increasing confidence'.[77]

After the matter was discussed at the Provincial Synod of 1859 and further recourse was made to Rome, the Oblates were finally withdrawn from St Edmund's in 1861. There is some confusion over whether this was a voluntary gesture of pacification or whether it had been ordered by the Holy See. Pius IX certainly admonished the English bishops when they gathered in Rome for the canonisation of the Japanese Martyrs in 1862 and spoke of the need to overcome their various divisions; 'his wish was, and he added later this must be considered a command – that we should take the highest and largest mountain in the Alps and put it over all past questions and dissensions without any tunnel through to get at them'.[78]

Above: A group of students and staff in the Pleasure Grounds in about 1869. These were formal gardens laid out in the 1850s for the use of the professors. The statue called Virgo Mater was replaced in 1897 by a new statue of Our Lady of Lourdes.

The Pleasure Grounds were levelled in 1922 to make way for the School Block.

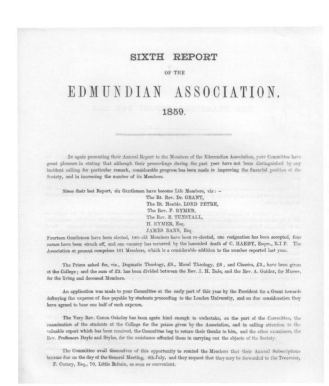

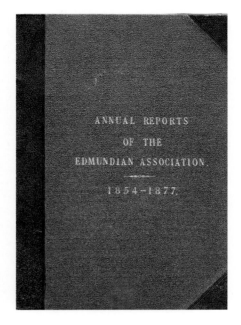

Above and below: The Edmundian Association produced detailed printed annual reports of its activities which were kept in bound volumes.

Above right: The Sablonière Hotel in Leicester Square, London, where The Edmundian Association was founded.

THE EARLY YEARS OF THE EDMUNDIAN ASSOCIATION

The Edmundian Association was founded in 1853, the year of the chapel's opening, and grew out of several previous attempts at keeping old boys in touch with each other, including the short-lived Edmundian Cricket Club (1852-53). The first General Meeting of The Edmundian Association was held on 23 September 1853 at the Sabloniere Hotel, Leicester Square, at which Weathers was elected as President and Canon O'Neal and Charles J. Pagliano (who had done much of the spadework in forming the new organisation) as the first two Vice-Presidents.

The Association's main event was the annual dinner, normally held in London. Locations varied, though a popular choice in the early years was the Castle Hotel, Richmond, which had an attractive terrace overlooking the Thames. 'In the early days at Richmond,' we read, 'when the meeting took place at two o'clock in the afternoon, and the dinner at three, there was much time left for friendly gatherings and companionship, and friends who met but once a year could gossip at will. After dinner, boating parties were formed, and most of the members went on the river, while a few remained behind for a quiet rubber of whist'.[79] However, professional commitments meant that it was soon moved to the evening, to the regret of older members.

Alongside this social dimension was the task of raising funds for the College. At first an 'Ecclesiastical Student's Fund' was set up to provide scholarships and exhibitions but in 1864 the emphasis was shifted to funding material improvements. Thus 'it was agreed that the Treasurer should pay to the President of the College £50 towards fitting up a room intended as a museum for Philosophical Apparatus'.[80] This would be the first of many important benefactions over the years.

AN EDMUNDIAN VC

One of two Edmundians known to have received the highest military decoration was Everard Aloysius Lisle March Phillipps. He was the son of the well-known convert Ambrose Phillipps de Lisle of Grace Dieu, Leicestershire, who was particularly associated with the foundation of the Cistercian monastery of Mount St Bernard and the work of the Institute of Charity in the Midlands. Born at Grace Dieu on 28 May 1835, Everard was a student at St Edmund's between 1847 and 1849, before completing his studies at Oscott and joining the army as an ensign. In 1854 he sailed for India to join the 11th Bengal Native Infantry. Everard continued to take his Faith seriously and tried to attend Mass whenever he could; on one occasion he even rode sixty miles, calling to mind his father's twenty-five mile ride each Sunday from Cambridge to Old Hall Green. Three years later his regiment revolted at Meerat during the Indian Mutiny and Phillipps, who had picked up the local language, was asked to read the Queen's proclamation against the insurgents. This he did in the face of gunfire; before he got to the end of the first sentence his horse was shot from under him and he himself wounded by a stray bullet. Undeterred, he only took cover once he had finished reading the proclamation.

He transferred to the 60th Rifles (King's Royal Rifle Corps). During the Fall of Delhi, on 14 September 1857, he managed to capture the Water Bastion with a small group of men but three days later was shot in the head on the streets at Bank House, aged 22 years. His date of death is often wrongly given as 18 September. Buried at the Rajpura Cemetery, he was not initially awarded the Victoria Cross since this was not given posthumously until the reign of Edward VII. On 15 January 1907, he became one of the first six people to be awarded the decoration after death.

A memorial to the Edmundian VC was only unveiled on 9 September 2007 by his great-great-nephew, Tim Phillipps de Lisle. The family gave the College a copy of Everard's portrait.[81]

The oldest known photograph of St Edmund's College was taken some time between 1863 and 1869. The main building was constructed by James Taylor of Islington between 1795 and 1799, but the barrack-like building was later dismissed by Augustus Welby Pugin as looking like a "Priest Factory". The appearance was enhanced in 1871, when a porch, ornamental balustrades and terraces were added.

CHAPTER VII

THE RULE OF CARDINAL MANNING
1865-1893

When the Oblates departed from St Edmund's, the disgruntled W. G. Ward continued to live beside the College but refused to enter its doors as a protest for twelve years. Meanwhile Dr Manning was prepared to bide his time before attempting again to reform the seminaries. In 1865 he succeeded Wiseman as Archbishop of Westminster and two years later managed to appoint an Oblate (and Old Edmundian), Henry O'Callaghan, as Rector of the Venerable English College, Rome.

The new Archbishop had long had his doubts about the dual education system at St Edmund's and wondered whether the College was sufficiently 'Ultramontane' in sympathy. He had tried to reform it through the presence of the Oblates during the time of Wiseman. Now as Archbishop, Manning had other ideas.

In 1869 the Divines left St Edmund's in order to study in a separate seminary in London. A student at the time and future bishop of Portsmouth, John Baptist Cahill, looked back to those days in a sermon preached in 1905, when the Divines were returning to St Edmund's:

I well remember the day – the 10th of June, 1869 – when the Ordinary of this diocese [Manning] announced to us, after the dinner by which we were keeping certain centennial festivals of this college, that the divinity students of the college should leave St Edmund's and go to London, and then he added, and the words have never left my mind: "It is now time that they should leave the gentle sway of St Edmund, and pass out into the sterner discipline of St Thomas." [82]

St Thomas' Seminary, Hammersmith was opened in August 1869 at the Cupola House, which had a venerable history. Formerly the country residence of the Portuguese Ambassador, an adjoining house boasted one of the only convents in England in penal times, founded during the reign of Charles II. In 1876 Manning began to appeal for money so that new buildings could be erected and even stated that 'if I can leave behind me a solid, simple, and adequate building for the Higher or Greater Seminary of the diocese of Westminster I shall feel that the work of my life is done'.[83] In 1879 the new buildings were ready and a chapel added in 1885, now used by Sacred Heart School. Designed by John Francis Bentley, later to become the architect of Westminster Cathedral, it was his first major commission.

Left: Part of the sixth panel of the Barraud Mural in the Ambulacrum. From the left are St Anthony of Egypt, St Francis Xavier, St Benedict, St Francis de Sales, St Philip Neri and St Anthony.

Above: The altar in the Scholefield Chantry.

Top and top right: The exterior of the Scholefield Chantry. This small chapel was originally to be built in Fulham, south west London.

Manning was following a dream common to most bishops and inspired by the Council of Trent, which envisaged the seminary being located near the cathedral and 'under the eye of the bishop'. Indeed, Manning asked that the seminarians would serve at the Pro-Cathedral, Our Lady of Victories in Kensington. Other dioceses soon followed Westminster's lead and the next fifteen years saw the foundation of St Bernard's, Olton (for the diocese of Birmingham); the Seminary of Pastoral Theology in Bishop's House, Salford; St Joseph's, Leeds; St Thomas Aquinas', Shefford (for Northampton); St Joseph's, Upholland (for Liverpool) and the Diocesan Seminary in Nottingham. It is interesting that none of these survived into the twenty-first century.[84]

Weathers followed the seminarians to Hammersmith and his Vice-President, Dr Frederick Rymer, succeeded him at St Edmund's. Like Weathers, Rymer had been at the College for most of his life as a student and teacher. His first appointment, in 1848, had been to teach algebra to students who were nearly the same age as himself. In 1857 he turned down Manning's invitation to join the Oblates and left the College for four years, before returning as Vice-President.

Rymer's arrival at St Edmund's led to the construction of the Scholefield Chantry, one of the most intriguing of the College's buildings. The chapel was built in memory of Edward Cotterill Scholefield of Westridge, near Ryde (Isle of Wight). This enigmatic figure belonged to a Yorkshire family that had settled in Birmingham; his father was Joshua, who served as the town's MP and his half-brother, William, was the first mayor. A nephew, Rev. Clement Scholefield, composed the well-known hymn, *The Day Thou Gavest, Lord, is Ended*. Edward was a convert to the Faith but had no known connection with St Edmund's. He died in Paris on 1 November 1859, aged 34. It seems that his widow, Isabella (known as Jane), decided to build a chantry and started making arrangements with the church of St Mary Magdalene, Mortlake, where Edward was initially buried. This fell through and negotiations were then made with St Thomas', Fulham, where Dr Rymer was Rector. When he moved to St Edmund's as Vice-President in 1861, the architect Edward Welby Pugin suggested that the proposed chantry be built at Old Hall Green instead. The chapel, dedicated to St Edward the Confessor and including a vault where Edward

GREAT TROUBLE WAS TAKEN WITH THE DECORATIONS, WHICH WERE OF AN EXTREMELY ELABORATE CHARACTER.

Scholefield's body was laid, was ready by 1862 although the interior decoration was never completed. It is a slightly smaller version of the same architect's De Trafford Chantry, built next to All Saint's, Barton-upon-Irwell in Manchester the following year. A Scholefield Fund was established at the College to provided Masses for Edward Scholefield and his widow, who went on to marry Alfred, Comte de Damas d'Hautefort in 1863 and moved to the beautiful Chateau de Hautefort in the Dordogne. Her new husband was equerry to the Comte de Chambord, grandson of Louis XVI and Legitimist claimant to the French throne.

The year of the departure of the Divines coincided with the centenary of the foundation of the Old Hall Green Academy. Three days of festivities were arranged, attended by many Old Edmundians, and included a cricket match between 'Past' and 'Present', an athletics day and the planting of jubilee trees. Both Canon Oakeley and Fr Francis Stanfield produced 'Centenary Odes', while a cantata was also composed with words by Thomas Hood and music by J. L. Molloy. The oldest Edmundian then living, Alvaro Camera, was able to provide recollections stretching back to 1806. Solemn Masses were celebrated in thanksgiving for the blessings of the preceding century, for the College Alumni and Benefactors and for deceased Edmundians. Bernard Ward recalls that 'great trouble was taken with the decorations, which were of an extremely elaborate character, and served to veil much of the bareness of the unfinished church'. Indeed, this bareness was soon to be improved by the arrival of The Edmundian Association Centenary Windows the following year. However, 'there was an element of melancholy, for it was the last time that the Divines were to take part in such ceremonies'.[85]

Many lamented the departure of the Divines. As Edwin Burton wrote,

They seemed interwoven with College life, filling as they had done for over seventy years many minor offices. Much of the College routine had to be reformed. Without their aid in choir and on the Sanctuary it seemed impossible to continue the complete observance of the Sacred Liturgy. Fortunately, this difficulty was overcome and the liturgical services were continued as before by priests and schoolboys.[86]

Top and top left: The Ambulacrum and the Refectory decorated for the 1869 celebration of the first centenary of Old Hall Green Academy.

Above: To mark the centenary, Cardinal Manning planted a clump of horse chestnut trees in the Front Field (the last of them died in about 2000). This sundial was amongst them but the cows kept knocking it over, so it was moved to its current position near the Crucifix in about 1963.

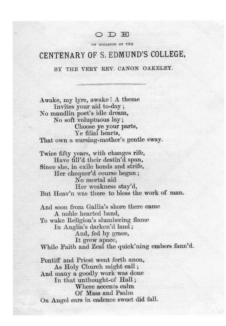

Above: A centenary ode written by Canon Frederick Oakeley, who was also responsible for translating Adeste Fidelis into English.

Below: Mgr James Laird Patterson was President of St Edmund's between 1870 and 1880

With their absence, the priests on the staff had to act as deacon and subdeacon at High Mass and the Church Boys wore surplices in choir. For the young Bernard Ward and many other boys, there was a more serious consideration:

When the Divines were removed from us in 1869, we looked on the state of affairs as very sad. For them it was sad, for how were they in future to get any decent cricket? For us it was sad, because the prestige of our eleven seemed irrevocably lost. To add to our misfortunes, the Archbishop (Dr Manning), had expressed a definite wish that the priests should no longer play. For a time we hoped that this might be evaded. It was said that one objection was that their names sometimes appeared in print. This might be obviated by their playing under assumed names. One suggestion was that they should spell their names backwards, and two well-known ecclesiastics were expected to appear in the score as "Rev. John Nanerb" and "Rev. Reginald Relwof" respectively. It soon transpired, however, that there were other objections than this, and that the priests would not, at any rate, play in the XI, and we were in the depths of despair.[87]

St Edmund's remained as a school, with both lay and (for the moment) Church Boys as well as the philosophers – indeed the lovers of cricket had to make do with matches between Church and Lay, and Westminster and Southwark. The lay and Church Boys were reunited and the old lay playroom abolished. The College was now divided into two 'divisions', with differing status, bounds and rules.

Students continued to go forward to seminary but, since Catholics were still forbidden to enter Oxford or Cambridge, many philosophers were prepared for external degrees from the University of London. The College thus continued to fulfil an important role within the Catholic community and to prepare future candidates for the Priesthood.

MGR JAMES LAIRD PATTERSON

Dr Rymer had several serious disagreements with Manning. He regretted the departure of the Divines and at the time of the First Vatican Council joined the likes of Newman in thinking it 'inopportune' to define papal infallibility as a dogma. The Archbishop wanted an 'ultramontane' as President and so appointed Mgr James Laird Patterson in 1870, the first non-Edmundian to hold the office, though rather appropriately he had been born on St Edmund's Day 1822. Patterson had studied at Trinity College, Oxford, and was much influenced by the Oxford Movement. Working for a while as an Anglican clergyman, he began to be plagued by doubts and went on a pilgrimage to the Holy Land to further his discernment. He was received into the Church in Jerusalem at Easter 1850. He decided to train for the Priesthood and, through the good offices of Mgr Talbot was given rooms in the Vatican Palace itself. Five years later he was ordained in the Eternal City by Cardinal Wiseman. He was highly trusted by the first two Archbishops of Westminster and, shortly before arriving at St Edmund's, was present as an official at the First Vatican Council.

St Edmund's was a conservative institution, delighting in its recusant tradition and its 'gothic' style, crowned by Pugin's chapel. It is no wonder that Manning questioned its 'ultramontanism' and was keen that the new President should introduce a more 'Roman' spirit. On an external

level, this involved wearing birettas for the first time and adapting some of the fuller gothic chasubles into Roman 'fiddlebacks'. Patterson made sure the church furnishings were all correct – he introduced tabernacle veils and altar frontals, added an extra sanctuary lamp and lowered the floor of the sanctuary. He also excluded the public from College functions, an exception being made for the annual Corpus Christi procession from the chapel to the parish church.

These 'Roman' sympathies caused uproar amongst the students. When the young Edmund Carroll entered the College, he remembered being asked 'whether I was a Goth or a Roman. When I replied that I was a Roman, imagining that they meant by the term a Catholic, I was taken to task by some of the students and warned that though I might curry favour with the superiors I would make myself an object of suspicion to my fellow students by joining the unpopular party. There was in the beginning real temper and party-feeling in the dispute'.[88]

According to Wilfrid Ward, even the Archbishop received a cool reception when he visited St Edmund's shortly after Patterson's arrival:

His solemn jokes, generally received with obsequious hilarity wherever he went, fell quite flat. The College band played dutifully to welcome him. He felt at once, I think, a want of real cordiality, and tried to introduce a more genial atmosphere by taking the conductor's baton when the music was over and with a furtive smile beating time himself, expecting much laughter from this stroke of humour. Dead silence ensued, and then a small boy at the back (whose identity was never detected) said slowly and distinctly "how funny." The sarcasm was withering; and I think the Archbishop blushed.[89]

Despite his unpopular policies, Patterson soon won the respect of the student body. His nature was genial and warm. 'Every day at dinner and supper,' recalled William Cunningham, 'as he came down the Refectory steps he would beam upon us all in his inimitable way, and his eyes would sweep round on both sides from the "Coffee-shop" upwards, never missing a face in its comprehensive greeting'.[90]

HIS SOLEMN JOKES, GENERALLY RECEIVED WITH OBSEQUIOUS HILARITY WHEREVER HE WENT, FELL QUITE FLAT.

Top: The Philosophy students in 1869.

Above: The choir in 1879.

Top: The first panel of the Barraud Mural. From right to left are Adam & Eve, Abel, Noah, Melchisedech, Abraham, Isaac and Jacob.

Above: Mark Barraud painted the mural in the Ambulacrum with help from his father Henry.

There were many improvements to the College under Patterson, including the foundation of St Hugh's (dealt with in a separate chapter), the construction of the Kitchen Wing and Terraces, and the decoration of the Refectory and Ambulacrum. The latter included 'a series of figures representing the history and triumph of religion by Mark Barraud aided by his father Henry Barraud, after the design of Prof. Führich of Vienna'.[91] It depicted the procession of the Church Triumphant, beginning with the Old Testament prophets and 'saints' and the pagan Sibyls, then with the figure of Christ in a chariot drawn by the Evangelists and pushed by the four Latin Doctors of the Church. Part of this mural was lost when the entrance aperture was extended and it is based on Führich's *Der Triumph Christi*. Behind the Lord are the Apostles and Saints of the 'new dispensation,' including St Edmund and the other College patrons.

The Franco-Prussian War had recently broken, which explains why St Boniface, Apostle of Germany, is leading a dog with the devil's tail and Bismarck's head (complete with spiked helmet or pickelhalbe). Henry Barraud's daughter, Margaret Mary, had recently entered the novitiate of the Sisters of Charity in Paris and experienced the Prussian siege, which created terrible hardships for the city's residents and led to the murder of the Archbishop. Bismarck was hardly thought of in a positive light. Mark Barraud also painted the walls of the chancel in a style that Patterson called 'medieval polychrome'. These were not deemed a success and were covered by curtains in later years, before being completely removed in 1893. It should be added that, as part payment for the Ambulacrum frescoes, no fees were charged for the education at the College of Mark's younger brothers, Francis and Philip. Both also became artists and the former produced the famous painting of his dog, Nipper, listening to a gramophone, which became the brand for 'His Master's Voice' (HMV).

Left: Part of the fifth panel of the Barraud Mural depicting, from left, St Christopher, St Edmund, St Thomas of Canterbury and St George.

Below: The despised Bismarck depicted as a dog, an unexpected conclusion of the Mural.

Above: A detail from the third panel of the Barraud Mural. The Three Wise Men are Caspar (with gold), Melchior (with myrrh) and Balthasar (with frankincense).

Above left: Otto von Bismarck, with his distinctive pickelhaube and walrus moustache, became the first Chancellor of Germany in 1871.

Top: The Fourth Provincial Synod of Westminster was held at St Edmund's in 1873.

Above: A lower light of a window in the Shrine Chapel shows Mgr James Laird Patterson bringing the Relic of St Edmund to a sick Cecil Heathcote in 1871.

Undoubtedly the most famous occurrence during the Presidency of Patterson was the miraculous cure of one of the students, Cecil Heathcote. According to the College Diary:

On Sunday, November 12, 1871, a student named Cecil Heathcote was so seriously injured by falling over a bench in the bounds that his life was despaired of. The President administered him, and going into the chapel before the Relic of St Edmund, made a vow of an altar to the Saint for the recovery of the youth, who was so ill that for several hours it was thought that every moment would prove his last. The Relic was carried to the Infirmary and applied to the youth's lips and forehead (he being apparently unconscious) and shortly afterwards a change for the better set in. the next morning the doctor, Mr George Covey, of Puckeridge, not a Catholic, was amazed to see the change, and both then and many times afterwards expressed his belief that it was unaccountable, except, as he expressed it, on the supposition of "our fellows' prayers."[92]

The President went on to fulfil his promise, building a new altar before the relic which, true to his principles, was solidly 'Roman' in style. It was consecrated by Bishop Weathers in 1872 and among those present at the ceremony was a very healthy Cecil Heathcote. The inscription on the altar referred to the President's vow: *S Edmundo voto solute*.

Students at St Edmund's included those from other countries and one of the most interesting of these, during Patterson's Presidency, was Camillo Siciliano di Rende, originally from Naples, who presented the College with a set of Roman vestments. Ordained in 1871, he worked for a while in London but his ecclesiastical career progressed rapidly; by the end of 1877 he was

Titular Bishop of Tricarico and in 1887 he was created Cardinal Priest of San Sisto. He died, aged 49, in 1897, by which time he was Archbishop of Benevento.

Between 21 July and 12 August 1873 St Edmund's was the location of the Fourth Provincial Synod of Westminster, a meeting of the English and Welsh Hierarchy and about fifty clergy, presided over by Archbishop Manning. The previous three Synods, which had met between 1852 and 1859, were held at St Mary's, Oscott. However, St Edmund's seemed a more correct location since canon law required the Metropolitan to convoke such meetings within 'his own Church'. *The Tablet* correspondent vividly described the scene at the opening:

The procession was truly splendid and excited the admiration of the representatives of the daily papers, several of whom were present, and who furnished lengthened reports that have appeared in their respective columns. The Morning Post and Daily Telegraph are especially diffuse. The coup d'oeil was in reality very striking: before the shrine of St Thomas of Canterbury the whole procession paused a moment and knelt. As the lengthened train of mitred prelates and of Religious and dignified clergy moved down the beautiful cloister of St Edmund's, along the esplanade in front, reaching the stately Gothic church by the western entrance, few sights of ecclesiastical splendour more magnificent have been witnessed in England during the last three centuries. Arrived at the church, and the Veni Creator, which was intoned in unison with solemn effect by the entire assemblage, being finished, all assisted at Pontifical High Mass, celebrated by his Grace the Archbishop of Westminster.[93]

The bishops and senior clergy remained in residence for three weeks, as they discussed liturgy, education, discipline and ecclesiastical life. For the duration of the Synod the 'Pontifical standard' (or flag) flew over the College and the arms of Pius IX placed over the outer door. Much to the students' delight, their return to the College after the holidays had to be postponed.

FEW SIGHTS OF ECCLESIASTICAL SPLENDOUR MORE MAGNIFICENT HAVE BEEN WITNESSED IN ENGLAND DURING THE LAST THREE CENTURIES.

Above: Old Hall Green Farm still operated until 1922, enabling the College to be largely self-sufficient.

Below: A ceremonial arch was erected to mark the 1869 centenary of Old Hall Green Academy.

Above: The Shrine of St Edmund at Pontigny Abbey in north-central France. The former Cistercian monastery was founded in 1114.

The 1870s saw the beginnings of large public pilgrimages from England to the shrines of Catholic Europe. In 1873 a 'great pilgrimage' was made to Paray-le-Monial in honour of the Sacred Heart. The following year it was the turn of the shrine of St Edmund at Pontigny. Several hundred pilgrims departed from Victoria on 1 September, including Mgr Patterson and staff and students from the College. At Newhaven a steamer was ready to greet them, flying the papal flag and that of St Edmund, and when they arrived at Dieppe the pilgrims sang the *Magnificat* and the hymn Iste *Confessor*. As they arrived at Pontigny they were met by Manning and a procession of the saint's relics, although the church bells were ringing not because of the English pilgrimage but because a well-known local priest had died suddenly of apoplexy. It was for this pilgrimage that Fr Francis Stanfield wrote the hymn *Sing, England's Sons*, which famously referred to St Edmund's as 'England's College home'. Other verses were written more particularly for the pilgrimage:

Edmund, bright Saint, the glory of our island,
Look on thy Pilgrims, thronging round thy shrine;
We left our shores for vine-clad, fair Pontigny,
Where still the halo of thy light doth shine.
Father St Edmund, Thy Pilgrims cross life's sea
Lead us home to Jesus, and home, sweet Saint, with thee.

Mgr Patterson retired as President in 1880. Despite suffering much from rheumatism in his final years, he was consecrated Titular Bishop of Emmaus at the Venerable English College, Rome. On his return from the Eternal City, he celebrated High Mass at St Edmund's and was welcomed by the College band, a triumphal arch bearing the words *Mane Nobiscum Domine* and carpets hanging from the front windows (which excited the attention of a local furniture dealer).

The new President was Fr George Akers, who had come to St Edmund's in 1877 as Prefect of Studies and Vice-President and, like his predecessor, was a convert. He had studied at Oriel College, Oxford (missing Newman by over a decade) and worked for a time as an Anglican clergyman. After ordination as a Catholic priest in 1870 he served as a curate in Hackney and founded a mission, built a church and established schools at nearby Homerton. He appears to have been something of an absent-minded professor and had a particular passion for the Scandinavian Sagas, 'in which he took such deep interest that he learned Swedish on purpose to read one of the Sagas, which had not then been translated into English'.[94]

Fr Akers only served as President for two years. His reign was relatively uneventful, although students rose to the then unprecedented number of 120. In 1882 he returned to parochial life, establishing a mission once again, this time at Hampton Wick. Although his time at St Edmund's did not coincide with the presence of the seminary, in 1896 Cardinal Vaughan moved him to St Mary and St Michael's, Commercial Road, where he was asked to set up a Pastoral College for what we would now call the 'on-going formation' of newly-ordained priests.

THE ILLUSTRATED LONDON NEWS.

REGISTERED AT THE GENERAL POST-OFFICE FOR TRANSMISSION ABROAD.

No. 1829.—VOL. LXV.   SATURDAY, SEPTEMBER 12, 1874.   WITH SUPPLEMENT | SIXPENCE BY POST, 6½D.

PILGRIMS AT THE SHRINE OF ST. EDMUND OF CANTERBURY, IN THE ABBEY CHURCH OF PONTIGNY.

THE ARRIVAL OF A FORMER VICE-PRESIDENT AS ARCH-BISHOP LED TO A FURTHER RETHINK CONCERNING THE SEMINARIES.

Above: The oldest known whole school photograph taken in 1871. Note the ball finials on the porch are not in place and the central path has not yet been constructed.

Below: The Refectory in 1876 had a grand balcony and staircase.

Fr Patrick Fenton succeeded as President. Belonging to a family that had moved to London from County Cork, he came to the College straight from the mission at Brook Green and had had vast experience in the diocese. He had served for some years as chaplain to the Hospital of St John and St Elizabeth, then in Great Ormond Street, and run by the Order of Malta, becoming the first Conventual Chaplain in England since the Reformation. His Vice-President at St Edmund's, Fr William Lloyd, was able to bring studies to a high standard.

Mgr Fenton (as he soon became) oversaw several changes to the decoration of the church, including the addition of the Ward Window. He removed the tabernacle veils and altar frontals introduced by Patterson. In 1887 it was decided to transfer the Church Students to other Colleges. Mgr Fenton disagreed with the policy and submitted his resignation. He went on to work at the church of St Thomas of Canterbury, Fulham, and was eventually consecrated Titular Bishop of Amycla and Auxiliary in Westminster. He remained a loyal friend to the College. In 1898, for example, he funded the complete re-tiling of the floor of the chancel and antechapel, the erection of new stations of the cross, the inlaid parquetry floor in the sacristy (soon afterwards destroyed in a fire) and the addition of new chancel gates and a brass stand for the eagle lectern.

The fourteenth President – and the sixth during Manning's reign at Westminster – was Mgr John Crook, who had previously spent some seventeen years at St Mary's, Cadogan Street in Chelsea. Bernard Ward recalled that 'he had not been long in office before his health began to break, and the last two or three years which he spent here, when I was his Vice-President, were in great part a record of his bearing up under physical trials and infirmities which eventually overcame him'.[95] By the time he resigned in January 1893, student numbers had declined and College finances were in a poor state. Mgr Crook, meanwhile, accepted the less onerous task of chaplain to Lord Petre at Thorndon in Essex.

THE CENTRAL SEMINARY

The arrival of a former Vice-President, Herbert Vaughan, as Archbishop of Westminster in 1892 led to a further rethink concerning the seminaries. Vaughan shared much of Manning's vision but was also painfully aware of the limited resources available to English Catholics. Some of the diocesan seminaries that had been recently founded turned out not to be viable and

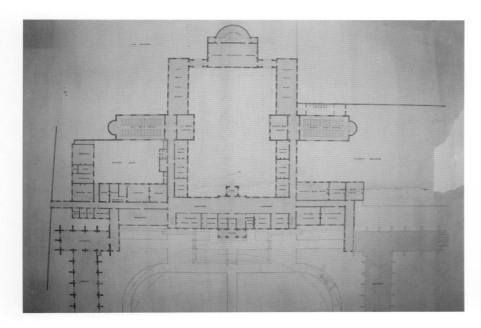

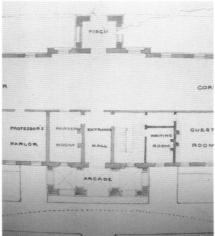

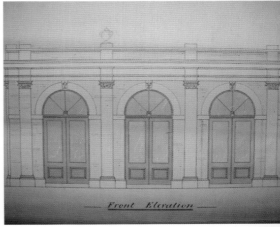

seemed to prove that it was virtually impossible for every English diocese to have its own institution with able teachers, spacious buildings and a well-stocked library. Surely it was best, Vaughan concluded, to combine resources; indeed the Council of Trent had recommended this in the case of poorer dioceses. He decided, therefore, to close the Hammersmith seminary and, accordingly, on 29 December 1892 the buildings were sold to the Sacred Heart Sisters, who opened a successful school on the site. It was a bold undertaking to terminate what had been referred to as the permanent monument of his predecessor's rule at Westminster, especially given the large sums of money spent on the project.

Hammersmith had suffered from declining numbers, caused partly by the absence of Southwark students after the opening of Wonersh in 1891. Moreover, a problem that Manning had not predicted was the coming of the London Underground, just opposite the seminary, in 1874 and the gradual transformation of the area into a busy suburb deemed unsuitable for ecclesiastical formation. Dr Rymer, rather unkindly, referred to Hammersmith as 'one of the noisiest, lowest, and most unhealthy suburbs of London' and spoke of 'the coldness, the dreariness, the poverty-stricken air of this new seminary and its surroundings'.[96] It seems not to have been a happy place and the regime was Spartan. One story recounted how a Carthusian staying the night there before ordination told Manning that his brother monks would have not put up with such fare. As a result dishes of prunes appeared the next night for supper.

In 1893 the Hammersmith students were sent not to Old Hall Green but to St Mary's College, Oscott, on the outskirts of Birmingham. Rome eventually ratified Vaughan's ambitious scheme and in July 1897 recognised Oscott as the central seminary for the dioceses of Westminster, Birmingham, Clifton, Portsmouth, Northampton, Newport and what was then the Vicariate of Wales. Of course, not all the dioceses joined with Vaughan. The northern bishops remained loyal to Ushaw, while Southwark had only recently established its own seminary at Henfield (1889) and then Wonersh (1891). One consequence of the 'central seminary' was that in 1895 the philosophers were withdrawn from St Edmund's so that they could join the divines at Oscott. As we shall see, they would return in 1904.

Top left: Plans for new buildings in 1870 are shown in red.

Top right: The arcade (front porch) and porch (at the rear of the building) were built in 1871. The grand central staircase between the entrance hall and waiting room was never built.

Above: The architect's elevation of the arcade (front porch).

Top: Cardinal Manning at the ceremony to plant horse chestnut trees to commemorate the first centenary of Old Hall Green Academy in 1869.

Above: Harvesting hay in the Front Field.

Right: The Chapel bell 'Great Edmund' which was purchased by The Edmundian Association in 1873. The blue door to the right leads to Dr William Ward's private staircase to the gallery on the Rood Screen.

Top left: The Chapel with ornate decoration that was introduced in the 1870s.

Top right: Livestock grazed right up to the wall of the front terraces.

Left: The 'New Wing' of 1858 showing, to the right, the small memorial chapel erected in 1875 by The Edmundian Association to commemorate the sacrilegious robbery of 1799.

Above: The Study Place in the 1890s, illuminated by gas lamps.

CHAPTER VIII

MGR BERNARD WARD

1893-1916

S oon after arriving in Westminster, Archbishop Vaughan appointed Bernard Nicholas Ward as President of St Edmund's. He was, of course, already part of the Edmundian landscape, having not only attended the school but being born and bred on the College estate. In 1882, the year of his ordination, he returned to St Edmund's from Oscott as Prefect of Discipline. Between 1885 and 1890 he was entrusted with establishing a mission at Willesden and teaching at Oscott, but he was then back as Prefect of Studies and Vice-President to Mgr Crook.

In 1892 Fr Ward was named Pro-President – a potentially temporary appointment for Vaughan was aware of the falling student numbers and financial problems at St Edmund's and was considering its future. In the meantime, Ward was given the opportunity to change the College's fortunes. This he managed to do and he was formally appointed President in 1893.

Here something should be said of this great Edmundian character. A vivid, though not entirely favourable, portrait was drawn by one of his teaching staff, Dr John Vance, who went on to become Headmaster of the Cardinal Vaughan Memorial School. He described Ward as 'tall, broad, bulkily heavy, of enormous girth' and 'walked heavily, in spite of a certain nimbleness, as his feet fell at a wide angle'.[97] He lived simply:

…habitually he went about in a rather greenish frock-coat, just on the decent side of shabbiness, and would refuse to take Joslan's "barouche" – Heaven alone knows the name of the ramshackle vehicle – to the station. He would walk the mile and a half switch-back road to Standon, though he disliked hurried movement, in order to realize his ideal of a "priest living as a poor man." His rooms, destitute of every comfort, were barrack-like in their unattractiveness. Much as he naturally cared for choice food, he would uncomplainingly eat anything. He drank no wine and never smoked.[98]

Ward was a noted historian and during his Presidency published a number of books, most notably his seven volumes on English Catholicism between 1781 and 1850: *The Dawn of the Catholic Revival in England, 1781 – 1803* (1909), *The Eve of Catholic Emancipation, 1803 – 1829* (1911) and *The Sequel to Catholic Emancipation, 1829 – 1850* (1915). These works are still referred to by scholars today.

Despite his many abilities, Ward was by no means easy to work with:

Traditions sprang into being at a touch of his hand and as readily vanished. Rules that had never been committed to paper, nor apparently to living memory, appeared at his call from the vast unknown…Ward was also singularly abrupt – almost an oddity whom Dickens would certainly have loved and rendered immortal. He would, for instance, meet guests on arrival at the College,

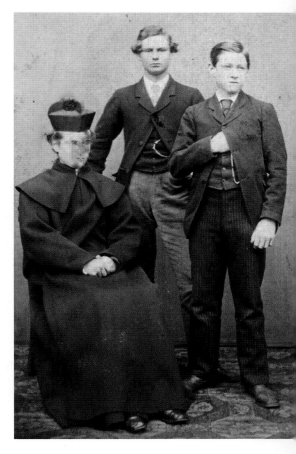

Opposite: A portrait of Bernard Ward that hangs at the College.

Above: The three sons of W G Ward. From left: Edmund, Wilfrid and Bernard.

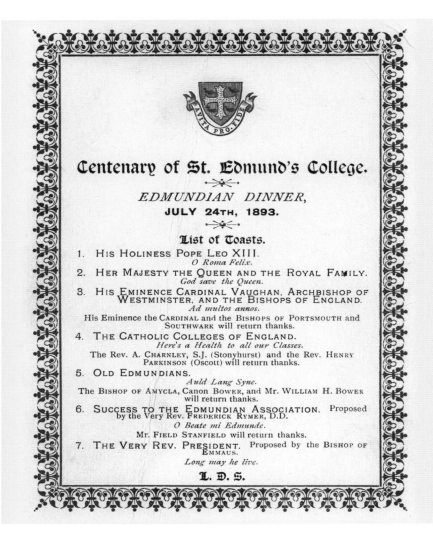

PROGRAMME.

Concert given on the Evening of the Feast of St. Edmund, 1893.

1	Pianoforte Solo	..	"Galop"	.. ..	*Wollenhaupt*
		Mr. W. H. ALLAN.			
2	Chorus	..	"Hark how for thee"	..	*Donizetti*
		THE CHOIR.			
3	Violin and Piano	..	"Lisette"	..	*G. Papini*
		J. COOK, G. BISHOP, F. FOUNTAIN, R. MARTIN, J. WHITMARSH, J. URBANI, R. DORAN.			
4	Solo and Chorus	..	"De ole Grey Mare"	..	*Scott Gatty*
		J. TYNAN.			
5	Sacred Song	..	"David singing before Saul"	..	*L. Bordèsi*
		Mr. BROADHEAD.			
6	Recitation	..	"He and she"	..	*Dreyfus*
		W. CASSON (angry wife), F. WOODS (Husband).			
7	Violin Solo	..	"Polonaise"	..	*C. Bohm*
		F. FOUNTAIN.			
8	Song	..	"Equatorial Line"	..	*W. Slaughter*
		P. HUGHES.			
9	Chorus	..	"Anvil Chorus"	..	*Verdi*
		THE CHOIR.			
		INTERVAL.			
10	Pianoforte Solo	..	"March in C"	..	*F. Ross*
		F. TORDIFFE (His first appearance).			
11	Violins	..	"Danse Negre"	..	*G. Papini*
		J. COOK, G. BISHOP, F. FOUNTAIN & J. URBANI.			
12	Solo and Chorus	..	"Daddy Won't"	..	*J. Tabrar*
		MASTER GONTRAN GOLDEN.			
13	Song	..	"Our Dinah"	..	*Scott Gatty*
		J. COOK.			
14	Violins	..	"Marche Triomphale"	..	*G. Papini*
		J. COOK, G. BISHOP, F. FOUNTAIN, J. URBANI, R. MARTIN & R. DORAN.			
15	Solo and Chorus	..	"Three Crows"	..	*L. Godfrey*
		J. GOGGIN.			
16	Chorus	..	"Dulce Domum"	..	*Reading*
		THE COLLEGE.			
17	Solo and Chorus	..	"Accidents"	..	*Osborn*
		R. MARTIN.			
18	Chorus	..	"Good Night"	..	*Scott Gatty*
		THE CHOIR.			

L. D. S.

Above and left: The 1893 centenary of the establishment of St Edmund's College was commemorated with a variety of events, including dinners and concerts.

give them a cold, reluctant touch of his large hand, and then, with emphasis, as he looked sideways over his glasses, demand when they were leaving. Not everyone could understand this mode of reception, more especially as Ward, a specialist in European and local time-tables, would mention the earliest available train. Adrian Fortescue, for instance, was, as he said: "Knocked speechless" and "only slowly recovered from the impact."[99]

Yet Ward managed to save St Edmund's, largely through his far-reaching vision and the benefactions provided by his family. 1893 was a fortuitous year to begin a new Presidency in such difficult times for it was the College's centenary. Ward cleverly used it to demonstrate to English Catholics the importance of the College both in the past and (potentially) in the future. To mark the anniversary, Ward published his *History of St Edmund's College*, based on years of research and his popular 'magic lantern' talks. It seemed to have an immediate impact. 'It is impossible to go anywhere, even into the cricket field,' wrote a First Division student, 'without seeing somebody diligently reading the *History* of the College, "getting it up," as one would be told, "for the centenary."'[100]

As a sign of the College's new-found confidence, Ward also inaugurated *The Edmundian* in printed form, which has become an invaluable source for the College's story ever since. As Canon Burton later put it, 'we were reminded that we had a noble past, and we were impressed with a spirit of hopefulness and confidence in the future,...he aroused the lasting interest of all Edmundians in the past life and fortunes of St Edmund's'.[101] This was also in line with many other Catholic schools that started journals around the same time.

The opportunity presented by the centenary was taken to heal old wounds. Dr Rymer was invited back to sing the Centenary Mass – his first visit to the College since 1870 – at which all the living ex-Presidents were present, except Mgr Crook. Sir John Stuart Knill, first Catholic Lord Mayor of London (whose father is believed to have given a major donation to fund the building of the College chapel), was escorted to a special prie-dieu on the sanctuary, his train being borne by his two nephews who were at the school. We are told by one witness that:

Fr Hopper, the acting procurator, had been at work for weeks decorating the front of the College with two triumphal arches, one by the Refectory and the other by the Church, linked up by an avenue of poles and Venetian flags and streamers. In the evening the whole of the front of the College was illuminated with rows of fairy lamps and Chinese lanterns on the trees. With a string quartette [sic] playing in the illuminated porch the guests and students paraded on the terrace and far down the park to view the illuminations. It was like a scene from fairyland and never before or since has the front of the College blazed with such splendour.

The only aspect that did not go according to plan was the arrival of the Cardinal: 'Vaughan, whose reception was planned with elaborate care – a carriage and pair waiting at the station, acolythes and crossbearer ready to receive him on arrival – defeated all the plans by walking from Ware and getting a lift in a greengrocer's cart in which to our dismay he drove up from the lodge. But that was Vaughan's way'.[102]

There were the usual toasts and speeches, one of which was given by the President:

The founders of this College came straight from the prisons of France, and are known as the Confessors of Doullens. Their spirit has been imitated here during the last hundred years, and Edmundians have shown an unostentatious devotion to duty and a solid piety worthy of the traditions of Douay, and a reproduction of the spirit of which St Edmund himself gave so illustrious an example. In looking forward to the second century of St Edmund's College, which begins to-day, what better can we hope, than that whilst we keep ourselves materially and intellectually abreast of the age and up to modern requirements, the same spirit of piety may continue to reign amongst us, and we may produce the same solid Christians, priests, and laymen, as we have during our first hundred years.[103]

Mgr Ward gathered around himself some able members of staff. Of particular importance was Fr (later Canon) Edwin Burton, who had qualified as a solicitor prior to entering the seminary and, like the President, was a keen historian. Burton arrived at the beginning of the autumn term 1898, having worked in the busy parish of Commercial Road, and from the first became

Above: The first page of the first printed version of The Edmundian in July 1893. All the printed versions have now been digitally scanned and can be purchased by decades or as a complete body of work.

Top: The ceremonial arch erected at the front of the College to mark the centenary of the establishment of St Edmund's College at Old Hall Green.

Above: An architect's design for an addition to the east end of the 'New Wing' which was never built. The Chapel of Reparation would have been through the arches

great friends with Ward; 'this was noticeable', recalled Mgr Collings, 'because they were seen constantly in each other's company in animated conversation, which was not the case with other members of staff'.[104] After Fr Kuypers departed from the College, Burton succeeded as Vice-President. The friendship between Ward and Burton grew and the two men often travelled together during the school holidays. Burton later reminisced:

As a travelling companion he gladly took all the arrangements on himself, thoroughly enjoying the mapping-out of a journey which was to last continuously for three weeks. For his idea of a holiday was to travel all the time. We would go from place to place, literally for the sake of the voyaging. His ideal day would comprise one or two train journeys, varied by steamer or a carriage drive, and ending at a hotel in some picturesque place where he was sure of being able to say Mass in the morning; and then he would dine and sleep, only to start off again on the morrow.[105]

Alfred Herbert was Prefect of Studies from 1904 to 1917. Like W. G. Ward, he was a layman and a convert, a former chorister of the Chapel Royal, Savoy. Received into the Church in 1873, he briefly studied at St Edmund's and returned as a member of staff in 1895. A gifted linguist, Pope Benedict XV awarded him the much-coveted doctorate in philosophy in 1917, in recognition of his long and distinguished service to ecclesiastical education. An impressive ceremony was held on the Feast of St Thomas Aquinas that year, at which he received the doctor's cap and ring from the President and then the kiss of peace from all the doctors present, who wore academic dress for the occasion.

Writing in 1926, Mgr Arthur S. Barnes stated that 'St Edmund's has been second only to the Oratory [School] in its devotion to the practice of producing Latin plays…These plays as produced at St Edmund's did not follow the severe traditions of Newman at the Oratory or of the plays at Westminster School, but a good deal of by-play was introduced, as also extra characters who had no speaking part'.[106] Newman's adaptations of Latin plays were generally used and Dr Herbert and Fr Burton directed well-received performances of Titus Maccius Plautus's *Aulularia*.

NEW BUILDINGS

Mgr Ward's vision encompassed the College buildings. In 1895 the architect A. E. Purdie drew up, at the President's request, an ambitious plan for extending the College, costing around £12,000:

The College will when completed form a quadrangle, with a cloister all the way round. At the back will be the exhibition hall, to be used ordinarily as the general study place, after the manner of the Northcote Hall at Oscott. The class rooms adjoin at either end, some of them being new additions, others being rooms already in use. There are to be ten in all, which would seem to be sufficient for all College purposes. This leaves the present senior study and the room adjoining the gymnasium free for play rooms, billiard rooms and boys' library; the exact arrangement of which may be safely left for time to unravel. The lavatories will project into the bounds and the swimming bath will be on the ground now occupied by the Professors' lawn tennis, for which latter purpose a new plot will be found in the pleasure grounds. It is proposed to cover in the space between the new lavatory and the Poets' Wing, to form a covered playground for wet weather.[107]

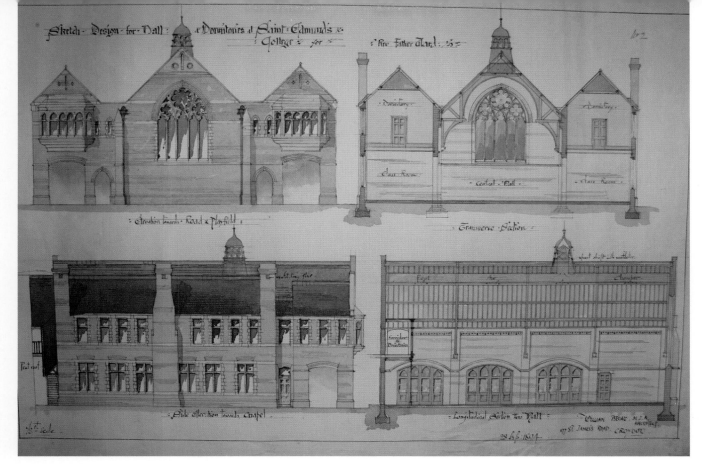

The foundation stone was laid on Exhibition Day 1895 by Cardinal Vaughan but the plan proved too ambitious and was never realised in its entirety. Nevertheless, the period saw much building work: the re-organisation of the Infirmary, music rooms and New Wing Dormitory and installation of new Chapel heating (1894), the erection of the Junior Study Place, Bounds Library, dormitory and lavatories (1895), the refurnishing of the Physical Science lecture room and Bounds playrooms (1896) and then the College Library, First Division Rooms and Laboratory (1897). He also oversaw the building of the Exhibition Room (1902) and 'Ward Wing' (1913).

The Pugin chapel was embellished. In 1904 a magnificent new Shrine Chapel was built to mark the chapel's golden jubilee. Paid for to a large extent by The Edmundian Association, it was solemnly opened on 24 May 1905, together with the new Divines' Wing. After High Mass, at which Bishop Cahill of Portsmouth preached:

Bishop Fenton and his ministers withdrew, and the Relic of St Edmund, which up to this time had lain upon a red velvet cushion, placed between the Altar-pillars on the gospel side, was brought by the Deacon to the Altar itself, where it was incensed. The procession now filed out to the new Shrine, while the Iste Confessor was sung, the Archbishop [Bourne] bearing the Relic which he wished to deposit for the first time in its new resting place with his own hands. The scene in the new chapel was both impressive and beautiful, when his Grace ascended the steps behind the Altar to lay the Reliquary on the outstretched arms of the well-known angels. The chapel itself was crowded with the clergy and students, the black and white of their choir-dress being relieved by the purple line of prelates and canons stretching clown the centre. The white reredos, with its delicate carving relieved by the crimson hangings of the Shrine and the green overhanging palms, formed a background against which the altar with its masses of lilies stood out boldly, and high over all stood the Archbishop in cope and mitre, alone, carefully fixing the Reliquary in the place where it will receive the veneration of future generations.[108]

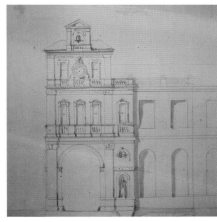

Above: The north elevation of the proposed addition to the east end of the 'New Wing'. A much less ornate building was created in 1904.

Top: A proposed 1894 design for a new school hall and dormitories which was never executed.

Top right: The swimming pool was built between 1895 and 1896 at a cost of £2,200. It was a personal gift to the College from Bernard Ward. It took almost seventy hours to fill the pool with water the first time. It had a 15 foot high diving ladder above just 6 feet of water at the deep end!

Top left: In the winter months starting in 1899, the swimming pool was converted into a gymnasium. The water was drained and a wooden floor was laid across. The floor was stored in a farm shed during the summer months.

Above: The Reading Room in 1906.

Mgr Ward also turned the Chapel into a sort of Westminster Abbey for the Archdiocese, collecting together the remains of many bishops and other worthies. This was facilitated in part by the announcement in 1899 that the historic church of St Mary Moorfields, near Liverpool Street Station, was to be demolished and rebuilt nearby, due to the redevelopment of the area. The bodies buried in its vaults needed to find a new home. Many were moved to Wembley but Mgr Ward arranged for the bodies of the Vicars Apostolic and former Presidents to be moved to St Edmund's. On 18 December the body of Bishop Poynter was the first to return. There was an 'imposing' procession down the Ambulacrum and, according to the Bounds chronicler, 'rumour had it that Dr Poynter's ghost walked about the house, which was so changed since his time that he lost his way. We certainly did hear footsteps about the house at a late hour, but we don't think that they were Dr Poynter's'.[109] He was buried in the cloister, although his heart remained in its original resting place in the chapel. A few weeks later, at the beginning of 1900, the remains of Bishop Bramston, Bishop Gradwell, Fr Francis Tuite (last titular President of Douay) and Fr Joseph Kimbell (President) were brought from Moorfields.

Indeed, 'the translation of the episcopal remains from Moorfields suggested the fitness of St Edmund's College as a resting place for the Vicars-Apostolic, whose special creation it was'. On 24 April 1901 the body of Bishop Talbot, founder of the Old Hall Green Academy, was transferred from the parish churchyard at Hammersmith:

On the eve of that day a long procession of priests and church students in cassock and cotta, followed by the lay boys, went in the clear light of a spring evening to meet the hearse at the lodge gate. The President, vested in black cope, received it with holy water and incense, after which the procession, chanting the Miserere, returned to the College Chapel where Vespers for the Dead were immediately sung. The coffin, surmounted by a Mitre and the Chalice and Paten, specially apt symbols of this Confessor of the Faith, lay in state in the centre of the choir. Late in the evening the Dirge was chanted by priests and students... The Bishop's family was represented by Lady Gwendolen Petre one of the last descendants of the Catholic Talbots, who was accompanied by her husband and daughter. On the following morning the High Mass of Requiem was sung by Canon White, Rector of the parish from which the remains had been brought. After a sermon by Rev. J. H. Pollen, S .J., the coffin was carried to the Chapel Cloister where the President performed the Burial Service, laying the Good Bishop Talbot to rest in that earth which he himself had given to the service of the Church.[110]

In 1907 Bishop Bonaventure Giffard was brought to the College from Old St Pancras Churchyard, together with his brother Andrew and his successor as Vicar Apostolic, Benjamin Petre. St Edmund's thus became the mausoleum of all the Vicars Apostolic of the London District, with the exception of John Leyburn (whose final resting place is unknown), Richard Challoner (buried at Milton and later moved to Westminster Cathedral) and Thomas Walsh (interred in the crypt of the cathedral he built at Birmingham).

In addition, in 1899 Mgr Ward obtained a collection of Sacred Relics from Narni, a small town in the Apennines, thanks to the local bishop who had rescued them from a church confiscated by the Italian State. These included the body of an unknown martyr who was venerated as 'St Ladislas'. At first the body was kept below the altar in the Douay Room but later translated to the Lady Chapel in 1902, near to the original shrine of St Edmund.

There were developments also on the domestic front. In 1902 a community of French nuns of the Institute of the Child Jesus arrived at St Edmund's and settled into the Old Hall, just as the Douay refugees had done in 1793. They were fleeing from anti-clerical laws. At the College they took over responsibility for the kitchen, laundry and infirmary.

AFFILIATION WITH CAMBRIDGE

It has already been mentioned that, despite improving conditions for English Catholics, for most of the nineteenth century Oxford and Cambridge were closed to them, at the request of the bishops and the direction of the Holy See. Manning in particular feared the contamination of the faithful at non-Catholic universities and tried to set up a Catholic University College in Kensington (1875-82), which ultimately failed due to poor administration and financial difficulties. With the accession of Archbishop Vaughan, the attitude changed and in 1895 permission was given for Catholics to attend the older Universities, on the condition they were provided with regular courses of lectures in philosophy, history and theology. A Universities Catholic Education Board was set up and plans were made to provide pastoral and intellectual care for Catholic undergraduates and to set up Catholic 'houses' at the Universities, no matter how small. Ideas were soon floated about a house of Benedictines at Cambridge and Jesuits at Oxford.

Around this time, Mgr Ward — encouraged, it seems, by Dr Herbert — raised the question of the affiliation of St Edmund's with Cambridge. His Vice-President, Fr Nolan, did much of the ground work and approached Anatole von Hügel, brother of the theologian Friedrich and, as Curator

RUMOUR HAD IT THAT DR POYNTER'S GHOST WALKED ABOUT THE HOUSE, WHICH WAS SO CHANGED SINCE HIS TIME THAT HE LOST HIS WAY.

Above: An 1899 sketch of the 'School in the Garden' by Leonard Longstaff (1893-95).

Above right: Leonard Longstaff's drawing of Bishop William Weathers' coffin in the College chapel in 1895.

of the Museum of Archaeology and Ethnology, the first Catholic don at Cambridge since the seventeenth century. Within a matter of weeks, at Christmas 1895, a *Memorial* was produced for the University Senate, outlining the College's history and its academic tradition:

The change from Douay to Old Hall, though welcome, brought one very serious disadvantage. Not only were the new beginnings necessarily very humble, but the valued privilege of forming part of a University was gone, and by reason of the stringency of the laws, then and long afterwards, there was no prospect whatever of entering into any relationship with the ancient Universities of the land.

Affiliation with Cambridge would thus be in continuity with the Edmundian tradition. The College was called 'a place of grave and serious learning' and the memorialist stressed that it had appreciated the long-standing link with the University of London. However,

the desire has been growing for something more than the direction of studies, their careful testing, and the crowning of successful work by an Academic Degree. There is the growing hope that our clerical students may be enabled to find themselves in that great current of life and thought which flows so richly at the two older Universities. This hope, moreover, is particularly cherished just now, when there is a serious endeavour to concentrate instead of dissipating the forces of clerical education.[111]

Affiliation with the University of Cambridge was duly granted by the Senate on 4 June 1896. This led to a more marked distinction between First and Second Divisions at Old Hall, henceforth styled the College and School Divisions, only the former being affiliated to the University and using the Cambridge Higher Local examinations twice a year.

Anatole von Hügel hoped that the Old Hall project, which he supported so keenly, would solve the problem of the care of Catholic undergraduates. A Catholic House could be founded, priests from Old Hall could look after the undergraduates and provide the lectures required by Rome, and – crucially – much of this could be bankrolled by St Edmund's. Fr Nolan was promptly appointed as Chaplain to the Catholics of the University and, with the financial assistance of the Duke of Norfolk, a property was purchased and St Edmund's House was founded in 1896. This was originally envisaged as a lodging house for Catholic students, mostly supplied by St Edmund's College. The Cardinal insisted that the new institution (initially referred to as 'Edmundshouse') should be clerical in nature and Rome stressed that the students should follow literary or scientific subjects with a view to a qualification in education. Thus, one of the first Cambridge students from Old Hall, Fr Myers (a future President), read Classics rather than Divinity; it is clear that his heart lay in the latter discipline, for he only managed to gain a iii, 3.

St Edmund's House would never become a fully-fledged 'branch College' of Old Hall, as the likes of Mgr Ward hoped. In 1898 it failed in its bid to be recognised as a Catholic Hostel by the University Senate. However, St Edmund's House continued as an important lodgings for Catholic students, many of whom were drawn from Old Hall and whose 'Cambridge Report' appeared regularly for many years in The Edmundian. Mgr Ward donated the chapel of St Edmund the year he became a bishop. In more recent years, the institution gained full Collegiate status and was renamed St Edmund's College, although it no longer has a direct link with Old Hall Green nor indeed a specifically Catholic brief.[112]

Mgr Ward became an influential voice in the world of English Catholic education. In 1898 he was elected Secretary to the Conference of Catholic Headmasters and sat for two decades on the Hertfordshire County Council Education Committee.

WAR IN SOUTH AFRICA

St Edmund's was, of course, fully aware of events beyond its walls. In 1899, for example, the Boer War broke out. According to the First Division chronicler:

October 11th. War declared – a Boer war. We are getting very excited about it. Perhaps we should not have known much about it but for the debate on the subject which made us all work it up. We most of us voted against England in the debate, but of course all this is quite different now war is declared. We have a large war map in the library and Father Ross comes in every morning to re-arrange little flags on pins which show us where the troops are. There seem a lot of striped flags (Boers) and not many Union jacks. But there are some Union jacks in the drawer, ready to be pinned on when our troops arrive.

The students followed the war via telegraph; indeed, 'the taking of Spion Kop...and the relief of Kimberley, were known at Old Hall within about an hour of the time when they were known in London'. However, 'it will be long remembered against him [the telegraphist] how he took down on February 21st a telegram from a friend of ours at the War Office, "Relief of Ladysmith confirmed," when the original was "Relief of Ladysmith unconfirmed." The result was much

Above: The College celebrated British victories in the South African War with great patriotism. 'Pretoria Day' – 7 June 1900 – celebrated the capture of Pretoria by British forces. The students decorated the College using flags and lamps that had been used to celebrate the centenary of 1893. Fireworks were purchased in London and the professor who purchased them arrived back at the College in grand style sitting on the box containing them!

A grand design in 1895 by architect
A E Purdie to enclose the Quadrangle and
create an exhibition hall, ten classrooms,
lavatories, a swimming pool, a covered
playground, two dormitories, a library for
the students and a billiard room for the
professors. From this plan only the
swimming pool was ever executed.

The design also shows the Chapel spire
which never existed.

A. E. Purdie,
FRIBA
Jan. 1895

Top: The laying of the foundation stone of the new Divines' Wing in 1904.

Above: The ceiling of the new Shrine Chapel. The chapel was built in 1904 at the suggestion of The Edmundian Association to celebrate the Golden Jubilees of the College Chapel and of the Association, both of which took place in 1903.

Opposite top: The opening of the Divines' Wing on 24 May 1904. The dignitaries and guests are seated in front of 'the elephant', the porch so named because it looked like the hind quarters of the animal.

Opposite bottom: The interior of the Shrine Chapel when it was built.

rejoicing and a holiday, all of a "previous" nature'. One student added, 'there is now a rumour that the telegraph clerk was in the employ of the boys, who wanted a play day. But this rumour is denied'.

The College kept a paternal eye on the old boys involved in the conflict and printed their letters in The Edmundian. There were several casualties, including Forrester Cunningham (killed in the battle of Elandslaagte) and Lieutenant Charles Thomas (who died of enteric at Kroonstad).

THE RETURN OF THE DIVINES

Francis Bourne, who had succeeded Cardinal Vaughan as Archbishop of Westminster in September 1903, decided to reverse the policies of his two immediate predecessors by returning the seminary to St Edmund's. This greatly pleased the octogenarian former President, Dr Rymer, who had disagreed with Manning's decision to remove the Divines in 1868. Visiting the College in 1903 for the chapel's golden jubilee, he had 'declared that he longed to lived and felt sure he would live, to see the College reconstituted in all its completeness'. His wish was indeed granted.

The return of the seminary, which took place in 1904, necessitated new buildings. The result was the Divines' Wing, designed by F. A. Walters, with its distinctive porch known as 'the elephant', and opened on 24 May 1905, along with the new Shrine Chapel. The local press described the Divines' Wing as it appeared at the opening:

It is entered by a handsome porch on the east side, which with the façade is executed in red rubbed bricks and Bath stone dressings. Over the porch is a massive pediment, on which are beautifully carved the College arms, and over the front door is another pediment adorned with Catholic emblems. On the one side of the large entrance hall are the lecture rooms for philosophy and theology, and on the other side the students' common room and sacristy. Beyond these rooms is the ambulacrum, which is connected with the south cloister and leads to the Oratory, which will be known as the "Chapel of St Francis de Sales." For beauty of design the altar in the Oratory, which is the gift of the Archbishop, demands attention. The altar is composed of alabaster and antique green marble with panels of red marble, and the altar-piece consists of three paintings on copper set in beautifully carved wooden panels adorned with 2,000 gold leaves. The carver was three months engaged on this reredos, and the work is a triumph of artistic skill... The lengthy south cloister is joined at right angles by the west cloister which communicates with the refectory and the library, the only two portions of the old building with the exception of the church that will be used by the Divines.

There is a lift from the ground floor to three upper stories where are the professors' and students' rooms, accommodation having been provided for fifty Divines. Jeffrey's "Ideal System" of heating and ventilation has been adopted, and as it can be easily controlled and regulated at will, it is certainly one of the most perfect systems in operation at the present time and quite a feature of the new buildings. The new building is lighted with acetylene gas, which claims to be superior as an illuminant to either coal gas or even electric light, as it gives an extremely soft and brilliant light, and its rays approach chemically more nearly to the qualities of sunlight.[117]

The altar in the Divines' Oratory had images of St Edmund, St John the Apostle and St Francis de Sales, all carefully chosen as models of the 'spirit' that the Archbishop hoped would be produced by the College: 'a spirit of gentleness, which is the perfection of strength, and the outcome of Christian self-restraint'.[118] The seminary was always kept separate from the rest of the College, with its own lecture room (now the Myers Room), common room (now the Griffiths Room), refectory (the current Music School), sacristy (later to become the Cardinal Hume Centre) and oratory (the present Staff Parlour). There was even a Natural History Museum, including about a thousand stuffed birds, collected by the biologist and convert, St George Jackson Mivart, which were transferred to St Edmund's after the closure of the ill-fated Catholic University College in Kensington. Many of these were later given to St Mary's Hospital, Paddington.

SOON, THE CHAPEL WAS ALL BUT DESERTED.... THE FIRE WAS ALREADY BEYOND CONTROL.

On 21 July 1907 the Divines' Wing was severely damaged by a fire originating in the attic, though the exact cause was never definitively established. It was a Sunday and High Mass was in progress when, during the singing of the creed, a worried sacristan approached the President to tell him the disturbing news. Soon, the chapel was all but deserted, except for the sacred ministers and choir, so that Mass could be reverently completed. The fire was already beyond control and boys were dispatched on their bicycles to summon the local fire brigades. In the meantime, the students tried to collect together as much water as possible to dampen down the flames and the College was evacuated. Much of its contents, including books from the Library and treasures from the Museum, were either carried or thrown out and left on the lawns. Stories were later circulated that one student had flung his much-loved type-writer out of the window and that a member of staff, who had carefully insured his personal effects, watched the fire with an expression of pleasure. Thankfully there were no serious casualties, beyond Fr James Reany suffering burns, the Head Boy being hit by furniture thrown from a window and William Foley having his cassock covered in molten lead. Fortunately the fire did not spread very far, thanks to the lack of a strong wind and a barricade consisting of wet mattresses and linen, which was erected on the first floor where the Divines' Wing connected with the rest of the College.

The fire brigades started arriving about an hour after the alarm was raised – not bad considering there were no telephones and the College telegraph office was closed. By this time, a considerable crowd from the local area had gathered to watch the unfolding tragedy. The throng included some unscrupulous types who freely wandered through the (safer) parts of the College, helping themselves to watches and other valuables from empty rooms.

Opposite: The cricket pavilion was built in 1894 at a cost of £90, the money being raised by subscriptions from Old Edmundians. By using the point at which two existing walls met, it was built economically and filled an ugly corner. In 1906 it was moved back slightly and extended.

Above: The cricket team of 1894.

Left: The 'Giant's Stride' was a popular item of playground equipment.

By evening, the fire had been contained, leaving the new extension severely damaged and roofless. Most of the College's treasures had been saved, although some of the geological and natural specimens, then being stored in the attic, were destroyed and the money claimed from their insurance went towards the rebuilding of the top floor. The new Mansard roof, completed by Easter 1908, actually enabled seventeen extra rooms with dormer windows.

The great fire of 1907 left a strong impression in the College psyche. A special red-covered supplement to *The Edmundian* in September 1907 recorded all the details of the College's almost miraculous escape from catastrophe for posterity. The Edmundian Association erected a window in the Shrine Chapel in thanksgiving. Forming part of a series of windows concerning the life of St Edmund, the new window showed various scenes in the saint's life that involved fire. Moreover, a memorial tablet was placed at the spot where the barricade had been built. A manual fire engine was also purchased, in case of future emergencies, and it promptly earned the nick-name of Manuale Clericorum.

GAMES AND PASTIMES

Mgr Ward had a great concern for the College's sporting tradition, particularly cricket – hardly a surprise given that his grandfather, William Ward, was a celebrated cricketer and proprietor of Lord's. His score of 278 for the MCC against Norfolk in 1820 had been the highest individual innings until W. G. Grace broke the record in 1876. By that time Fr Ward himself was a proud member of the MCC. He persuaded 'Bill' Caffyn to coach the College XI in the 1884-85 season, the first former professional to do so. Caffyn had played for Surrey and spent some time in Australia where, in the words of the *The Edmundian*, 'he became practically the father of Australian cricket'. However, by the time he was helping at St Edmund's he ran a barber's shop in Hertford.[119]

SEPTEMBER, 1907.

THE EDMUNDIAN.

Special Supplement

WITH

AN ACCOUNT OF THE LATE FIRE.

CONTENTS.

Fire at St Edmonds College July 21st 07

Opposite top: The playing field in the early 1890s. The building in the centre was known as the 'Poets' Wing'. On the ground floor were a gymnasium, carpentry workshop and billiard room, and on the first floor were rooms for students.

Opposite bottom: The football team in 1911.

Above: The cricket team in 1914.

Right: The cast of the Latin play the 'Sumbolaria' in 1909, directed by Dr Alfred Herbert (seated centre).

Left: The Bounds Prefects in 1908.

Below left: The school uniform in 1905.

Below right: A tug-o-war in 1908.

Opposite top left: Long Dormitory was built in 1913.

Opposite top right: The Divines Refectory was also built in 1913.

Opposite below: Mr James Dobson in the science laboratory in the early 1900s.

St. Edmund's College, Old Hall, Ware. Allen Hall, Refectory.

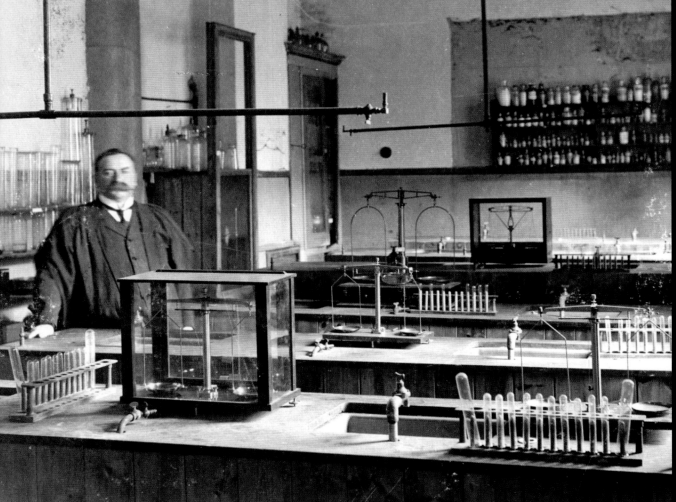

Above: The Professors' Cycling Club.

Top: The football team in 1894.

In 1901 Ward traced the history of Edmundian cricket in the College magazine, noting that in its early days 'the chief rule seems to have been that it was in every way subservient to the interests of farming on the College land' so that 'the games were arranged on whatever part of the park happened to be in best order that particular year'. The method was 'entirely unscientific' and 'underhand bowling of course reigned supreme,'[120] until the MCC rules were introduced by Mr Tunstall, a future Procurator.

Ward made sure that in the summer two afternoons were set aside each week for cricket and in 1894 erected the new Cricket Pavilion to serve the now extended Cricket Ground. It also functioned as a tuck shop, raising funds for the public games. Reports of matches were carefully written up in *The Edmundian*, in which the College XI encountered such opposition as 'Priests of the South of England' and 'Zouaves' (those who had volunteered to fight for the Pope during Italian Unification in an international regiment called the Pontifical Zouaves), as well as local teams.

In 1895 Mgr Ward built the Swimming Bath as a personal gift. Tragically one of the workmen, a College tenant, was crushed to death when an old wall suddenly collapsed during the building work. The pool was opened in Easter Week 1896 and the first official dive made by an old boy, Charles Rymer. At first the 'Syntaxians' were given the responsibility of looking after the pool, with the special privilege of using it whenever they pleased. During the winter months, a wooden floor was laid over the pool, transforming the space into a gymnasium.

Football was also an important part of Edmundian life and by the time of the 1893 Centenary, Association Football was replacing the rougher 'Bounds' Football, in which the ball could be carried and punched as well as kicked: 'Woe to the hapless youth who picks up the ball. He is greeted with angry shouts of "put it down!" "No hands! no hands!"'[121] Internal matches included 'Church v Lay', 'Irish v the World', and 'Gospel v Epistle Side' (referring to the two sides of the chapel).

Rugby, hockey and lawn tennis also proved popular and in 1894 it was reported that golf was 'now being played by a few enthusiasts in the College Park. They are experiencing the usual difficulties of beginners with the additional one of dealing with the bullocks which are wont to graze there, especially as the latter seem inconveniently attentive to the red flags that mark the holes'.[122]

There were other pastimes, including chess, billiards, cycling (into which the President enthusiastically threw himself) and paper chases, where those designated as 'hounds' would spend some energetic hours pursuing the 'hares' around the local countryside. During the winter, play-days were granted for skating on nearby lakes and rivers, just as students had done in the early days at Old Hall and before that at Douay. There were also elaborate snow fights, as the First Division chronicler recorded in 1895:

Jan. 22. As this was a half-play day, it was determined that a snow fight should take place down in the Park. The First Division challenged the house to mortal combat – to do or die. The disorderly army of the Bounds was the first in the field, and having selected a site, set to work to erect a fort. When the First Division mustered in the Ambulacrum, it was thought that the numbers were very uneven, there being about 18 of us to some 60 or 70 of the enemy. After a conference between the opposing leaders, it was decided that the Second of Rudiments should fight for us. This business satisfactorily settled, we also proceeded to erect fortifications. The sides were now augmented by the arrival of some of the masters. Dr Driscoll and Fr Kuypers fought for us, while Mr Connelly threw in his lot with the Bounds.

When the forts were finished, and a stock of ammunition laid in, we sallied out and assailed the enemy's position. So fierce and irresistible was our onslaught, that in a couple of minutes from the start, we had pulled down the walls of the fort, and rolled the component snow-balls far away from the original site, afterwards retiring joyfully to our own redoubt. The enemy, now left without a place of retreat, poured down in a confused horde upon our stronghold. They had difficult work to approach us, and had to be content with rolling parts of our walls a few yards away. Time was now called, to end the first attack, and each party retired to repair (in the one case) or to rebuild (in the other) their forts.

In the end, the result of the 'battle' was inconclusive, 'each side loudly proclaiming its glorious victory to Old Hall Green at large'.[123]

Above: The stars of 'Dick Whittington, without much of a cat', a school play in 1905. Dick Whittington was played by Bobbie Shone (1901-08) and the cat by Cyril Hume-Wright (1903-06).

The Last Years of Mgr Ward

Examination of New Boys

There was a College tradition of an 'Examination' for boys who joined the school after term had started:

A new boys' examination was always a great occasion: three or four Rhetoricians dressed in cassock and biretta or master's gown, spectacled and sometimes bearded, would assemble on the platform of Ruds II class room, while the whole school packed into the remaining space. The victim was placed in front before the dais and subjected to the most harassing and embarrassing as well as the most impossible questions and then finally required to sing. At this the gas lights went out and a complete and general pandemonium ensued from which the "masters" made it their business to be "first out".[126]

Mgr Ward saved St Edmund's from closure and created the modern College, including many of its traditions. According to Dr Vance, the College became 'more like a private gentleman's house or a private academy' and for his many achievements 'Ward, not of any set purpose or caprice, but by his very nature, demanded personal recognition'.[124] He could be forgiven for thinking it was 'his' College, his little empire. However, the last years of his Presidency were overshadowed by the First World War (dealt with in the next chapter), personal bereavement, poor health and disagreements within the College.

In 1908 rumours abounded in the press that Ward was about to be appointed bishop of Northampton and consequently he received letters and telegrams of congratulation. Indeed, it seemed also to be 'an opportunity of terminating Mgr Ward's presidency with honour, on the principle of promovetur ut amovetur'. However, in the end, the mitre was handed to Frederick Keating, who had formerly been Ward's colleague at Oscott. According to Mgr Collings, a confidante of Cardinal Bourne:

When the names of the candidates for the vacant see of Northampton were submitted by Propaganda to the Pope for his final selection, Mgr Ward's name appeared first on the list. While the Holy Father was considering the question Cardinal Gasquet had one of his routine audiences and was consulted as to the appointment. The Pope had no personal knowledge of either candidate. The Cardinal, remembering what Mgr Ward had told him some time before, and not knowing that in the meantime he had changed his mind and was quite willing to leave St Edmund's if promoted to the episcopate, conveyed his previously express wish to the Holy Father. The Pope thereupon appointed Canon Keating.[125]

Ward was acutely embarrassed. He seemed to lose some of his enthusiasm towards the College and found increasing solace in his historical research. Relations became strained with other members of staff and his health visibly began to decline.

In September 1915 the President was severely shaken by the death of his brother, Edmund Granville, who had been a generous benefactor to the College. Mgr Ward was forced into convalescence after being taken ill on St Edmund's Day 1915. Although some advised the immediate appointment of a new President, Ward was back in harness the following March. By this time, Burton was also in poor health and much of the day-to-day running of the College fell to Fr Myers, the Professor of Dogmatic Theology. A further blow for the President came in April 1916 when he lost his other brother, Wilfrid, editor of *The Dublin Review* and biographer of Wiseman, Newman and his own beloved father.

The staff now came to the conclusion that they could no longer work with the President and Fr Burton was deputed to present these feelings to him and request his resignation. As can be imagined, their friendship was never the same again, although the President saw Fr Myers as the head of an anti-Ward faction. On 19 July 1916 Mgr Ward finally resigned and accepted a new appointment as Rector of Holy Trinity, Brook Green. Before departing St Edmund's, he told his successor (Burton) that he thought he had been the victim of a plot.

Father Byles, the Hero of RMS Titanic

Father Byles was born Roussel Davids Byles on 26 February 1870, the eldest of seven children of a Congregationalist minister. He studied at Balliol College, Oxford, and intended to study for Orders in the Church of England. However, he was received into the Catholic Church in 1894, taking the name 'Thomas'. He spent a brief time at Oscott, before becoming a Professor at St Edmund's, Ware, while continuing his studies (1895-99). During this time he published *A School Commentary on the Second Epistle of St Paul to the Corinthians* (1897) and reorganised the College Library, burning unwanted books on a large bonfire. He was later sent to the Beda College in Rome and was ordained in 1902; his priestly ministry was revolved around the newly-founded Catholic Missionary Society (1903-05) and the Essex parishes of Kelvedon (1905) and Ongar (1905-12), then part of the Archdiocese of Westminster.

On 10 April 1912 he set out on the Titanic to officiate at his brother William's wedding in New York. Fr Byles was initially scheduled to travel on another White Star liner but switched at the last minute. In a letter, he complained about losing his umbrella on his way to Southampton and said that he found the ship's vibrations unpleasant. He also mentioned meeting two other priests on board: the Lithuanian Fr Juozas Montvila (whose beatification cause has been opened) and the German Dom Josef Peruschitz (who had been staying at St Augustine's Abbey, Ramsgate and was on his way to a Benedictine school in Minnesota). Fr Byles said Mass on the morning of the sinking (14 April) for both Second and Third Class passengers in their respective lounges, and preached in English and French. The sermon, rather appropriately, was on the need for a spiritual lifebelt in the shape of prayer and the sacraments when in danger of shipwreck in times of temptation. Byles was reciting his Breviary on the upper deck when the Titanic struck the iceberg. As the ship was sinking, he assisted many Third Class passengers up to the Boat Deck to the lifeboats. He reputedly twice refused a place on a lifeboat. He was last seen praying the rosary, giving absolution and calming the passengers who remained trapped on the stern of the ship after the lifeboats had been launched. His body was never found. Later that year his brother was received in audience by the pope, St Pius X, who referred to Fr Byles as 'a martyr for the Church'. He has twice been portrayed on the silver screen in *S.O.S. Titanic* (1979) and *Titanic* (1997) and there is a brass plaque in his honour at St Edmund's in Monument Lane.

Above: RMS Titanic was a British passenger liner that sank in the North Atlantic Ocean on 15 April 1912 after colliding with an iceberg during her maiden voyage. The sinking of Titanic caused the deaths of 1,502 people in one of the deadliest peacetime maritime accidents in modern history. Over a century after the event, the Titanic disaster is still a focus of great interest.

CHAPTER IX

'A CATHOLIC WINCHESTER': BOURNE AND ST EDMUND'S
1916-1932

The summer term of 1914 was noted for its fine weather and several colourful events that punctuated life at St Edmund's. In May, for example, the foundation stone was laid for the new Catholic church of St Richard at Buntingford, the occasion of an impressive procession along the village street consisting of the College Divines, clergy, Mgr Ward, who 'walked with Mgr Benson in the dress of a Papal chamberlain, thus bringing the Roman purple into the long line of black and white,' and finally Bishop Butt, in cope and mitre. The aforementioned Mgr Benson of Hare Street, the famous convert and writer who would die unexpectedly just a few months later, preached a memorable sermon.[127]

Then, in June 1914, the College was visited by an Irish saint and two English cardinals: Blessed Columba Marmion, the Abbot of Maredsous (Belgium) and an esteemed spiritual guide, preached the General Ordination Retreat, while the annual Speech Day was attended not only by Cardinal Bourne but also Cardinal Aidan Gasquet, a monk of Downside recently elevated to the Sacred College. *The Edmundian* reported that 'the scene on the Terrace on the arrival of Cardinal Gasquet, and his reception, accompanied by the cheers of the assembled students, with Cardinal Bourne waiting him at the threshold of the College, was bright and picturesque: still more was that after lunch, when the visitors sat watching the Indian Club Drill, and the colours of the Ladies' dresses lent additional brightness to the view'.[128] The 'displays' included human pyramids: these were in three groups, 'in the centre one of which the President seated himself on a board resting on the knees of two athletes, while the Vice-President and Prefect of Studies took corresponding positions in the groups on the right and left respectively. Meanwhile the band played "God save the King."'[129] The fine weather was such that the speeches took place on the terrace.

THE FIRST WORLD WAR

No one expected that four years of hardship and bloodshed were about to begin. Indeed, political events moved so quickly that many Edmundians were caught unawares:

The suddenness with which the war broke out, in the early days of the vacation, when our masters were scattered in different lands, holiday seeking, necessarily led to their being in some cases in positions of discomfort and even anxiety; but on the whole less inconvenience was caused than might easily have been the case. The President [Mgr Ward] was on the eve of leaving for Switzerland via Alsace; but fortunately had not actually started. Dr Tynan was in Belgium, but succeeded in getting home without much difficulty. Father Cameron set out with the pilgrimage to Lourdes, and had to turn back at Paris, on the day of the declaration of war.

Left: The Cadet Corps (8th Hertfordshire Cadets) in 1917.

Above: Old Edmundians serving in the Great War wrote regular letters which were published in The Edmundian.

He had a very difficult journey home. Our French Master, M. Heer, by nationality a Swiss, was called to the colours, and had to resign his position with us. Father Myers was in Belgium during the early weeks of the war, and only came home after the Germans had overrun the country. Dr Vance was taking his holiday at Fiesole, outside Florence, and appeared to be stranded through not being able to get any money. It was fortunate, so far as he was concerned, that the Conclave brought Cardinal Bourne to Rome, and by his kind help Dr Vance was rescued from his disagreeable position. He had a slow and uncomfortable, but safe journey home.

There were immediate changes to College life. By the end of 1914, the editor of *The Edmundian* stated:

All outside matches at Football have been cancelled, and an effort has been made to revive the shooting range, which became popular during the South African war, but has of late years fallen into disuse. Then we have the weekly short Exposition, as well as the Miserere at the Sunday Benediction, to remind us of the duty of prayer; while the two alms boxes at the bottom of the church carry on a friendly rivalry between the Prince of Wales' Fund and that for the Belgian Refugees.[130]

The celebration of St Edmund's Day in 1914 was more restrained than usual, although much was made of the presence of Mgr de Wachter, Auxiliary Bishop of Malines, who represented 'heroic Belgium' and the many refugees who had come to England. These included Belgian seminarians who found a temporary home at St Edmund's; by September 1916 there were two students from the diocese of Bruges and one from Ghent. Cardinal Bourne presented an altar of Our Lady of Perpetual Succour to the Divines' Oratory in 1915 as a way of commending the country and Empire to her maternal protection during the anxieties of conflict.

In February 1917 the College responded to a Government appeal to adopt a Voluntary System of Rationing, which allowed 4lb of bread, 2½ lb of meat and ¾ lb of sugar per week for each person. This necessitated drastic changes in the provision of food and Burton was open-minded enough to ask that

the men of each year should choose two representatives thus forming an advisory committee of eight to sit under the chairmanship of the Senior Deacon and report on two points: (i) the best way of reducing the consumption of bread, meat and sugar, and (ii) the substitution of other articles of diet.[131]

Fortunately, the new rationing measures did not prevent the traditional pancakes on the Shrove Tuesday play-day. *The Edmundian* noted that 'after some months experience of the revised dietary, we can only state that whatever our enforced mortification may have cost us, we have rarely had so little illness in the house, and the healthy appearance of the boys, taken with a chronically empty infirmary, is the best testimony that their health has not suffered'.[132]

The College anxiously followed the progress of the war and, quite naturally, had a special interest in Old Edmundians serving at the front, including many Church Boys who had reached military age. At the end of January 1916, for instance, six Rhetoricians were summoned to the Colours and told by Fr Myers in the brief ceremony that marked their departure:

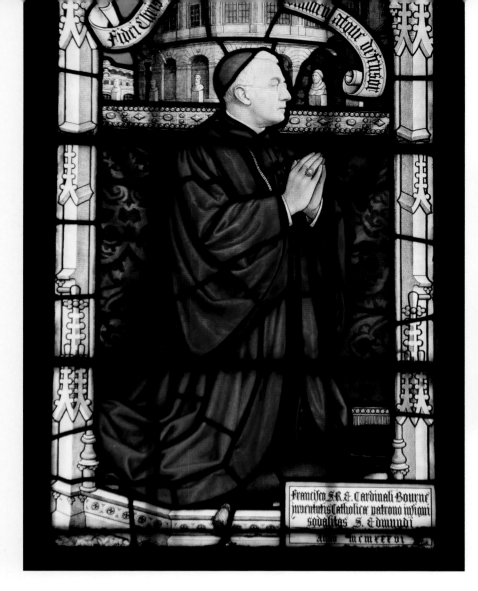

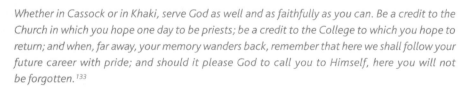

Whether in Cassock or in Khaki, serve God as well and as faithfully as you can. Be a credit to the Church in which you hope one day to be priests; be a credit to the College to which you hope to return; and when, far away, your memory wanders back, remember that here we shall follow your future career with pride; and should it please God to call you to Himself, here you will not be forgotten.[133]

Sadly, one of their number was killed in action in March 1917: Joseph Leopold Mann of the Honourable Artillery Company, formerly a Rhetorician. His friend, Frederick Dixon, wrote that 'he died as he lived a good and brave Edmundian', his body being found 'with his Prayer book clasped in his hand'. He had remained focussed on his desire to be a priest and 'always used to say that one of our greatest helps and consolations came from the prayers that were said for us at College'.[134] A Requiem was held for him at the College and for the first time both the Khaki cap and Church student's cassock were placed together on top of the catafalque.

By mid-1917 there were twenty Church Boys fighting for King and Country and the lectures in philosophy were suspended until the end of hostilities. Throughout the war there had been some apprehension about whether the Divines or even those in Major Orders would be called up, as they had been in France. The Military Service Act of 1916 listed clergymen as a reserved

Above: The first Edmundian conscripts to the Great War, taken on 19 January 1916, the morning of their departure from the College. Standing from left: Henry Merrifield (1910-16), Patrick Murphy (1912-16), Reginald Hatton (1913-16) and William McCormick (1912-16). Seated: Joseph Mann (1910-16) and Frederick Dixon (1909-16 & 1920-23).

Sadly Joseph Mann was not to return. On 15 March 1917 his platoon was ordered forward to test the strength of the opposing force. He was shot in the side and, unable to move, he lay on the ground under fire, reading the prayer book he carried with him. He was later killed by a bullet in the head. He is buried at Gommecourt British Cemetery in France.

occupation and Bourne and his fellow bishops worked hard to ensure that this continued to be the case. However, rumours to the contrary persisted; in March 1917 the papers reported that 'the Army Council intended to recall the exemption granted to theological students'. The President sent his deputy to London to find out more. On his return, he gathered the Divines together and assured them 'that the matter was in hand and there was no need for anxiety, that all men in major orders were exempt, that the others would be called up for medical examination and if passed as fit would be placed on the reserve with leave to continue their studies at the College'. They were even given a day-off since they had become 'very unsettled and anxious'.[135]

There was also a need for army chaplains and the Cardinal encouraged his priests to consider their positions; three College professors had joined up by the summer term 1917 and as a result supervision in the study places was now undertaken by Divines, so that the staff had time for the additional classes. Several Divines also assisted in teaching.

Old Edmundians home from the front or invalided could often be found visiting the College; on one occasion the President recorded that 'Mr F. L. Crowley home on short leave from his regiment gave an address to the boys in the exhibition room...on his experiences of training in trench-digging, bomb-throwing, etc'.[136] *The Edmundian* contained regular updates, letters and, with a depressing regularity, obituaries of those who had fallen; 'we have become sadly accustomed,' the editor wrote in July 1915, 'to seeing a new name placed on the Church door, and the announcement on Sunday, before the sermon, of yet another Edmundian being read out as "killed in action."'[137] An Annual Requiem was held for those fallen in battle: 'the Church was draped in black and a laurel wreath was placed round the names of the dead at the foot of the catafalque which was covered with the Union Jack and bore an officer's cap and sword... After the Absolutions the buglers and drummers of the Cadets Corps sounded the Last Post'.[138]

The College took great pride in its old boys who were decorated for bravery. In October 1916 Fr Burton wrote in his Diary of a visit from Lieut. Edward Villa, who 'joined the army as a private, at the age of 15, obtained a commission in the Notts and Derby Regiment, won the Military Cross and was wounded twice, the second time severely in the arm when escaping from Germans who had taken him prisoner. He is still in his nineteenth year'.[139] Then there was Francis Knapp, who had left St Edmund's as long ago as 1878 and joined the Carmelites, being ordained as 'Fr Simon Stock'. Despite poor health, he served as a military chaplain during the Boer War and joined up again in 1914. He was attached to the Irish Guards and awarded both the Military Cross and DSO. He died on 1 August 1917 after being struck by a piece of shell. On being hit, he said to a fellow officer, 'It's come at last'.

Fr Lancelot Long, who had formerly served as Master of First Rudiments and Choir Master, wrote that his experience in France was:

made up of violent contrasts. On the same day one would visit the trenches and give a catechism class to village children. From a festive gathering one would pass to spend an hour flat on the earth, praying the while that the German gunnery might not be too "deadly accurate"...One

Above: The Divinity students 1916-1917.

remembers the wounded coming in, the smell of gas, the streams of blood, the piteous cries for water, the shrieks of the men as their wounds were dressed, and the silent bodies awaiting burial. Then, too, one remembers the lanes fresh in their green and spring-time glory, the larks that sang just before zero hour, the bands of happy children, the laughing infants in a catechism class, and the quiet of our Sunday Mass. Life in France was lived in contrasts. It was a thing not of subdued harmonies but of crashing discords.[140]

In 1916 the College itself got a taste of the action. The President wrote on 1 October that 'shortly after Benediction the noise of Zeppelins was heard, and continued from 9.30 till midnight, but none seemed to come very near the College. Just before twelve o'clock many of the professors, Divines and servants saw a Zeppelin fall in flames in the direction of north London. There was much cheering both from the College and from villagers in the roadway'.[141] In the early hours Stevenage was bombed and a Zeppelin brought down at Potter's Bar, which caused much noise and vibration. A year later, Zeppelin raids were still disturbing the College community at night. The school chronicler reported on 1 October 1917:

On three consecutive nights the local guns put up a noisy barrage, for the benefit of enemy planes, attempting to reach London from the north. Apprehension of falling shrapnel caused us to assemble in the ambulacrum, which served as our cellar. Naturally, most of us said that we were not in the least afraid, but I feel sure that a few, at any rate, felt a little uneasy. Not only was it exciting, but also to a certain degree fascinating to watch the star shells. One would almost have imagined that they were a display of fireworks but for the distant rumble of the guns, in the direction of London.[142]

ONE STUDENT WAS HEARD TO SAY, 'I WISH THEY'D HAVE AN ARMISTICE EVERY TERM'.

In February 1917 great excitement was caused when a British plane crash landed in West Ley Field, not far from St Edmund's: 'the officer Lieut. Knight-Austey came to the College for assistance and telephoned to St Alban's for lorries to remove the aeroplane. Meanwhile the 4th platoon of the Cadet Corps mounted guard during the afternoon'.[143] The pilot took great pleasure in showing the boys the different parts of his plane and how they worked.

It was, of course, a great relief when the Armistice came in 1918:

Nov. 11th — About midday today arrived the news of the signing of the Armistice and the consequent cessation of hostilities; studies were immediately suspended and the day was given over to rejoicing. In the evening all the shades were removed from the gases in Church and for the first time for five long years the Church was lit up as in prewar days. At Benediction a solemn Te Deum was enthusiastically sung and after the Adoremus all stood and sang "God save the King."

A play day was promptly declared and after a High Mass of Thanksgiving, the boys were treated to a huge bonfire ('what struck a casual observer as being rather extraordinary was the number and variety of the latest revue songs which everyone seemed to know and accuracy with which they were sung') and, after supper, a 'patriotic concert'. One student was heard to say, 'I wish they'd have an Armistice every term'.[144]

THE PRESIDENCY OF CANON EDWIN BURTON

Against the backdrop of war, as already mentioned, the long Presidency of Mgr Ward came to an end. This had been a delicate moment and the authorities were careful to show the long-serving President their appreciation. At St Edmund's Day 1916 a telegram was sent to Mgr Ward at Brook Green: 'The Cardinal and bishops of the province of Westminster, many old

Edmundians, professors, Divines, and boys, celebrating the feast of St Edmund, have you in their thoughts and gratefully recall your long years of work for the College'.[145]

Ward's successor as President was his trusty deputy, Dr Edwin Burton. He had been on the teaching staff since 1898, becoming the longest-serving Vice-President (fourteen years). He was also a generous benefactor to the College, donating as early as 1893 the stained glass windows of the Lady Chapel, now in the Shrine; followed by the Akers Window (1900) and, in conjunction with Mgr Ward, the Douay Martyrs' Windows in 'Monument Lane' (1903). He contributed to the building of St Edmund's Shrine and gave the carved Statues in the Divines' Ambulacrum. A keen historian, like Ward, his magnum opus was the two volume life of Bishop Richard Challoner (1909), which contained a substantial section on Standon Lordship. He also managed to reorganise the College Museum and catalogue the Archive.

Mgr Ward's departure was the end of an era. It also saw the start of a new one, as Cardinal Bourne was able to bring to fruition various schemes he had for St Edmund's. He has been described as the College's 'second founder'[146] and once declared: 'I was a student here, both as a lay boy and afterwards as an ecclesiastic, and I can say fully that there is no interest that I have more keenly at heart than the welfare of both classes of students at St Edmund's College'.[147]

An immediate change introduced by the Archbishop was the setting up of a Cadet Corps. This had been vigorously opposed by Mgr Ward, who discouraged any signs of a martial spirit at the outbreak of war and thought a Corps entirely unsuitable for an institution that was, in part, an ecclesiastical seminary. Bourne, on the other hand, was supremely aware of his role as a national leader in wartime and thought that the training in arms and military discipline was not only a sign of the College's patriotism but an important part of the public school curriculum. Thus, the 8th Hertfordshire Cadet Corps was formally established on 22 September 1916, under the command of Fr Austin Askew, the Prefect of Studies, and with the assistance of Sergeant-Major Roberts.

In a circular letter to parents, Burton stressed that the Corps undertook 'to provide elementary military training' and that this would promote 'self-control, combined with initiative and intelligent application of whatever demands particular circumstances may make upon him, as well as confidence in his own power of action, endurance and command...his character and physique are, therefore, trained, developed and strengthened'.[148] The Corps' debut was at St Edmund's Day 1916, when they formed a guard of honour for the Cardinal and were later inspected by him.

As can be imagined, Mgr Ward was furious at this development, though there was little he could initially do, especially since Bourne had insisted the retired President should not be involved in College affairs. However, in 1917 he was appointed first bishop of Brentwood, a diocese formed out of Westminster's eastern territory. Bourne encouraged this appointment but there were already tensions between the two prelates and these were now exacerbated by the inevitable growing pains as the new diocese was established. Chief among these were the questions of funding for Brentwood and the position of the new bishop with regard to the College. There was also the issue of which Westminster students would be transferred to the embryonic diocese.

Above: Dr Edwin Burton was President of St Edmund's between 1916 and 1918.

Opposite top: Windows in the Shrine Chapel that were donated by Dr Burton.

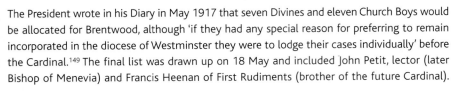

The President wrote in his Diary in May 1917 that seven Divines and eleven Church Boys would be allocated for Brentwood, although 'if they had any special reason for preferring to remain incorporated in the diocese of Westminster they were to lodge their cases individually' before the Cardinal.[149] The final list was drawn up on 18 May and included John Petit, lector (later Bishop of Menevia) and Francis Heenan of First Rudiments (brother of the future Cardinal).

Canon Burton, meanwhile, was struggling with the material condition of the College. As Dr Vance later recalled,

Roofs leaked, floors fell away, ceilings hung in dubious suspension, the gas system leaked in pipe and joint and gave but a feeble spluttering light, the gates and posts of the property were crumbling below the paint, the farm buildings were falling to pieces and the thatch of the barns might be carried off by any frolicsome wind. The sanitary system was defective, the water supply in places uncertain. Much of the woodwork of sashes and stair-ways was rotten, the furniture was broken, and the whole College both within and without, needed that thorough overhaul and decoration which was ultimately to cost many thousands of pounds.[150]

Student numbers were low, income was limited and there was hardly any capital available. Overcome by these administrative challenges and coping with poor health, Burton decided to resign at the end of 1918. He went on to found a new mission at Hampton Hill and in 1924 he moved to Harrow as Chaplain of the Visitation Convent. He died on 13 December 1925, by which time he was partially blind and suffered from Bright's Disease.

The Presidency of Mgr Edward Myers

Canon Burton was succeeded as President by Fr Edward Myers, who had previously gained a reputation as a strict though popular Prefect of Discipline, 'usually carrying a bunch of rather large keys which he used, not for opening or locking doors, but for rapping students on the elbows, should he chance to catch them with their hands in their trousers' pockets'. Few members of staff, it was said, administered the 'paddycock', that peculiarly Edmundian instrument of punishment, with 'more deadly accuracy or with more telling effect'.[151] His new Vice-President, Dr Vance, wrote:

He was a scholar, and a lover of all things concerning the history, dogma, moral and law of the Church, and from that point of view an admirable head of a Seminary. He was a great personal friend of mine to the last and he trusted me implicitly. But he was a poor administrator and found it terribly difficult to decide anything. He might even allow an important letter, drafted for me, to which he had agreed fully, to lie on his table for two weeks and only sign it after repeated and – to me – embarrassing requests to sign.[152]

Myers faced enormous financial challenges, as had his predecessor, who, in his farewell speech, noted that he would go down in history as the shortest-reigning President, involving the College in greater debt than any of his predecessors. In an attempt to battle the deficit, it was decided in 1919 that the pension for students was increased from £75 to £100 a year. It perhaps was not helped by the Myers' tendency of using the cheques paying boys' fees as bookmarks.[153]

Above: The paddycock – a peculiarly Edmundian instrument of punishment.

Top: Edward Myers was President of St Edmund's between 1919 and 1932.

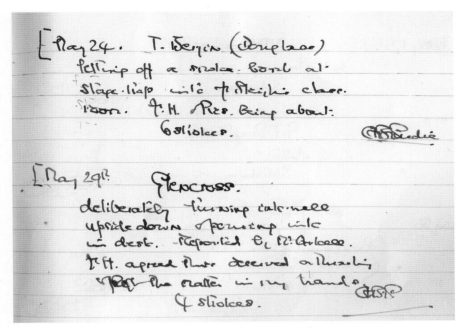

Left: An extract from the book in which punishments were officially recorded. In May 1928, Thomas Bergin (1927-29) received six strokes of the paddycock for letting off a water bomb in the School Block, and Nicholas Glencross (1925-28) received four strokes for turning an inkwell upside down in a desk.

Myers' Presidency would see many important changes, although it began with a major disagreement with Bishop Ward. On 31 December the former President wrote to Mgr Myers requesting that 'our Brentwood students may with advantage cease to join the Cadet Corps'.[154] In a previous letter to Burton, Ward wrote that such an organisation was not suitable for seminarians and that 'it seems to put it into their heads that military service is part of a Church student's or priest's career in normal times, whereas it is I imagine not even permissible except under compulsion, or in times of extraordinary danger to the country like the present'.[155]

The dispute over the Corps soon became emblematic of deeper disagreements between Ward and Bourne. Much ink was spilt over the issue and both bishops went to Rome to seek support. Indeed, Ward received some sympathy from Mgr Arthur Hinsley, the Rector of the English College who would one day succeed Bourne as Archbishop.

As tensions worsened, Ward withdrew the Brentwood students from St Edmund's in April 1919 and transferred them to Wonersh and other seminaries – a bold and painful step for a past President to make. Later that year, the Congregation of Seminaries in Rome ruled that the formation of Cadet Corps was forbidden in seminaries or, in the case of a mixed institution like St Edmund's, for church students.

More happily, in 1922 Bourne opened the impressive Galilee Chapel, in thanksgiving to Our Lady for the preservation of the country during the war. Based on the fine example at Durham Cathedral and designed by Frederick A. Walters, the chapel had a more practical purpose: as a chapel, indeed a veritable 'parish church', for the lay boys. It would also serve as the Cardinal's final resting place, just as the Durham Galilee housed the tomb of Cardinal Langley, and there was even a shrine to St Pudentiana, whose basilica in Rome was Bourne's titular church. However, some of the clergy thought the ambitious project inappropriate given the financial situation of the times, and it was said that Myers only heard of the project by letter the day the workmen first arrived.[156]

FROM THE PARK   Joseph Pike

THE REORGANISATION
OF SAINT EDMUND'S COLLEGE

THE recent reorganisation of S. Edmund's College at Old Hall certainly marks a very important and decisive moment in the history of that school. I have been asked by some of my Clergy to explain more in detail the history and precise nature of that remodelling for their own niformation, and for that of their lay friends who are interested in all that belongs to the education of Catholic boys. I very gladly endeavour to meet their wishes.

To understand S. Edmund's College, its history and development, we must have constantly in mind its twofold origin. It is at one and the same time the representative in the South of England of the venerable English College of Douai, first in date and dignity of all our post-Reformation foundations, indeed the forerunner of all the rest; and the continuation of the secondary school for boys founded by Bishop Challoner at Standon Lordships in 1749, and transferred by Bishop James Talbot, after a brief sojourn at Hare Street, to Old Hall Green in 1769.

The College at Douai was founded by Dr. William Allen distinctly and specifically as an Ecclesiastical Seminary for the training of candidates for the Priesthood. It has indeed the signal honour of being actually the first Seminary ever established as the outcome of the legislation of the Council of Trent, which had concluded its long and frequently interrupted sittings only five years before the foundation of Douai College. It is known that the great S. Charles, justly regarded as the initiator of Seminaries, looked to Douai for guidance and inspiration as he set about the work always associated with his name. But from force of circumstances, and in the absence of

THE HOUSE SYSTEM

Cardinal Bourne, like many others over the previous century, realised that the mixed nature of St Edmund's had both advantages and disadvantages. It was indeed good for Church Boys to mix with those who were destined for 'the world' and for the lay students to benefit from a solidly ecclesiastical environment. He recognised, however, that 'parents undoubtedly often hesitated to send their boys to Old Hall because they regarded it as too ecclesiastical, while those who were most concerned about the training of candidates for ordination were at times anxious as to the sufficiently ecclesiastical character of the school'. The Cardinal was also clear that the poor condition of many of the buildings and a deficit of £15,000 on the current account meant that some drastic reorganisation was needed, allowing St Edmund's to attract large numbers of students.

Dr Vance claimed that, following a pilgrimage to Lourdes, the Cardinal believed 'Our Lady had told him to establish a house system at St Edmund's College. In this belief he never wavered. He encouraged himself by reading the story of Winchester and Eton, where boys designed for the Church studied side-by-side with others who profited by the same masters'.[157] Bourne thought that William of Wykeham, the medieval founder of Winchester, fulfilled in anticipation the requirements of the Council of Trent on seminaries. Students destined for the priesthood mixed with lay boys, though they were kept separate through the House System. This idea had been followed in other institutions, including Eton, which was in the fifteenth century 'distinctly a junior seminary, the cassocked or "togati" boy inmates being the Collegers; and the fame of learning generously imparted brought the "oppidani" clustering round the College to share in

IF ROME WAS SATISFIED BY
THE NEW ARRANGEMENTS,
NOT ALL PROFESSORS,
PARENTS AND STUDENTS
WERE.

the teaching of that great school'. Indeed, had the Reformation not occurred, surely all Catholic schools would have used this model and 'had Allen, or those who came after him, been able to return to their own country to open seminaries and schools therein, would not they too have embraced with eagerness the tradition already created by Wykeham and enabled clerics and laics to be taught and to play together in their boyhood while in their separate houses they were being assured all that their different aspirations demanded'.[158]

Thus, in 1922 the College was reorganised into 'houses' named after three great Edmundian figures: Bishops Challoner, Talbot and Douglass. The last of these was intended for Church Boys – effectively constituting a Junior Seminary - the previous two for those hoping to embark on a military or professional career. The boys of Douglass enjoyed several privileges, much to the resentment of the other students. Meanwhile, the Divines' Wing for those studying theology was formally re-named 'Allen Hall', after the founder of Douay.

The Edmundian expressed the hope that the reorganised College would 'offer the advantages of the English public school, with its insistence on manliness, initiative, character and responsibility, together with its old significant advantages of Catholic training and ancient tradition'.[159] Pope Pius XI himself wrote to Bourne and was 'specially anxious to express to you Our warmest congratulations on the raising up of the Junior Seminary, where students who seek to become priests will receive a special training in harmony with their holy vocation'. In fact 'the education of young clerics is indeed too important and too delicate a matter not to call for special rules and special spiritual and intellectual guidance distinct from that given to other young men who are also Catholics indeed, but who are not preparing themselves for so sublime a dignity'.[160]

If Rome was satisfied by the new arrangements, not all professors, parents and students were.

CHALLONER HOUSE
SHEWING CORNER OF SCHOOLS.

The new Schools were blessed and opened
Michaelmas 1922. Challoner's is one of the
first houses arranged exclusively for laymen.

Joseph Pike

Opposite: The Talbot House photograph of 1926.

Above: To coincide with the introduction of the House system, a new building was erected to provide 'hand-lavatories', change-rooms and drying rooms for the boys after their games, and what was described as 'a whole system of splash, douche and ordinary baths'.

Right: In 1923 the artist Joseph Pike was commissioned to produce a set of sixteen contemporary views of the College. These were published in a book entitled 'Pencil Sketches'. The original drawings still hang at the College.

According to Vance, who privately opposed the scheme, Myers was so concerned with putting the College back on its feet that 'he accepted passively the whole plan of the House System'. The Vice-President thought that 'to run the place as a public school, it would need a new and effective staff, a new standard of equipment, and an overhaul which was far beyond the means of the Cardinal. We also needed an experienced and efficient Bursar'. When Vance told Myers the proposal was misconceived, the President answered, 'Yes, Yes!! But what can I do?'[161] Mgr Stephen Shaw, who entered St Edmund's in 1917, later referred to the '1922 calamity' and stated that many of the boys 'preferred the Bounds (Ruds to Grammar) and First Division (Syntax to Rhetoric) that we'd grown up with'.[162] The reorganisation of the College was partly made possible by a sizeable bequest made to the diocese by Mary Fitzgerald for the purpose of education. Bourne syphoned much of this off towards St Edmund's, much to the annoyance of some of the clergy who were desperately trying to establish schools in their parishes and felt they were in greater need of funding.

It took time for the new system to get established. Each House now had its own housemaster, refectory, play room and dormitories. The former College refectory was transformed into a library, while the old library became the refectory for Douglass. The initial lack of electric lighting in Talbot house turned out to be a blessing in disguise 'at least as far as prep was concerned for we were able to do much less work by lamp light than we do now'.[163]

Top right: The School Block was built in 1922. It contained new classrooms, laboratories, an armoury, a shop, music practice rooms and an exhibition hall.

Above: The Chemistry laboratory in the School Block.

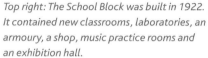

Right: Each House had its own Refectory. This is the one for Challoner.

The house system led to much re-building work, including, perhaps most notably, the School Block, with its new classrooms, laboratories, music rooms, an armoury and exhibition hall, which were shared by the different Houses. The works necessitated the levelling of the Pleasure Grounds, the formal gardens laid out in the mid-nineteenth century for the use of professors, although the statue of Our Lady was retained in a prominent position. Later, in 1932, the former parish church, next to the Old Hall, was extended to make a gymnasium.

AN APPEAL TO ALL EDMUNDIANS FOR A MEMORIAL TO OUR MEN WHO FELL IN THE WAR

ST. EDMUND'S COLLEGE, OLD HALL WARE, HERTS 1920

St. EDMUND'S COLLEGE,

Old Hall, Near Ware, Herts.

1921.

FEES.

ENTRANCE FEE.—Five Guineas (in lieu of plate and linen).

PENSION.—At the College the annual Pension is **£100**, payable in advance at the beginning of each term.

At St. Hugh's Preparatory School the annual Pension is **£90**.

EXTRAS. — College Books and other School requisites, including Laboratory Charges, **£2** per term, payable in advance.

Medical Fee, including Doctor, Trained Nurse and Medicines, and use of Infirmary, **£1** per term, payable in advance.

Laundry, Mending, and Repairs in Wardrobe, **£1 5s. 0d.** per term, payable in advance.

INCIDENTAL EXPENSES.—(*Not* payable in advance).

Music Lessons (piano) when required are charged for at three guineas per term.

Each boy will be charged **5/-** a term subscription to the Public Games for the Autumn and Spring Terms, and **8/-** for the Summer Term.

College Cadet Corps.—Entrance Fee, **£1 10s. 0d.** Subscription per term, **12/6**.

St. Hugh's Boy Scouts.—Entrance Fee, **£1**, Subscription **2/6** per term.

College Magazine.—Subscription **2/-** per term.

Haircutter.—**1/6** per term.

Tailoring Repairs and Boot Repairs are charged for as incurred at low rates.

A FULL TERM'S NOTICE IS REQUIRED FOR THE REMOVAL OF A STUDENT FAILING WHICH ONE TERM'S FEES WILL BE CHARGED.

PROFESSORS

In 1926 the separate post of Headmaster was created and the first to hold the office was the popular Fr Francis Dolores Healy (known as 'Tim'), who had previously been Prefect of Discipline and Housemaster of St Hugh's. He combined firmness and gentleness and was known for his wise counsel; Fr Ronald Knox, then a young convert, recalled that 'he read through every sermon I preached while we were at St Edmund's together, and his suggested alterations nearly always won the day, if not in the manuscript, at least in the pulpit'.[164] A story that Fr Healy often told against himself recounted how,

he was walking up and down [in the Senior Study Place] saying his Office when he noticed a boy laboriously carving his name on his desk. Fr Healy merely pointed and passed by. On his return journey he had to point again. Yet a third time it was necessary to point, but this time the culprit also pointed — to a neatly carved F. D. Healy two or three inches above his own effort: no words were spoken.

Fr Healy combined the new role of Headmaster with being Housemaster of Douglass and Secretary of The Edmundian Association and the heavy load of these responsibilities led to a breakdown in health, necessitating his resignation in 1929. He died four years later, aged only 51, while working as Rector of St Mary Moorfields.

Above left: In memory of Edmundians who died in the Great War, an appeal was launched to repair the crumbling fabric of the College Chapel. This led to the sum of nearly £2,000 being raised.

Above right: In 1921 the annual school fee, known as a 'Pension' was £100 (or £90 in St Hugh's).

Above: The Galilee Chapel, to the right of the photograph, was commenced in 1921.

It was the gift of Cardinal Francis Bourne as a thank-offering to Our Lady for her preservation of the College during the Great War. The Chapel had long been in need of more accommodation for special occasions. Having been inspired by the Galilee Chapel at Durham Cathedral, the Cardinal instructed the architect Frederick A Walters FSA to design a similar building for St Edmund's.

The combination of lay and church students continued to present challenges. Mgr Collings recalled that 'on at least one Speech Day the Divines were ordered to go out for the whole day so that the visitors would not see a large number of clerics milling around, giving the impression that the College was really a Seminary and not an ordinary "Public" School, which might deter parents from sending their sons to the College'.[165]

However, if St Edmund's was to stand alongside the older public schools, it needed excellence on the teaching staff. Living conditions for professors were harsh. According to Vance, the Cardinal thought that '£40 per annum was sufficient for the clergy (let them "supply" during a large part of their holidays); that fires in the priests' rooms were a "luxury"; that beer or Algeria wine were totally unnecessary; that the clergy should live with the Divines and share their food, etc, etc'.[166] Despite these austere instructions, which were never fully followed, the period saw some highly able figures on the staff.

Between September 1919 and his untimely death in February 1923, Dr Adrian Fortescue was Professor of Church History at Allen Hall, as well as teacher of German. Once a fortnight he travelled to St Edmund's from his parish at Letchworth, which he had founded – he considered his church the most beautiful west of Constantinople. Fortescue combined these roles with his celebrated writings on the ceremonies of the Mass and the Eastern Churches and it is little surprise that Edmundians remembered 'how he would weave so much of his wide knowledge into his inspiring talks, lectures and sermons'.[167]

Between 1919 and 1926 the College was home to Ronald Knox, the son of an Anglican Bishop of Manchester and one of the brightest of his generation at Oxford. Following his conversion, he was ordained a Catholic priest on 5 October 1919 and, we read, 'on the following day a

St. Edmund's College, Old Hall, Ware. The Galilee.

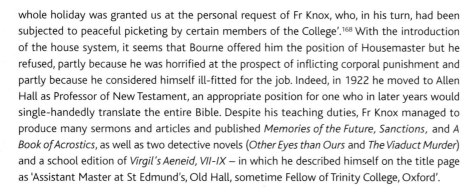

Top left: The interior of the Galilee Chapel was depicted on one of a set of College postcards.

Left: Ronald Knox came to St Edmund's in 1919 and was Professor of New Testament in Allen Hall between 1922 and 1926.

Above: Dr Adrian Fortescue was Professor of Church History in Allen Hall between 1919 and 1923.

whole holiday was granted us at the personal request of Fr Knox, who, in his turn, had been subjected to peaceful picketing by certain members of the College'.[168] With the introduction of the house system, it seems that Bourne offered him the position of Housemaster but he refused, partly because he was horrified at the prospect of inflicting corporal punishment and partly because he considered himself ill-fitted for the job. Indeed, in 1922 he moved to Allen Hall as Professor of New Testament, an appropriate position for one who in later years would single-handedly translate the entire Bible. Despite his teaching duties, Fr Knox managed to produce many sermons and articles and published *Memories of the Future, Sanctions,* and *A Book of Acrostics*, as well as two detective novels (*Other Eyes than Ours* and *The Viaduct Murder*) and a school edition of *Virgil's Aeneid, VII-IX* – in which he described himself on the title page as 'Assistant Master at St Edmund's, Old Hall, sometime Fellow of Trinity College, Oxford'.

Knox was fully involved in the life of the College. At Easter 1923 he gave a retreat to the Challoner boys, who recorded 'he has a wonderful knack of keeping us all interested, and really we feel ever so much better after listening to him'.[169] The following year he wrote English and Latin hymns in honour of St Edmund (including 'By English hearts too long forgot'). With the help of Fr Purdie, he was responsible for two Latin plays performed at Speech Day: *Thesauropolemopompus* (1924) and *Londinium Defensum* (1925). In the first of these, everyday phrases like 'Well I never!' became *Bene ego nunquam* and 'Righto', *Rectum O*. Amusing though they were, A. S. Barnes commented that these farces 'had not quite the educational value of the older plays'.[170]

Above: Canon Edward Mahoney taught at St Edmund's between 1919 and 1954. Despite his stern demeanour, he was considered to be one of the leading Moral Theologians in the entire Catholic Church.

Laurence Eyres (a fellow convert and teacher at St Edmund's) wrote that:

He could punt with dexterity, and when Pogo came into fashion he could prance about on this sprung stilt as nimbly as any Hugonian. On this subject he wrote some amusing Latin elegiacs for The Edmundian, entitled Omnes Eodem Pogimur. He could walk on a rotating garden roller, and could cuckoo convincingly enough to elicit a reply from any genuine cuckoo in the vicinity. He used to amuse the small daughter of some friends of ours in this way, and when she eventually heard the real thing, she pointed to the tree and said, 'Father Knox !'[171]

Evelyn Waugh further recorded that Knox had 'a habit of lighting his pipe outside the cricket pavilion with a burning glass'.[172] No wonder he was so popular with the boys.

Another brilliant mind to be found at St Edmund's was Canon Edward J. Mahoney, appointed Professor of Moral Theology in 1919. Thanks to his methodical teaching and his contributions to *The Clergy Review*, he was eventually recognised 'as perhaps the leading Moral Theologian writing in the English Language, and it is no exaggeration to say, one of the leading authorities in the whole Church'. He continued teaching at the College until his death in 1954, although he eventually moved to the parish of Buntingford and then Poles Convent. In his obituary, Mgr Butcher wrote: 'the humour that was such a marked feature of his lectures and his writing was not wanting in his ordinary conversation. Many of us must have gone along to see him merely because we wanted him to help us through a period of depression. There must have been many more interesting tasks at his hand; but, however interesting they were, he would always put them aside for our benefit'.[173] He donated his extensive library to the College and his papers form a large part of the College archive.

A close friend of Mahoney was Mgr Canon George Smith, who taught dogmatic theology from 1918 and eventually became Vice-President (1947-52). The two men had been students together and were now united not only in teaching at their alma mater but in contributing to *The Clergy Review* and serving Catholics in the locality. Indeed, before the foundation of the parish at Puckeridge, they would preach open-air Missions and answer queries placed in the 'Question Box'.

With a double doctorate from Rome, Smith had a truly European outlook and, unusually for the times, would typically spend his summer in his adopted Italian village, Baveno on Lake Maggiore, where 'he made firm friends with the padrone and with many of the villagers, who always had a warm welcome for Don Giorgio; there he returned again and again, to while away the weeks of the summer vacation, swimming in the lake, basking in the lovely Italian sun, enjoying the local wine, before returning with renewed vigour to his desk and to the endless academic round of lectures, articles, book reviews, conference cases, pastoral letters, and other tasks which his theological learning imposed upon him'.

One evening Smith was rushed to hospital after colliding his motorcycle with a hay wagon. It was thought that his academic career might come to an end:

Myers considered that extraordinary measures were called for. Sparing no expense, the best experts were summoned, and the patient blessed with the relic of St Edmund, while the Divines maintained watch day and night before the Blessed Sacrament exposed in the Oratory. The patient

THE EXPLOSION INSPIRED
FR KNOX TO WRITE HIS
FAMOUS LATIN POEM, NOX
ERAT, WHICH OPENED THUS:

'Twas night; the College all in silence lay,
The boys, fatigued from working hard all day,
Were deep in slumber; Rhetoricians snored
As if by Virgil's Aeneid wholly bored.

rapidly improved; in Myers' words, all at the hospital said, "there is something more than human agency at work." Smith went to Italy to recuperate, there receiving the experts' bills. The mark of the accident remained on his forehead until the end, and it was not unknown for some unruly Divines to make practical use of the belief that it had deprived George of his sense of smell.[174]

A surprising presence among the staff of Allen Hall in 1924-25 was a young priest from the diocese of Peoria, Illinois: Fulton J. Sheen. He would later win global fame as an Archbishop, author and 'televangelist'; his series *Life is Worth Living* (1951) was watched by 30 million every week. However, St Edmund's constituted his first experience of teaching, while working for his agrégé at the University of Louvain, and he was still learning the tricks of the trade. In his autobiography Sheen mentioned meeting an Old Edmundian five years later who expressed surprise that he was now teaching at the Catholic University in Washington and commented, 'I hope you are a better teacher now than you were then'. The cause for Sheen's beatification was opened in 2002.

At 2.14am on 17 March 1925 an explosion rocked St Edmund's, involving the 'starlight' equipment. Fr Sheen recalled that 'it was some kind of illuminating gas which was stored in the large toilets. The starlight used to leak into our butter and bread so that we were constantly eating it. Of all the nights when the starlight plant should blow up in an English seminary, the one chosen by the starlight gods was the eve [sic] of St Patrick's Day. We heard the explosion during the night. When we looked out on St Patrick's Day, we found the lawn of the seminary strewn with toilet bowls'.[175] A few days later, on the Feast of St Joseph, the President sang High Mass in thanksgiving that there were no casualties or extensive damage to the buildings.

The College had long been devoted to the memory of its martyrs. In 1927 what was left of the English College, Douay was demolished as part of a bold town redevelopment scheme. During the work, a well-preserved body was discovered in a leaden casket. This was identified as John Southworth, who had studied at the College, won fame for his pastoral labours in London during the 1636 plague and was eventually hanged, drawn and quartered at Tyburn in 1654, the last secular priest to be put to death in this way and only martyr to suffer under Cromwell's regime. The Cardinal sent a member of the College staff to France as his representative: Fr Albert Purdie, the first Housemaster of Challoner (1922) and then Headmaster (1929-36) in succession to Fr Healy. A talented classicist, he had been awarded the O.B.E. for his services as Senior Catholic

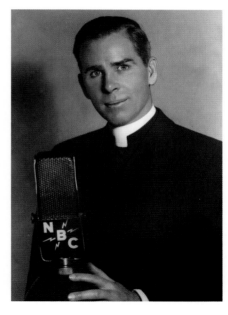

Above: Archbishop Fulton Sheen preached on 'The Catholic Hour' radio programme in the 1920s, and later became its most popular host. He moved to television in the 1950s with 'Life is Worth Living'. He was named a bishop in 1951 and became an archbishop in 1969.

Top left: Outside the cricket pavilion in July 1931.

THE MEMBERS
OF
CHALLONER HOUSE
Present

VICE-VERSA
(A Play by F. A. ANSTEY).

CHRISTMAS, 1922.

Dramatis Personæ :

Mr. BULTITUDE	J. Hall
DICK (his son)	D. Appleton
Dr. Grimstone (Headmaster of Crichton House)	E. Hazel
Clegg (a coachman)	P. Tierney
Mr. Shellack (an old gentleman) ...	G. Pritchard
Tipping (a big boy)	L. Measures
DULCIE Grimstone	K. Kershaw
Eliza (a maid)	E. Hazel
Chawner (a sneak)	E. Cowell
Jolland	A. Hawks
Biddlecombe } Boys	F. Baillie
Coggs	G. Doyle
Kiffin (a new boy)	R. Leborgne

Act I. Mr. Bultitude's Dining Room.

Act II. The Schoolroom at Crichton House.

Chaplain of the British Forces at Salonika and Constantinople during the War. He was a strict disciplinarian and a queue of nervous boys could often be seen outside his office after the evening meal, awaiting canings from 'Wackford Purdie'.

Fr Purdie arranged for the body of the martyred priest to be brought back to St Edmund's in 1927 and stored in the Douay Oratory on the President's Gallery. Southworth was included in the group of 136 English Martyrs beatified by Pius XI on 15 December 1929, at which Mgr Myers represented the College. That evening the body of the new beatus was taken in procession out of the Douay Oratory along the Ambulacrum and into the chapel. The casket was placed in the Lady Chapel, 'draped with a red pall, and over the head was placed a beautiful crown of flowers, reminiscent of the old Douay days, when according to a contemporary account the body of the Martyr lay exposed in "a little roome" and had a "croune of flowers" upon the head'.[176] In 1930 the relics were taken to a new shrine at Westminster Cathedral and he was later canonised as one of the Forty Martyrs in 1970.

Judging from *The Edmundian*, College life was seldom dull. The Divines organised a Shakespeare Society, during which the bard's plays were read, and a more light-hearted Glee Club. The Literary Society of St Edmund of Canterbury continued to flourish, with many distinguished speakers from both within and without the College: Hilaire Belloc on 'Historical Evidence' or 'The Position of Catholics under James II', Ronald Knox on a variety of subjects including 'Sherlock Holmes', and Adrian Fortescue on 'Devil Worshippers', a 'strange but harmless Syrian sect, almost unknown, with its mild propitiatory worship of the devil'.[177] His untimely death in 1923 left a series of talks on Mormonism unfinished.

It also seems to have been a relatively happy place. Each individual boy would have had his own reflections on the subject, of course, but as far as John Whitney was concerned, 'there was little violence at the school except on the rugger field, and no real bullying. Cliques were formed from time to time but they contented themselves with verbal abuse or, what was worse, deadly silence!' Students were given responsibilities from an early stage and there were no restrictive rules. Indeed, 'there were no bounds beyond which we were not allowed to venture, any expedition being limited by the time available and the one rule that it had to be on foot – no transport allowed. The 400-acre College estate gave us plenty of room to roam but there was no ban on longer walks'. Modern students would find the living conditions harsh. The dormitories, for example, situated on the top floor of the respective House, were normally equipped

with bed and a cupboard, but each boy also had a washbasin, with a basin and a jug of cold water…Lavatories were not convenient and one learned to avail oneself of the facilities before retiring. There was one prefect in charge of each dormitory - he had a door and an individual light. Though radiators were installed they were almost useless as the dormitories had sash windows on opposite long sides of the room. It was very cold in the winter but there was no shortage of blankets, and exhaustion made sleep almost immediate.[178]

Despite the undoubted quality of many of the professors and the best of intentions, the scheme to make St Edmund's into a 'Catholic Winchester' was ultimately a failure, largely due to the College's limited resources. Fr Denys Lucas, for many years Housemaster of St Hugh's, wrote that Bourne's plans for the College had 'even given rise to ridicule and have been a source of embarrassment to subsequent administrators'.[179] Mgr Butcher, who was a student during the 1920s, recalled that 'the maintenance of the buildings once again had to be cut down and the appearance of the College became very shabby. Morale also declined'.[180] By September 1931, a bleak economic year, there were only 45 Church students and 64 lay boys.

OFFICERS' TRAINING CORPS

The 8th Herts Cadets Company, affiliated to the 1st Hertfordshire Regiment and commanded by Captain Askew, was set up at St Edmund's in 1916 amidst a storm of controversy, as already noted. Once the dust had settled, military drill, parades, inspections and the rifle range became a familiar part of Edmundian life.

In November 1924 the 8th Herts Cadets was disbanded and replaced by the Officers' Training Corps (O.T.C.). This, indeed, was the original intention of Cardinal Bourne although in 1916 the War Office only allowed the creation of a Cadet Corps as a first step. The O.T.C. was placed under Captain Headlam, formerly in charge of the O.T.C. at the Oratory School and known as 'Bones' on account of his physique. It initially consisted of one company with three platoons, one from each House, and the training was designed to qualify the boys for commissions in the Territorial Army or National Army in case of emergency. Francis Ford remembered: *We had to dress up in First World War uniforms, designed for horse-riding with puttees and peaked caps. We had SMLE .303 rifles and huge bayonets. We were taught the next war would be a war of movement but always practised suicidal frontal assault. Flanking movements were unknown. We fired .22 in the gym and 5 rounds .303 on the range. I remember receiving pack drill with bricks for barging one of Captain King's NCOs. We were instructed in First World War Lewis guns. As it happened this was useful as many were brought out of store to replace Brens lost at Dunkirk.*[181]

'Hal' King directed the O.T.C. for many years – with such efficiency that within five years of its foundation the Corps of Drums won the band competition at the summer camp at Tidworth Pennings. Indeed, the name 'Captain King' quickly became synonymous for a generation of students 'with the Army and with clipped, concise, clear orders'.[182]

The 1940s saw two changes of name: the Junior Training Corps (1941) and then the Combined Cadets Corps (1949), but the work remained essentially the same. But times were changing. Although 'on a bleak but rainless day in December 1967,... Harold Wakefield – School Staff Instructor, ex-regular Battery Sergeant Major, with campaign medals from the Second World to Korea – was buried with such military respect as the College could not have given more smartly or more sincerely to a Cardinal,' the C.C.C. was deemed increasingly irrelevant and unnecessary.[183] On 31 January 1968 it was disbanded by the Army Council.

After nine years of absence, the Combined Cadet Corps was re-founded in 1976 by Dr Cecil Friedlander, then the Director of Studies and Careers Master. The recently retired Bursar, Major King, who had formerly been so involved in the O.T.C., initially acted as unofficial Quartermaster. It remains an important part of life at St Edmund's.

Above: The garden party on 20 July 1929. Tea served on the front terraces was arranged by Harrods, and a programme of music was given by the Band of the First Hertfordshire Regiment.

CHAPTER X

FROM BICKFORD TO BUTLER
1932-1984

MGR FRANCIS BICKFORD (1932-46)

Mgr Myers left St Edmund's in 1932 to become an Auxiliary Bishop in Westminster and eventually coadjutor to Cardinal Griffin, with the title of Archbishop. Meanwhile Fr Francis Bickford succeeded to the Presidency. The son of an Admiral and both an Old Hugonian and Edmundian, he had been awarded the Military Cross while serving as a chaplain to the 47th Lancer Division during the First World War. His most recent work before coming to St Edmund's was as Rector of Edmonton, where there was a house for late vocations.

Bickford's early years at the College were energetic. At his first St Edmund's Day, the Cardinal blessed the Douay Hall that had been built by his predecessor. Soon afterwards the new President arranged for the Chapel to be renovated and the front drive to be resurfaced, for 'until the year 1934, motorists had become inured to the experience of arriving half blinded by the dust of the avenue and with their bones jolted by the ruts and bumps of an uneven road'.[184] Perhaps his proudest achievement, as an Old Hugonian, was the extension to the Preparatory School, opened in May 1939, which led fortuitously to increased student numbers at a critical period.

As time went on, Bickford's health began to decline. Between 1937 and 1943 he served as Vicar General for the diocese in addition to his duties at St Edmund's. Mixed with his sense of duty was an inability to delegate, making the strain on his constitution enormous. Added to this were the anxieties caused by the outbreak of War in 1939.

THE SECOND WORLD WAR

The Bursar, Fr Leo Straub, recalled that after hearing Chamberlain's famous broadcast on 3 September 1939, 'many in the College stood at east-facing windows; expecting to see at any moment, hordes of enemy planes approaching to drop bombs on us. But all was quiet, and no enemy planes appeared'[185] – at least for the time being. When the bombing campaigns did intensify, the only damage sustained at the College was from a parachute mine, which fell near the main road in the autumn of 1940. It failed to explode and the following day it was examined by military personnel, who arranged a controlled explosion. The resulting blast shattered a number of windows on the front of the buildings and the chapel. The crater that it created was in subsequent years used by some Divines for the purpose of sunbathing!

Left: An aerial photograph of the College in 1962 looking north east.

Above left: Mgr Francis Bickford was President of St Edmund's between 1932 and 1946.

Above right: Cardinal Bernard Griffin planting the first of what was intended to be a new avenue of trees.

Below: Derek Worlock (1934-44) (later Bishop of Portsmouth and Archbishop of Liverpool) in his rugby kit in 1938.

All Edmundians were affected by the shortage of staff and supplies and the curtailing of many activities. It was decided from the beginning that all Houses should dine in the Douglass Refectory, though 'House tables' maintained their separate identity. The other refectories were turned into dormitories, as was the School Hall, from which there was direct access to the main College shelter (the music rooms under the stage, which became known as the Refugium peccatorum). All evening services were held in the Galilee Chapel, where blinds were fitted for the 'black-out'. A branch of the Home Guard was set up in May 1940, comprising of members of the O.T.C. as well as local ex-service men, and soon they were digging trenches in strategic positions around the College. It was reported by a Challonerian that 'stray German planes on one or two occasions set into motion our plans against air attack. Boys, in dressing-gowns and slippers, went calmly and in high spirits to the shelter; L.D.V.s [Local Defence Volunteers] went to their posts, and a section of the Allen Hall Fire Brigade manned the buckets in various parts of the House'.[186] When a Hurricane crashed into a field near the College, Mass was offered for the Polish pilot who lost his life. Fortunately he was fortified by the sacraments.

The irregular supply of coal during the winter meant that the seminary lecture hall was no longer used and that hot baths became a much-lamented thing of the past, the seminarians now going to the school for a fortnightly scrub. The Divines were given permission to listen to Churchill's broadcasts and a 'telephone guard' was arranged to monitor the coming of air-raid warnings. Many became A.R.P. wardens and took care of necessary tasks such as sandbagging. Canon Brian Frost, then a schoolboy, remembered the black-out as 'an ideal chance for a bit of chaos,' so beloved by any child:

There was the blackout curtain to be pulled back just a little to show a chink of light. It was always possible that a passing Heinkel would spot it way up in the sky and that would bring a bit

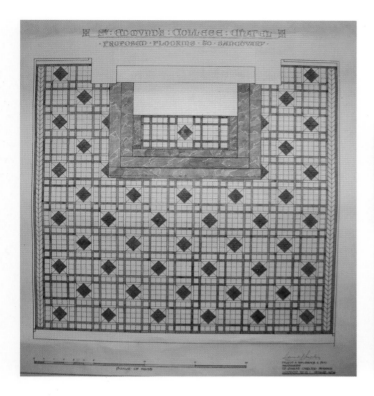

of excitement. Usually it prompted a bang on the window as a helmeted member of Allen Hall outside (they acted as College Air Raid Wardens) would shout, "I can see the light" – in retrospect, maybe, an insight much to be desired by any member of that august and pious community; though the impious layboy might not have considered that so philosophically.[187]

Rationing caused headaches for the College authorities, especially Fr Straub:

There was one Ration Book for every resident in the College, over 400 of them! And each month, the coupons for that month had to be cut out of the books, counted (what a job!), and sent to the "Food Officer" in Ware. In return, he then sent us an authorisation to buy the various kinds of food; but the quantity that he allowed was very strictly calculated, being limited to the precise number of coupons that we had sent him... Once food rationing began, it became obvious to the Bursar that shortage of food to feed the 400 plus residents could become a problem. He therefore brought a trailer for his car, and scoured the surrounding countryside and farms for food. Not every kind of food was rationed from the beginning; and the Bursar always tried to be one step in front of the Food Ministry, thinking, "Now what is likely to be rationed next?" he then bought in quantities of it. Thus, after meat was rationed, he thought the eggs would be rationed next. They were; but he had already bought in about 10,000 of them, and preserved them in great earthenware containers, in a liquid, called, if I remember rightly, Oteg.[188]

When a camp was set up for German prisoners of war near Much Hadham, Fr Straub (who spoke German) was deputed to visit each Sunday and celebrate Mass. When they were moved away and replaced by Italians, Fr Kelly took over chaplaincy duties. He liked to recount how he reproached one prisoner for not being a good Catholic since he never came to Mass. The Italian drew himself up and answered, 'Father, I am a good Catholic. Back in Italy, my wife goes to church every Sunday!'[189]

Top left: Drawing for a new sanctuary floor in 1934.

Top right: Students were issued with gasmasks during the Second World War.

Above: A ledger showing staff salaries in the Lent Term in 1934 totalled £1,054 16s 11d.

Above: Athletics in the 1930s. Note the shotgun being used as a starting pistol.

Right: January 1935. Robert Bowman (1933-35), Denis Calnan (1934-37), David (Pat) Gower (1926-35) and Victor Moverley (1933-36) with their giant snowball.

Opposite: Easter 1936. Four boys in Douglass. From left: Peter Amato (1934-39), Stanley Seamen (1935-42), Evelyn Aubourg (1933-38) and John Widdicombe (1934-39).

Top: Some of the academic staff in 1937.

Above: A French class in the School Block in about 1936. From left: O'Neal Segrave (1934-37), Brian Bayliss (1931-39), Joseph Manning (1934-38), Brian Hick (1929-39), David Thomson (1935-45), Gerard Barry (1934-39), Anthony Roberts (1934-45) and Keith Barnes (1935-38).

Although members of staff had, in many cases, left for military service, a Maltese Dominican friar who had been teaching at Rome's Angelicum University found refuge at St Edmund's while Italy was at war with Britain: Fr Paul Zamitt. Not only did he act as Professor of Philosophy, imparting to the seminarians an impressive knowledge of the works of St Thomas Aquinas, but he was also confessor to several local convents and looked after the public chapel attached to the Archbishop's house at Hare Street. We are told that 'nothing was too much trouble for him'. When a certain parishioner said she was unable to get to Mass without some means of conveyance, he undertook to get her a bicycle, then considered unobtainable. He bought a wreck off the scrap-heap for a few shillings, brought it back to the College, and set to work on it. In a week or two, after buying some spare parts and paint, he produced practically a new bicycle. He went to bed late and rose early but, when he did sleep, his neighbours were more than aware: 'there is a story that in the early days of the war, some of the Divines on nightguard heard a strange sound which they took to be that of enemy planes overhead. They went to investigate, but on discovering that the said noise proceeded from Fr Zamitt's bedroom they returned to their post'.[190]

Much excitement was caused when the College was taken over by the Headquarters of Southern Command for two days in September 1941; 'the Ambulacrum a labyrinth of telephone wires, the Douay Hall a barrack room, the garages transformed into field kitchens, and the whole College as active as an ant's nest – with the constant arrival and departure of despatch riders, the transmission of wireless messages and the continual movement of lorries and Bren gun carriers'.[191] However, despite these dramas, life continued as normally as possible. The 150th anniversary of the College's opening was marked in 1943 with a Pontifical High Mass and a play, 'The Amazing Dr Clitterhouse', produced by one Derek Worlock (later Archbishop of Liverpool).

Left: 'Rex' King (left) with Cardinal Heenan.

Below: 'Rex' King outside the School Block.

Above: Parts of a Mustang fighter aeroplane which crashed in Kings Wood, north of the College, during the Second World War salvaged (illegally) by Bernard Hypher (1942-48). These comprise a propeller feathering gearbox and 0.5" ammunition.

'REX' KING

At the end of 1940 the Headmaster, Fr Thomas Sherlock, was forced to retire after four years in office, due to poor health, and for the first time a layman was chosen: John Haldane Walton King, popularly known (for obvious reasons) as 'Rex'. Not only did he prove ideal for the job, but his appointment helped maximise the number of priests available as army chaplains. A Cambridge graduate, Mr King had been on the staff since 1930 but had only recently been received into the Church by Fr Arthur Reys, who taught philosophy in Allen Hall. In his years as assistant master he made his mark on the College community, editing *The Edmundian*, producing a book, *Rugby Football for the Learner-Player*, which the Welsh international Wilfrid Wooller recommended as a standard text book for juniors, and directing the O.T.C. with much aplomb.

As Headmaster 'Rex' faced a daunting challenge. With little experience of housemastering and still comparatively new to the Catholic Faith, he had to direct a teaching body made up mostly of priests, one or two of whom may have reasonably expected to hold his position. He persevered through these difficulties and managed to increase student numbers during a difficult decade overshadowed by war and financial anxieties. He made the house system more fluid and mixed Church and lay students in each house, leading to many vocations which may otherwise have been missed. In September 1945, Junior House was opened for eleven and twelve year olds, under Fr Nicholas Kelly. The same year Rex married Joan Brabazon, Assistant Matron at St Hugh's and the first Headmaster's wife at St Edmund's, who remained a pillar of support. 'By the time he is thirty,' he would often say, 'a man needs another sacrament, either Holy Orders or matrimony'.[192]

Mgr John Bagshawe (1946-52)

Above: Monsignor John 'Baggy' Bagshawe. He enjoyed shooting in his leisure time, and on one occasion discharged the barrels of his shotgun at a rabbit through the open window of his room at the front of the College!

During the summer vacation of 1946 an ailing Mgr Bickford resigned as President and returned to his former parish of Edmonton. Canon Smith took care of College administration until a new President was announced in October: Mgr John Bagshawe (affectionately known as 'Baggy'). Given the various post-war challenges faced by the College, he seemed an ideal candidate since he had worked as a banker before entering Allen Hall and more recently had acted as Diocesan Financial Secretary. Shortly after his arrival, Canon Smith was appointed Vice-President.

Under Bagshawe's careful stewardship, much of the College was repainted, new playing fields laid out, the Infirmary rebuilt, a new 'wash block' erected and the church windows that had been damaged during the war repaired. Aspects of College life that had been put 'on hold' during wartime were restored, such as The Edmundian Association and the annual festivities for St Edmund's Day. The President managed to deal with these tasks with calmness and good humour. Indeed, he was always willing to join in jokes about his portly figure. However, there were still serious financial problems and a growing deficit. 'Under present conditions,' he wrote, 'trying to make ends meet is a most disheartening business! Everything tends to go up in price, and invariably one finds that a saving effected in one direction is promptly cancelled by an increase in cost of some other item'.[193]

Cardinal Griffin maintained a keen interest in the College, despite periods of ill health. He encouraged the priests on the school staff to get a Diploma of Education (though it was difficult to fit the required studies into the life of a priest schoolmaster) and in 1949 he decided that the Headmaster should once again be a priest. He accordingly appointed Fr Denis Britt-Compton, who had been on the staff since 1947. Mr King accepted his relegation with humble graciousness. Indeed, Mgr Bagshawe reported that 'he did not seem a bit surprised, and indeed had been expecting it for some time'.[194] Despite being offered St Hugh's, he continued as an Assistant Master, until he was made Bursar three years later.

Up until 1949, the Little Company of Mary had been looking after the domestic arrangements. The four sisters announced they would withdraw from the College during 1950 and the President was faced with the problem of finding a replacement community. The Cardinal wrote: 'My suggestion to you is that you should send your Procurator [Fr 'Jack' Halvey], who is a good stout Irishman, over to Ireland to look out for a suitable community for the work, but the obvious thing is to start a novena and have the whole school praying'.[195] Eventually, on the fifty-fourth attempt, a new congregation was found: the Istituto Suore Missionarie della Consolata per le Missioni Estere, who took charge of the kitchens and domestic services in December 1950. They remained until June 1974 and, all in all, twenty-eight Sisters served the College under four different Superiors: Sister Beatrice (1950-58), Sister Luisita (1958-65), Sister Mariana (1965-68) and Sister Eusebia (1968-74). Their presence would come to signal the changes that came to St Edmund's within a decade or two. Mr King wrote:

At a time when English domestic staff were virtually unobtainable, the Sisters initiated the employment of Italian staff through their contacts in Italy with signal success. In many respects the Sisters brought a breath of fresh air to the then somewhat conservative Edmundian scene, and as we watched them taking part in games on the playing fields with the Italian girls, we realised, not without amazement, that we were at last moving into modern times.[196]

Left: Mgr Reginald Butcher was President of St Edmund's between 1952 and 1964.

Above: An examination in the 1950s.

Below: The CCF Corps of Drums marching past Buckingham Palace in 1952.

MGR REGINALD BUTCHER (1952-64)

In 1952 Mgr Bagshawe left St Edmund's for Our Lady of Victories in Kensington, where his main task was rebuilding the church destroyed by German bombs. In his final year he had the pleasure of seeing the Ministry of Education recognise the school and St Hugh's. He was replaced by Fr Reginald ('Reggie') Butcher, educated at Downside and previously (like Dr Vance) headmaster of the Cardinal Vaughan Memorial School in Kensington. Derek Worlock described him as follows:

Exemplary in his spiritual duties – as we used to call them – he showed and expected high standards. Intensely loyal to Church and State, he based his relationships on mature trust and if he was let down by colleague or student he did not hide his distaste, though he seldom complained. They just knew that they should have done better. If this suggests a degree of intolerance, we should not forget the saving grace of his own brand of humour: on learning that a boy had been caught thieving from Woolworths, his classic comment was "Oh, not Woolworths!" Which put everything in its right proportion.[197]

Despite the progress made under Mgr Bagshawe, the new President faced many difficulties. The College had a deficit of over £8,000 and essential repairs needed to be made – indeed, the maintenance staff had been reduced from sixteen to six over the previous few years and when the Ministry of Education announced an inspection in 1952, three priests gave up their Christmas

Above: The Centenary Dinner of The Edmundian Association on 29 September 1953 – exactly 385 years after Cardinal Allen had opened the English College at Douay – with some 173 members and guests in attendance.

Top right: A group of Divinity students in May 1955.

holidays in order to undertake much-needed painting work. This was deemed necessary for the school had failed the previous inspection and further failure would threaten its very existence. It was largely thanks to the Headmaster, Fr Britt-Compton, that the outcome was successful. A memorable scene was provided during the inspection fortnight when news reached the College of King George VI's death; the Inspectors joined the whole school community on the cricket field for the Last Post.

Shortly after his appointment, Fr Butcher sent his observations while still a relative 'outsider' to the Cardinal. He thought St Hugh's was too small and that the older boys went to the Lay School too quickly, depriving St Hugh's of its leaders and placing 'the [sports] teams at a great disadvantage when meeting other schools. The small boys grow very depressed if their school cannot put up a reasonable show against other schools (this is quite an important factor with small boys) being liable to grumble at home and in consequence to be sent to other schools than St Edmund's'. He noted that the professors were devoted and hard-working but in many cases lacked experience; 'very few of the masters have taught elsewhere – many have been boys at St Edmund's'. He also suggested that Allen Hall's 'proximity to the school and the comparatively large number of students who come straight from the school tend to make for a rather schoolboy mentality'.[198]

A large part of the debt was paid off thanks to an increase in school fees and in 1955 for the first time no deficit was reported; 'this however has been achieved by the most rigid economy and by a niggardliness which has occasionally caused me most painful embarrassment'.[199] In

1951 Fr Butcher appointed Mr King as Bursar. Given King's long association with the College, his experience as Headmaster and his gift for friendship, it was an astute move. He was kept busy in his new job. The College was re-roofed and re-wired and the heating system completely overhauled within the first two years. Further projects followed, including the building of the Godfrey Wing at St Hugh's in 1960.

Mgr Butcher (as he became in 1954) had been told by Cardinal Griffin to improve the 'spirit' among the Divines. He was keen to involve them in service to the wider community. The SVP had provided an opportunity for this since the mid nineteenth century but now the scope of activity was widened to include volunteering for the Hertfordshire Family Welfare Department, which involved getting old houses ready for the homeless. When the Carmelite sisters arrived at Ware in 1958 the Divines provided much manual labour in the Carmel before the Enclosure was officially erected. Many continued their friendships with the sisters after they had left the College to serve as priests.

In addition to this was manual work about the College, which also had the advantage of saving money: 'distinctions of order or social background disappear rapidly when a group of students is engaged on cleaning out the chicken house or painting the rooms. The Divines certainly show much more interest in the College, they learn how to do jobs for themselves, they undoubtedly look after the property on which they have worked'. In fact, the President thought there was greater loyalty to St Edmund's among the students when compared to his own youth.[200]

Above: Fr (later Canon) Denis Britt-Compton was Headmaster between 1949 and 1968.

Left: Members of staff enjoying their leisure time. From left: Fr Denis Britt-Compton, Fr Daniel Higgins and Fr Peter Phillips in a makeshift punt on the pond at Rigery Farm, Colliers End, which was owned by the College.

Below: Members of SECMEC (St Edmund's College Motor Engineering Club) in the early 1960s.

However, Mr King and others had their doubts about the scheme. A member of staff, Fr (later Mgr) Frederick Miles, recalled:

On "President's Gallery", the most prestigious of all galleries, there was, of course, the President's Room, and a place called the Cardinal's Room, which the visiting Archbishop of Westminster would occupy when he came to the College. The Bursar persuaded the President that the Cardinal's Room needed re-decorating. "That'll be just the work for Mr Heekin and his fellow students", said Mgr Butcher. "Well, if you think so", said the Bursar, unconvinced. The work duly went ahead, and on its completion the Bursar, who hadn't at all approved of the scheme of using students for this, announced to the President that the work had been done. "Would you like to see it?" asked the Bursar. He took Mgr Butcher into the freshly decorated room. The good Monsignor looked around and said, "My God! It looks like a brothel!" King's comment in a dry, deadpan, how-would-you-know voice was "Does it Monsignor?"[201]

HE WAS STRICT, BELIEVING THAT 'SHOES TELL A PRETTY BIG STORY'.

Another important development was the introduction of day boys in the mid-1950s. It was by no means easy including day pupils within a boarding school and some objected to the change. In March 1956 Mgr Butcher wrote to Cardinal Griffin:

It is rather distressing to learn, as I have just done, that three boys are being withdrawn at the end of the year because we are admitting day boys. Even so I cannot think that we are doing anything other than what is our duty to the Catholics of the neighbourhood. It would be a terrible thing if we were to stand aside and see these boys go to non-Catholic Grammar Schools. We must trust that our policy will have the blessing that it surely deserves.[202]

A word should be said about several members of staff at this time. The Headmaster between 1949 and 1968, Fr Britt-Compton, had read Geography at Downing College, Cambridge and retained a passion for geology and the natural sciences. He established a meteorological beehive and dug a pond for newts and frogs in the College grounds. He memorably began a St Edmund's Day sermon (1969): 'St Edmund came from Canterbury and died at Pontigny in France. By a remarkable coincidence both Canterbury and Pontigny are built on a substratum of chalk'.[203] He was strict, believing that 'shoes tell a pretty big story', and had to deal with such notable schoolboy stunts as the 'mysterious' appearance of Fr Peter's Bourne's car in the Ambulacrum one morning. The perpetrators were only revealed years later in the St Edmund's College *Bicentenary Book*.

In 1956 Fr Bernard Lagrue joined the staff, having served in the submarine division during the Second World War and more recently studied Natural Sciences and Astrophysics at Christ's College, Cambridge. He remained at St Edmund's for some thirty-seven years. A gifted teacher, it was noted at the time of his death that his 'dedication to and interest in the boys (and later the girls) in his charge was total'.[204] He managed to find redeeming features in all students and spent many years running the Hobbies Club.

In 1963 Mgr Butcher was suddenly laid low by a stroke that struck him during Cricket Week; Mgr Miles recalled him getting up from his chair after watching a match and falling to the ground. In due course he was forced to resign as President, though he continued to live in retirement at the College. A second stroke came three years later, which left him virtually unable to speak, but he lingered on, impressing generations of students through his holiness and courage, until his death in November 1975. Bishop Worlock noted:

Who knows what effort was required of the man when, five minutes before the bell would ring, he would rouse himself and the sound of his irons would echo along President's Gallery and down those stairs to the Ambulacrum. New standards had to be set. When he celebrated Mass in the old rite, he would recite the Orate Fratres and then, for the sake of rubric and his server, he would somehow effect his liturgical circle to include the whole world in his invitation to share in his sacrifice. If priesthood and sacrifice are related, then in these last years Reggie the invalid achieved a fullness of priesthood which at an earlier age we might have expected to take the form of episcopate.[205]

Top: Fr Bernard Lagrue ran the school Hobbies Club for many years.

Above: 10 June 1960: The Ceremonial Parade held to commemorate the centenary of cadet forces. The salute was taken by an Old Edmundian, Group Captain (later Air Chief Marshal) Neville Stack. He had then just returned from Rhodesia and Nyasaland, where he was in attendance on the Queen Mother during her tour. The Parade was watched by many parents and former leaders of the CCF Contingent. From left: Fr Denis Britt-Compton (Headmaster), Group Captain Stack, Sergeant-Major Harold Wakefield (Staff Instructor) and Patrick Foort (Training Officer).

ACTIVITIES IN THE 1960s

Above: Tug-of-war.

Top right: Erecting a tent near the cricket field.

Below right: Fr Alec Wells, the choirmaster, invigilating an examination in the School Hall.

Opposite: Members of SECMEC messing about in the College grounds.

*Above: From left: Adrian Gilbert (1962-67),
Tony Simpson (1963-68) and Peter Hughes
(1962-67) in 1967. Alastair Emblem (1958-67)
is in the window to the left. All were members
of student bands called 'The Shades' and 'The
Nazz'. In the late 1960s the school uniform
jacket was standardised to a green worsted
material.*

MGR MAURICE KELLEHER (1964-68)

During Mgr Butcher's illness, Fr Hubert Richards looked after the running of the College until the
new President, Mgr Maurice Kelleher, arrived during Holy Week 1964. Having worked as Rector
of the Shrine of Our Lady of Willesden, a busy parish founded in 1885 by the young Bernard Ward,
he must have been struck by the contrast provided by the fresh air and green fields of Hertfordshire.

However, Mgr Kelleher's brief Presidency was to be a difficult one, set against the aftermath
of the Second Vatican Council with all its opportunities and challenges. On 11 October 1962
the whole College had watched the opening ceremony on television and The Edmundian
proudly noted that there were four alumni among the Council Fathers: Bishops Grant (Auxiliary
in Northampton), Petit (Menevia), Rudderham (Clifton) and Scanlon (Dunkeld). In 1964 it was
announced that a member of staff, Fr Charles Davis, had been appointed as a peritus or
theological expert at the remaining sessions. On his return visits to the College he gave talks
on what was being discussed in Rome.

The proverbial windows of the Church were opened, letting in a mixture of fresh air and stormy
weather. Old certainties were questioned and traditions scrutinised for their 'relevance'. Fr
Denys Lucas, the outgoing Housemaster of St Hugh's, summarised this 'spirit' in his St Edmund's
Day sermon of 1964:

*Tradition may well have its value as a stabilising force; but if we allow its letter rather than its spirit to
become the object of reverence, then tradition may well be an obstacle to progress, clouding men's*

minds, hindering clear judgment and vision… The church cannot afford to sit back brooding over the basic truths of God's revelation as though they were china eggs. No, they are real eggs, with life within them to be developed by the warmth of Christ's love for his bride. This is indeed an exciting age in which we live – an age of challenge and adventure, an age for youth and for young ideas.[206]

Following *Optatum Totius*, the Council's *Decree on Priestly Training* (1965), alternative approaches were tried at Allen Hall and the traditional curriculum broadened. The Divines remained separated from the rest of the College, as had long been the case; more 'distant cousins' to the school than brothers. However, the whole Edmundian community came together for special occasions and seminarians occasionally found themselves helping the school when there were gaps in the rugby team! A new programme of studies was introduced in September 1967, with an emphasis on pastoral formation, a more active diaconal year and visits to families, parishes and institutions beyond St Edmund's. Lay lecturers were brought in, such as Dr Jonathan Gould, who taught clinical psychiatry, arriving 'inconspicuously in his Rolls Royce and smoking a large cigar'. Since he had been involved in high profile murder trials at the Old Bailey, students purposefully distracted him from the abstract subject of his lectures so that he could talk more of his experiences.

Despite these changes, the 1960s witnessed a period of discontent in most seminaries. In the summer of 1965 Cardinal Heenan contacted his eventual successor, Abbot Basil Hume of Ampleforth, requesting that a monk act as spiritual director at Allen Hall (a plan that never went ahead). The Archbishop wrote revealingly:

All seminaries are undergoing a period of turmoil. This is understandable in view of the amount of writing being done about the need to transform the whole seminary regime. The restlessness has led to a loss of students greater than in normal years… Seminarians are in many ways more serious than in former years and they certainly are in much greater need of direction.[207]

Divines of the period recall the sense of mistrust between professors and students and the feeling that the President was constantly scrutinizing their motives in order to eliminate unacceptable candidates for Holy Orders. Anton Cowan, for example, who was at Allen Hall between 1966 and 1973, asked permission to help his elderly parents move house, necessitating a night spent away from seminary. Mgr Kelleher 'remained silent for several minutes, equivocating with "hums and haws" and a rather strange high-pitched noise – and then replied: "Well, you know, Mr Cowan, we must not keep trying to invent ways of getting away from this place. But I leave it to your decision and conscience'.[208]

In 1965 three prominent professors left Allen Hall for other academic appointments: Fr Charles Davis (Professor of Dogmatic Theology), Fr Hubert Richards (Professor of Sacred Scripture) and Fr Peter de Rosa (Lecturer in Metaphysics). Within ten years they had all left the Priesthood.

ST. EDMUND'S COLLEGE

OLD HALL, WARE

Rule of Life

for

Students in Allen Hall

1964

Above: The rules were very strict for seminarians. The Rule of Life published in 1964 listed 88 regulations that students had to follow, ranging from singing, praying, appearance and recreation.

DRAMA IN THE 1960s

Fr Austin Garvey was on the staff at St Edmund's between 1954 and 1966, having previously been in the seminary between 1945 and 1951. He taught Classics between 1954 and 1966, and was Housemaster of Talbot for his last two years at the College. As an enemy of the shoddy and the third-rate, he instilled into the boys a pride of giving of their best, and the result was a series of successful productions on the stage.

Above: The Affair, 1966.

Opposite top: Macbeth, 1965.

Opposite bottom: Two Ridiculous Misses, 1960.

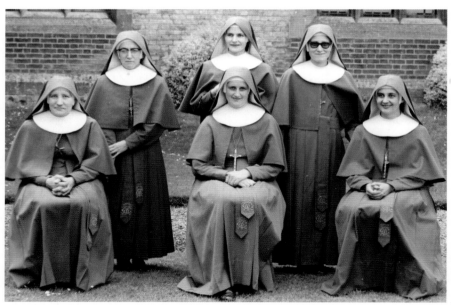

Right: The Consolata Sisters of Turin, a missionary congregation with extensive activities around the world, were at St Edmund's between 1951 and 1974. They carried out selfless and untiring work quietly behind the scenes, supervising the kitchen, linen room and domestic staff.

Below: The Garvey brothers Austin (left) and Michael were prolific in the 1960s. They are shown here officiating at a sports day.

In particular, the dramatic resignation of Fr Davis in 1966 was compared at the time to the 'secession' of Newman from the Church of England in 1845. When he left St Edmund's, Davis was described as 'one of England's greatest theologians and one of our own most respected and best-loved professors'. Indeed, The Edmundian continued,

For four or five years no one noticed anything extraordinary in this professor. Eccentric perhaps, incredibly studious, but no signs of the future peritus, still less of the source and centre of heated discussion in theological circles. In those days his effect on the student body was unremarkable, his lectures more trying than stimulating. But gradually a change came. His course was streamlined, much historical erudition was eradicated, and a new approach to eternal truths emerged in the lecture hall. Theology became exciting and – that word again – relevant! The students were infected with the enthusiasm of Fr Davis and the crime of talking shop was quietly erased from the unwritten law-books of the seminary.[209]

The exodus of priests like these greatly troubled Cardinal Heenan and he made sure he visited Allen Hall at regular intervals to meet with staff and students.

There were changes also in the school. Throughout the 1960s the number of day boys increased; ten years after their advent, day boys constituted more than a quarter of the total student body (1965-66). Fr Britt Compton reported that there were complaints that 'the College is becoming more of a grammar school than a smaller public school, and yet public school fees are being charged'.[210] Major building works were also completed: namely the new convent wing and garages (now no longer extant). Such initiatives led to an angry anonymous letter in The Tablet from a 'local resident' insisting that 'lovers of the countryside' and 'admirers of the Catholic Church' should unite in opposition against these characterless buildings at St Edmund's.

In February 1966 Mgr Kelleher suffered a mild heart attack after attending an episcopal consecration in Liverpool. Two years later he asked to return to parochial work and was appointed parish priest of Our Lady of Victories, Kensington (following in the footsteps of Mgr Bagshawe).

HIS BOOKED-LINED STUDY
WALLS EXUDED SCHOLARSHIP,
SOMETIMES THROUGH A
HAZE OF SWEET-SMELLING
TOBACCO SMOKE.

*Left: Bishop Christopher Butler was President of
St Edmund's between 1968 and 1986.*

THE BUTLER ERA (1968-84)

In 1967 a Benedictine monk arrived to take up residence at St Edmund's: Bishop Basil Christopher Butler, the newly-appointed Auxiliary Bishop of Westminster, who would be given special responsibility for the county of Hertfordshire. He was no stranger to ecclesiastical leadership, having been Headmaster, then Abbot of Downside and Abbot President of the English Benedictine Congregation. He was also a well known theologian, a peritus during the Second Vatican Council (like Fr Davis) and Vice Chairman of the Anglican-Roman Catholic International Commission (ARCIC). The College authorities must have wondered how easily such a renowned prelate would fit in but, as Fr Garvey later recalled with obvious relief, 'our distinguished guest proved to be an unassuming man with a friendly smile, a lively interest in what was going on, but with no wish to interfere'.[211]

Bishop Butler succeeded Mgr Kelleher as President in 1968 and the following year also became Chairman of Governors. The bishop lived at St Edmund's for nearly twenty years and the College quickly became for him a 'second Downside'. He had rooms and a private chapel on the President's Gallery and normally ate alone in the Bickford Dining Room (now the Careers Office), although he liked to join the rest of the staff for post-prandial coffee and afternoon tea in the Common Room, often 'arriving in habitually somewhat begrimed cassock with a cheerful gesture of the hand that seemed part-wave and part-blessing to those already assembled in the further reaches of the room'. An early riser, he could normally be seen at dawn 'taking a meditative stroll, along the terraces and drive in the summer, or through the Ambulacrum and sometimes upstairs when the weather was inclement'.[212] John Gillham, himself a hard working Chairman of Governors, wrote:

I think he found the peaceful Hertfordshire country environment and his attractive study, overlooking the parkland in front of the College, conducive to his contemplative thinking and theological writing. His book-lined study walls exuded scholarship, sometimes through a haze of sweet-smelling tobacco smoke wafting from his beloved pipe. He was, however, no recluse. His study door was always open to those who wished to consult him.[213]

SPRY AND USUALLY BECASSOCKED, HE WAS A TRUE FATHER TO THE COMMUNITY.

Above: Fr Michael Garvey was Headmaster between 1968 and 1984.

Below: A statement of policy and future plans, which described changes to the structure of the College and its curriculum.

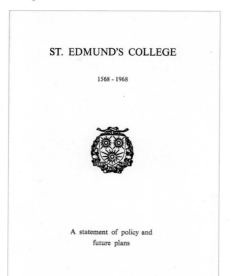

ST. EDMUND'S COLLEGE

1568 - 1968

A statement of policy and future plans

Butler certainly had plenty of issues to deal with as President. The fourth centenary year of the foundation of the English College, Douay, 1968, was to be one of great change. Not only was there a new President but, after nineteen years and faced with serious illness, Fr Britt-Compton passed on the reins of Headmaster to Fr Michael Garvey. Like his younger brother, Fr Austin Garvey, the new Headmaster had had a long association with St Edmund's and greatly loved the College's heritage, penning a guide to the College Chapel. As a master he was noted, among other things, for introducing athletics as a mainstream College sport. In order to accomplish this, he had sacrificed six weeks of his vacation one year to attend an intensive athletics summer school. In 1967 he had actually petitioned the Cardinal to be allowed to undertake full-time ministry with the physically disabled and so it was to his comparative dismay that he was named Headmaster. However, he dutifully flung himself into the job and one colleague later wrote, 'spry and usually becassocked, he was a true father to the community, regarded by many as a faithful and sympathetic friend'.[214] Others experienced his sterner side; 'a sure sign of something being wrong,' a member of staff, Cecil Friedlander, recalled, 'was the harried looking black-clad figure, head down, scurrying along the corridors or sitting at his desk, staring hard at the blotting pad and, most seriously of all, drumming with fingertips on the desk'.[215]

A final important appointment was that of Fr James O'Brien, formerly of the Catholic Missionary Society, as Rector of Allen Hall – a new office for this had formerly been the task of the President. He was popularly known as 'Big Jim' and brought with him solid pastoral experience, humour and a sense of purpose. One of his students, Fr Brian O'Shea, remembered how 'he had the gift of treating everyone even-handedly' and 'at the end of term concert he would don a Beatles wig and entertain us with his "letter home to mother". This gave him the chance to voice his observations and perceived eccentricities about staff and students alike. As always he made his point with self-deprecating humour, thereby giving us all a sound preparation for parish life'.[216]

MOVING THE SEMINARY

In 1968 it was announced that the seminary was actively seeking a new home in order to be nearer to the London parishes and universities – essentially a return to Manning's policy of 1869. The new Rector had the aim of moving the seminary by 1970. In actual fact the great move took place in July 1975; as one seminarian put it, 'like the Austrian Empire in the 19th century, Allen Hall always seems to be passing away into its new existence but never quite makes it'.[217]

There was, of course, opposition. At the end of 1969, the Westminster Chapter agreed unanimously that seminarians should not cut themselves off completely from the Edmundian tradition and doubts were raised about the appropriateness of future priests attending lectures at a 'secular' university. Even Bishop Worlock was not convinced of the advisability of the move, 'because of noise and health problems' in the great city.[218] In his Presidential Address on St Edmund's Day 1973, Bishop Butler said:

I said it was sad. But what is really happening? The Seminary is grasping its new vocation in the Church of Vatican II, a Church which sees the world not as an enemy to be shunned, so much as a fellowship of humanity to which we all belong: from which we Christians have much to learn, and to which we have to offer the incomparable treasure of "the faith of our fathers".[219]

OFTEN THE HOUSE CONFERENCES GIVEN BY THE RECTOR IN THE ALLEN HALL ORATORY WOULD BE INTERRUPTED BY GUNFIGHTS EMITTING FROM THE CANON'S TELEVISION.

Various locations were suggested for the new Allen Hall. These included St Pelagius', Highgate, the convent at West Hill, the former Calvary Nursing Home in Sudbury and new buildings in the parish grounds at Bow. The Cardinal liked the latter idea because of Bow's proximity to the East End and the presence of its parish priest, Fr William Brown, who had been one of the altar boys at Barking when Heenan was curate. With the diocese buying a large former Anglican convent at London Colney for use as a Pastoral Centre, it seemed that an additional option was that Allen Hall could share this site.

A special meeting was even arranged in May 1972 'to discuss the future of Allen Hall, Ware and St John's Seminary, Wonersh', following the bishops' decision to look at the rationalization of the seminaries. However Mgr McConnon and the Wonersh staff seemed particularly wary of an amalgamation: 'to commit the Southern Bishops to a project which is costly and of doubtful value is a proposal which the Staff at Wonersh could not recommend'.[220]

At a meeting held at St Edmund's on 15 November 1972, Mgr O'Brien 'announced that a further matter had now to be taken into consideration, namely, the possible availability for use as a Seminary of the Convent in Beaufort Street, Chelsea'.[221] This quickly became the favoured option. It was near the centre of London, close enough to the Cathedral to fulfil the Tridentine vision for a diocesan seminary which was closely under the bishop's eye and it stood on the former grounds of St Thomas More's 'great house'. Soon, those studying at Heythrop began to reside in the convent building during the week, returning to St Edmund's at the weekend.

Top: Canon Clement Parsons edited 'The Edmundian' magazine between 1968 and 1973.

Above: The long-planned move of Allen Hall to Beaufort Street, Chelsea, took place in the summer of 1975.

Amidst all this discussion, life at St Edmund's continued as usual. There were inspirational lecturers, such as the Jesuit Fr Philip Caraman, remembered not only for his scholarship in Church history but his sense of humour and kindness towards students. He was the Vice-Postulator of the cause of the English Martyrs and accompanied many of the students to the canonisation of the Forty Martyrs in 1970, twenty of whom had trained at Douay.

There were College 'characters' such as Canon Clement 'Pop' Parsons, the founder of Finchley Grammar School, who was living in retirement at St Edmund's and for a time acted as Spiritual Director and editor of *The Edmundian*. He disapproved of modern developments, including the Allen Hall move, and communicated a sense of balance to enthusiasts of the latest Church reforms: 'once asked about "lay participation", when everyone was raving about Parish Councils and Commissions, he replied, "There's nothing new; how do you think I got anything done in the past? Fat lot of help I got from some of my brother clergy."' A veritable College institution, 'often to be seen with pipe firmly clenched in teeth, cutting the grass and trimming the hedges of the graveyard next to the parish church, or walking up College Lane from Chestnut Drive back around the pitches and in past the parish church,'[222] he was also addicted to cowboy westerns. 'Often the house conferences given by the Rector in the Allen Hall oratory would be interrupted by gunfights emitting from the Canon's television. His room was directly above the oratory'.[223]

Above: A scene from The Edmundian Association's dinner dance in 1972, held at the Rainbow Room, Derry & Toms, in Kensington High Street, London. Nearly 500 Edmundians and guests attended. From left: John Vaughan-Shaw (Social Secretary), Bishop Christopher Butler (President), Mrs Kitty Muggeridge, Malcolm Muggeridge (guest of honour) & Fr Paul Bidone. Malcolm Muggeridge was a journalist, author, media personality and satirist. During the Second World War he was a soldier and a spy, and in his early life a left-wing sympathiser. He later became a forceful anti-communist, was credited with popularising Mother Teresa and in his later years became a Catholic and moral campaigner.

By the summer of 1975, one seminarian recorded that 'genuine "last" historic events occurred – last exams at St Edmund's, no more school to squash us in, no more of the College favourite meals of soya bean, meat and beef burgers! No more walks over the country fields (a favourite of the Rector), no more quiet country lanes to bike down'. In due course, 'about 650 empty tea chests appeared one afternoon in two Pickford vans. Volunteers had been asked for and the usual people turned up to help form a chain gang from van through the College office door and along the floor into the now almost empty "Ward Library."' The seminarians then retired for the pre-ordination retreat, after which they were given two days for personal packing: 'tea chests again began to move out of the library, the headmaster asked "where was the big tea-party?"'[224]

CHANGES AT THE SCHOOL

The 'migration' of Allen Hall not only allowed the seminarians to enjoy closer contact with London's parochial and intellectual life but also, crucially, allowed the school to expand and flourish. On the down side there was also an urgent need for money to meet the increased expenses. Fr Garvey made a number of important changes to bring St Edmund's safely into this new era. He had set up a Governing Body and arranged for the College to join the Governing Bodies Association of independent schools. He himself was elected to membership of the Headmasters' Conference.

Left: 'Rex' King being presented with a gift by Cardinal Basil Hume, Archbishop of Westminster, at a dinner in the Douay Hall to mark his retirement, on 12 June 1976.

Below: The 'Language Laboratory' was installed in 1968 as a contemporary aid to modern languages teaching. It allowed the teacher to listen to and manage students using analogue tapes from a master console connected with sound booths. Reliability issues and changes in teaching methods led to its demise in the 1980s.

There were some notable departures and arrivals: 'Rex' King retired in August 1976 after forty-six years at the College and was replaced as Bursar by Captain Joseph Phillips. Stalwarts of the subsequent chapter of Edmundian history joined the staff, such as Duncan Gallie (1976). The period also saw the further decrease in the number of priest masters and their replacement with dedicated lay teachers. Soon only two priests remained: Fr Bernard Lagrue (who stayed until 1993) and, of course, Fr Michael Pinot de Moira, whose remarkable stint at St Edmund's would continue well into the twenty-first century. Lay housemasters were appointed to Challoner in 1967 (Paul Ketterer) and Douglass in 1968 (John Vaughan-Shaw). Soon the first female teachers arrived. One of these worked in the French Department (Margaret Hasler) and, as Canon Paschal Ryan (then a pupil) noted,

I am not sure which was the more astounding aspect of her advent, that she was a woman or that she was not Roman Catholic. One could almost hear the rumble of generations of Old Edmundians turning in their graves. But that was just the start, male Protestant teachers were hired to teach science and maths. The odd thing was that two of them were Irish, but apparently they found the treatment they got from the RCs in this country very different to their experiences back home.[225]

Fr Garvey broadened the curriculum to include Biology and managed to attract increased numbers of students. In 1969 there were around 260; by the time he retired as Headmaster in 1984 there were about 430. To accommodate the rising numbers, further Houses were established: Poynter House in 1970, with Brendan Cannon as Housemaster, followed by Griffiths two years later, under William T. Gribbin, who remained Housemaster until it was disbanded in 1984, and Stapleton in 1975, under Stephen Blake. In September 1979 the last intake of County day boys was received but the school successfully took part in the Assisted Places Scheme, which ensured that the College continued its service to the local Catholic community. Denied his chance to exercise ministry to the disabled, the Headmaster regularly took students on pilgrimage to Lourdes and fostered links with St Elizabeth's Home and School for epileptic children in Much Hadham.

Above: Hockey was introduced as a sport with the arrival of girls in the 1970s.

The most dramatic change was the first tentative steps in co-education. This had been on the cards for some time and the policy was being followed in other prominent Catholic schools. Not surprisingly, it filled some Old Edmundians with considerable apprehension. In 1970 a former Headmaster, Fr Purdie, had written to Canon Parsons, 'I have an awful fear that the College may go co-educational and that girl boarders will take over Allen Hall and all its amenities. O di immortales!'[226] For several years girls from Poles came to St Edmund's once a week to join the General Studies class. Then, in September 1974, five girls, three of whom came from Poles, joined Rhetoric as full-time students. *The Edmundian* noted that 'their arrival is, it seems, the thin end of the feminine wedge: more girls are expected to join our sixth forms next September, including a number of boarders'.[227] From 1975 the girls formed Margaret Pole House, the name keeping the link alive with the convent. It is fitting that the girls' boarding areas on the upper floors of the main building eventually became known as Garvey's, after the Headmaster who introduced co-education.

In May 1978 St Edmund's launched its first major appeal, with the goal of transforming the Allen Hall refectory, old staff accommodation and the area below the Masters' Common Room into a Music Centre and the adaptation of the Douay Hall as a theatre and gymnasium. A target of £150,000 was set and by the end of June £136,000 had been raised, which meant that plans could be adapted to include a covered playground. The Music School and Douay Hall Theatre were ready for use by the Michaelmas Term 1979 and the covered playground was completed the following spring. A College Chapel Appeal quickly followed, due to the deterioration of much of the stone work and roof, and once again this was successfully met by the generosity of old boys and benefactors.

There were deeply felt changes not only in society at large but also within the Church, following the Second Vatican Council, and an apparent split between 'traditionalists' and 'progressives'. In one editorial for *The Edmundian*, Gavin Dorey prayed that St Edmund's would be 'preserved always both as a witness to the truths our Lord teaches and as a place where the Christian life is genuinely lived':

[The plain, bewildered Catholic] will share at least one thing with the traditionalists (it belongs to the Church, not to them): their clear-sighted assurance of the primacy of the spiritual and of the permanence of Catholic teaching on faith and the moral law. He will share at least one thing with the progressives (it belongs not to them but to the Church): their zeal for the Works of Mercy and their desire to bring both the Gospel and social justice to the world. If he is not helped in the present time by the lack of clear direction from lesser ecclesiastical authorities, he can look instead to the See of Peter in the certain knowledge that that authority at least will not fail him. Above all he must assure himself that to be a Catholic (which is not to be either of the right or of the left), and to eschew the bogus partisanships that make their voices heard so insistently, is the most positive and most real of all positions to adopt. Taken seriously it means nothing less than the imitation of Christ.[228]

Above: The former Allen Hall refectory was converted into a Music School in 1979. The citation, composed by the Head of Classics John Vaughan-Shaw, reads:

THESE ROOMS, FORMERLY THE REFECTORY OF ALLEN HALL, NOW RESTORED THROUGH THE GENEROSITY OF BENEFACTORS AND DEVOTED TO THE ART OF MUSIC, WERE DEDICATED BY BASIL CARDINAL HUME ARCHBISHOP OF WESTMINSTER ON THE 2ND DECEMBER 1979.

CHAPTER XI

THE PREPARATORY SCHOOL
1874 – Present

When W. G. Ward left St Edmund's in 1873 for his substantial estates on the Isle of Wight, it was decided to use his former residence, 'Old Hall House', as a Preparatory School dedicated to St Hugh of Lincoln. This was not, of course, the first 'preparatory school' at Old Hall Green. Dr Stapleton used the Hermitage for this purpose. After the erection of the New Building, the 'children' moved to the Old College and the chapel there was used by both the boys and the local Catholics. By 1808 there were some thirty or forty boys in the preparatory school. The early Masters included Francis Tuite, Lewis Havard and, between 1814 and 1816, Thomas Griffiths, the future President and Vicar Apostolic. This early institution stood in a long tradition stretching back to the school at Esquerchin, once used as a feeder for Douay.

However, the history of the modern preparatory school began in September 1874, when boys from second and third Rudiments were transferred to the new St Hugh's. Some simple adaptations had been made to the house: Ward's drawing room would serve as the Refectory and his library the chapel; the first floor became dormitories. The new school was initially known colloquially as 'Ward's'.

The first Headmaster was John A. Evans and his wife acted as matron until a more permanent appointment was made. After four years, Mr Evans departed and was followed by a succession of priest Headmasters. Fr Fenwick Skrimshire, 'a cultivated and kindly priest,' was there between 1880 and 1884, assisted by Aubrey Ansell, whose gentleness earned him the (affectionate) nickname 'Sister Mary'. Mgr Ross, one of the early Hugonians, recalled:

There were just over twenty boys then, and in the refectory Father Skrimshire and Mr Aubrey Ansell sat at the top of one table, and the capable Miss Rowan [the matron] at the bottom of the other, so that the boys were "under a crossfire of observation"... In the bounds there were all the facilities for secret robber caves; there were trees to climb; and in the copse and the field below, good birds-nesting in the Spring. In theory, the copse and the field were out of bounds, but "Sister Mary" being gentleness itself, a certain latitude was observed in these matters. The result was that the boys were more free to roam than their elders in the College, and conceived a great love of the open air and the countryside.[229]

After Fr Skrimshire's departure, it was the turn of Fr Edward St John (1884), Cardinal Bourne's great friend, and Fr Frederick Hopper (1884-88), one of the original Hugonians. He did his best to ensure St Hugh's felt like a real home for the boys, adding carpets and house plants to the interior and building a conservatory. Fr Cyril Shepherd (1893-97) divided the study-place into two, provided a reading room and chess room and inaugurated concerts and pastoral plays.

Left: The St Hugh's football team in about 1897.

Left: Fr Tunstall, the Bursar, outside St Hugh's in 1893.

Above: The rear of Old Hall House.

Below: The original dining room in St Hugh's.

These took place in the Bounds on a long summer evening: 'a platform was erected, the piano was carried by some of the older students at the College from the playroom, the trees and shrubs, which formed a fitting background, were decorated with fairy lamps. Then the entertainment opened with light, soft music sung by the boys, followed by a short play, recitations and songs. The masters from St Edmund's were invited as well as the brothers of the Hugonians'.[230]

There was a quick turnaround of Headmasters – eight in the school's first two decades – but some stability was provided in 1903 with the coming of Fr Ernest J. Nolan, who stayed at St Hugh's for an unprecedented fifteen years. Although a stern disciplinarian, he delighted the boys by reading to them after supper in the Senior classroom: Dickens, Scott, even The Adventures of Sherlock Holmes. He was, like the President (Mgr Ward), rather corpulent and a Hugonian later recalled that 'one of the great jokes about 1906 was when Fr Nolan purchased a very heavily built bicycle which had been specially made for "Bunny" Ward. I think he had been advised to take more exercise for health reasons. We used to watch him learning to ride; he would put one foot on the back step and ponderously hop perhaps half a dozen times before he could make up his mind to launch himself on to the saddle. He would sometimes accompany us when we went for walks, and as he could not ride very slowly for fear of falling off we used to trot beside him to keep up'.[231]

The boys contributed to the wider College community, although their day-to-day existence was essentially independent. On Sundays they went to the College chapel for High Mass, as they did for grand occasions such as St Edmund's Day and the General Ordinations. The tradition emerged that St Hugh's provided train-bearers for visiting bishops and that during the Corpus Christi procession they scattered flowers in front of the Blessed Sacrament. The chapel at St Hugh's was the scene of First Holy Communions. Mgr Ross wrote:

The tone of piety at St Hugh's was truly admirable. I made my First Communion on St Joseph's Day, 19 March 1884, and so carefully were we prepared by Father Skrimshire, that I count it the turning-point in my life...I count it the greatest blessing of my life – the priesthood was the outcome – that I went to St Hugh's at the age of ten. [232]

The First World War brought with it changes to the timetable, extra prayers and the advent of rationing, although many regular aspects of Hugonian life continued unaffected – sport, rambles, bathing, paper chases, lantern lectures (many on wartime themes) and, of course, outbreaks of illness. The chronicler for mid-1917 was even able to write that 'the Weather has had more direct effect upon us than the War' and that rations had some benefits: 'true, there has been no tuck-shop since Christmas, but that only means that we have more money for other things'.[233] However, some of the boys had to deal with harrowing experiences of the war:

Feb. 6th [1915]. A new boy, Ian Monro, came last Monday. A pathetic story attaches to this boy. On the morning of the German attack on Hartlepool two of his aunts who lived on the front there,

Above: St Hugh's Preparatory School in about 1894. At around this time the refectory, study place and library were all refurbished. According to The Edmundian of the day, a lavatory 'of the most approved type' was installed at the same time.

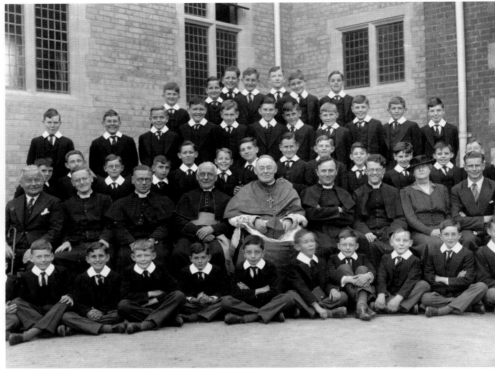

Top Left: The Bickford Wing was built in 1938.

Right: Cardinal Hinsley in 1938 on the opening of the Bickford Wing.

Below: A view from inside the Bickford Wing.

were making ready to go to Mass. One being ready, went to call her sister. Just as she entered the doorway a cannon ball came through the window and killed the two ladies on the spot. Their uncle, who had preceded them to Church, received so great a shock that he had to go to bed, and to the grief of all, died next day.[234]

While the College was inaugurating the Cadet Corps, St Hugh's set up a Troop of Boy Scouts, under the Scout Master Mr F. R. Stanes, and the first boys were enrolled on All Saints' Day 1916. Four days later Bishop Butt came to inaugurate the Troop:

At 3pm the ceremony of blessing the Troop Colours took place. Unfortunately the weather was too bad to allow the proceedings to be held in front of St Hugh's as had been intended. The Scouts were drawn up at the north end of the Divines' Ambulacrum with their colours, the Union Jack and the Troop Flag (St Hugh's swan on a background of blue and brown). The Cadet Corps paraded at the south end of the Ambulacrum. Many professors and Divines also attended. The Bishop, vested in cope and mitre, and attended by deacon and subdeacon in white dalmatics took up his position at the junction of the corridor and the Ambulacrum, facing the front door. He then addressed the Scouts drawn up before him. After this the colours were held crossed before him by two kneeling scouts, while he recited the prescribed blessing from the Roman Ritual. He then formally handed the colours to the Troop. The Cadets then marched past, saluting the colours. After this, His Lordship gave Benediction in the Divines' Oratory.[235]

*Left: The foundation stone for a new wing
was laid by Cardinal William Godfrey on 10 May
1960. He was assisted by Mgr (later Archbishop)
Derek Worlock.*

Above: The Godfrey Wing as completed in 1961.

*Below: King Manuel II of Portugal reigned until
1910 when the monarchy was abolished. He lived
in exile in Twickenham, south west of London.*

From 1920 the Headmaster of St Hugh's (also known as Vice-President) became known as the Housemaster. The first of these was Fr Francis Healy, later to become the first Edmundian Headmaster, who immediately made some changes to the school interior: the refectory became the chapel and there was also a new sitting room, playroom and scoutroom. More revolutionary, 'upstairs, basins with hot-water supply have been provided, and as this has done away with the old washstands, we have a new dormitory over the old chapel'.[236]

The daily routine was enlivened by special events and visitors. During the mid-1920s the exiled King Manuel of Portugal was often a guest at the College. At the St Edmund's Day celebrations of 1923 he addressed a few words to the boys of St Hugh's, saying that 'they could do nothing in their lives without faith and religion, and in their lives it would be even more necessary than it had been in those of their predecessors'.[237]

During the Presidency of Mgr Bickford, himself an Old Hugonian, a new wing was built consisting of a new chapel, study hall, class rooms and, upstairs, a bright and airy dormitory. This was largely thanks to the vision of Fr Sherlock, the Headmaster, who realised that any improvement at St Edmund's must begin with the Preparatory School. The President himself took great pleasure in laying the foundation stone of the extension on 17 October 1938 and by the following year it was ready to be opened by Cardinal Hinsley. According to Mgr Butcher, the new building effectively 'enabled the College to struggle through the war years. Parents wanted their children to be out of the big cities, so St Hugh's became fairly full and the numbers in the school also increased'.[238]

St. Edmund's College

A Dormitory (St. Hugh's)

The Second World War necessitated several changes. In the Autumn Term of 1940 it was decided to hold classes upstairs in the dormitories and to move the sleeping accommodation into the classrooms, library and sacristy. The same year, Fr Denys Lucas arrived, thinking he was filling a temporary vacancy. He remained twenty-four years and became Housemaster in 1949. He speedily introduced a number of changes affecting timetable and studies (namely, the Common Entrance Exam) and developed the school's sporting tradition, introducing cricket and rugby matches against other prep schools. Due to the somewhat cramped conditions at St Hughes, he planned a new wing, which was opened by Cardinal Godfrey in 1960 and ready for use the following year – a bold enterprise since the Bickford extension had only recently been erected. At one stage there was even a proposal to move to a separate building away from the main College site – Blakesware, placed on the market by Lord Gerard – although this was deemed too expensive and impractical.

Fr Lucas – or 'Lukey' as he was called – was a larger than life figure. A colleague, Canon Peter Phillips, remembered the 'tall, aristocratic figure striding through the College grounds, faithfully accompanied by Paul, his springer spaniel'. Furthermore 'Denys was large in every sense and in all he did, stalking deer and fly-fishing in Scotland, coaching cricket and rugby, instilling discipline and learning into those in his charge'.[239]

Appropriately perhaps for a keen cricket fan and a member (like Ward) of the M.C.C., his favoured instrument of corporal punishment was 'The Bat', a half-size trophy bat that had been signed by England and South Africa test teams and was always administered before Lights Out. Canon Paschal Ryan recalled:

We had a rule book issued on arrival, and the infringements (e.g. fighting, talking in class) could – almost always did – result in being beaten with a trophy cricket bat. Every evening there would be a line of boys in dressing gowns and pyjamas waiting to be beaten – lined up on the stairs outside "Lukey's" room. In order of seniority, of course. "Seniores priores" was one of the first bits of school lore/law one learnt. One memory: a small boy, possibly the youngest in St Hugh's, too young really, went in to be beaten by Lukey. It was the umpteenth time, he was scared, Lukey was scary (six foot tall and a loud voice). Small schoolboy sadists that we were, we waited outside, silently listening. The boy went in. We heard nothing while inside Lukey's study the boy told of whatever infraction of the rules had brought him there. Pause. We all imagined some stern words of admonition being given, and the boy bending over while the Headmaster's hand raised the bat, poised to strike, as the boy lifted his dressing gown. Instead of the expected "thwack", there was a scuttling sound as the boy tried running behind the desk and chairs to escape. An exasperated and infuriated adult voice boomed out: "Are you a man or are you a mouse?" Silence. A "Who wants to be a Millionaire"-like moment of truth as the frightened boy prepared his response. A millisecond seemed like an hour. Answer there came, as a high pitched squeal replied – "A mouse, Sir!"

Fr Lucas had a gentler side. He had a great love of nature (though a keen shooter of rabbits, even while in the driving seat) and was well known for his hospitality. He added several social functions to the yearly timetable, including the Fathers' cricket match, the match against the Old Hugonians and the annual Hugonian Dinner in London. We read in The Edmundian, that 'his most spectacular innovation, however, was probably the foundation of the Thursday Club,

"ARE YOU A MAN OR A MOUSE?" SILENCE... "A MOUSE, SIR!"

Opposite top: The St Hugh's refectory in the 1950s.

Opposite bottom left: A dormitory in the Bickford Wing (from a College prospectus).

Opposite bottom right: A classroom in the Bickford Wing.

Below: Fr Denys Lucas was Housemaster of St Hugh's between 1949 and 1964.

THE CHAPEL IS THE HEART OF THE COMMUNITY AND THE TUCK SHOP IS THE STOMACH.

Above: The art classroom in the Godfrey Wing in St Hugh's.

Right: These miniature cricket bats, carrying the signatures of the England and South African teams for the Lords Three Day Test in 1935, were used as instruments of punishment.

an institution shrouded in mystery in boys' minds, but in fact a weekly dinner party at which members of the staff can relax and enjoy their own company and that of their guests'.[240] Especially in the early 1960s the Thursday Club was the scene of much discussion about the Church. Eventually, inspired by the 'spirit' of the Second Vatican Council, Fr Lucas volunteered to become a missionary in Uganda in 1964. Indeed, there was an obvious 'contrast between Denys the top-drawer bon viveur and Denys the devoted priest caring for the poorest of the poor in conditions of increasing danger under Idi Amin'.[241]

Also on the staff at St Hugh's during the period were Fr Anthony Potter and Fr Michael Pinot de Moira. Fr Potter used to say, rather perceptively, that 'the Chapel is the heart of the community and the Tuck Shop is the stomach'. Speaking about Fr Pinot, Canon Paschal Ryan remembered:

Above: Fr Michael Pinot de Moira was an assistant teacher in St Hugh's between 1958 and 1971

he was an incredibly vibrant presence, whether in the classroom, on the rugby pitch or in the swimming pool... We "mugs" as he called us would not dare to put a foot wrong in his presence. At the same time his classes were always fun. Whether it was French or Maths, or latterly Chemistry, he always kept us on the go. The Chemistry was fun, as he was quite frank about the fact that he was finding his way as he taught us. Apparently the authorities had looked at the syllabus, noticed we lacked Chemistry, built bench for experiments in the upstairs Art Room, and told Pinot to teach it. He never did a teacher training course, just gifted... Some parents were a little taken aback if they visited Fr Pinot's room, to find this smoke-filled den with boys playing roulette, card games, and in the middle of it all the becassocked (always in a cassock) Pinot. For all that, we knew our place, and if we were told to get lost, nobody would have dared moan more than under their breath. The "boundaries" may have been invisible, but they were very real.[242]

A feminine presence was provided by members of the Faithful Companions of Jesus from Poles Convent who 'commuted' to St Hugh's between 1949 and 1972. This was a definite boost, not only because of their dedication to the pupils but because they were all qualified teachers. Links were also built up with Poles. On 8 December 1949, for example, the boys were invited over to the Convent by Reverend Mother for a tour, which the Hugonian chronicler declared 'most revealing – there is something in being a girl after all, at least, when it comes to being educated'.[243]

In 1964 Patrick Foort, a former Anglican minister, became Housemaster and moved into a specially constructed house nearby. Fr Potter remembered:

We all make mistakes, and hopefully learn from them. Patrick was no exception and this endeared him to all. He was one of us. He once told the boys at an assembly that now the apples were appearing on the trees in the orchard lining the bounds play area no one was to touch them. He even pointed to where the orchard was! Matron was none too pleased with all the "tummy" aches she had to deal with in the next few days.[244]

He managed to increase student numbers but the need for a new structure was also felt. In 1971 it was decided to amalgamate St Hugh's into the College, ending its relative independence. On 9 September 1971 Fr Garvey formally established a Junior School, made up of St Hugh's and Junior House. The idea was that boys were given a gradual introduction into the larger world of St Edmund's:

In the first three years a boy's life centres entirely round St Hugh's. In the first two forms his work is teacher centred with our two assistant mistresses completely committed to them. In the 3rd form his work begins to be subject based, but the different masters usually come to him. The 4th year boys are beginning to share their curriculum with the College. They have to become familiar with classrooms and laboratories further afield, but they are setted together, so that throughout this broadening of their experience they are sharing it with their friends. By their final year at St Hugh's, boys are ready to take a further step, being setted in each subject. In every set, they have familiar friends, but they are not an exclusively Hugonian group. Once classes are over they still come back to their known surroundings.[245]

Top and above: Two photographs taken in St Hugh's by a professional photographer in the summer of 1956.

The upper photograph includes Stuart Janion (1955-60), Chris Slade (1953-63), David Norbury (1953-61), Chris Ryan (1953-64), Martin Hubner (1954-57) and Robin Lindsay (1955-62).

In the lower photograph are, from left: Fr John O'Callaghan, Ian Stobbs (1952-62), Mike Jenner (1951-60), Philip Cauvin (1952-61), Patrick Peel (1951-61), Peter Ward (1953-61), Chris Knight (1951-61), Mike Lloyd (1952-60) and Joe Swift (1951-59).

The pupils no longer followed a course leading to Common Entrance but, at the age of 11, started studies that would lead, after five years, to G.C.E. 'O' Levels. The transition to senior school became a matter of natural continuity.

Mr Foort was succeeded by Anthony Hollington-Sawyer (1974-81), Peter Nicholson (1981-88), Richard Poole (1988-89) and Robert Maidment (1989-96). The 1990s saw the evolution of St Hugh's from a single-form school (one class per year, ages 7-11) to a two-form-entry school. Major changes occurred in April 1996, when a new Nursery and Infants' Department was opened in the renovated old wing, with its own play area, and in September 2000, when St Hugh's became an exclusively day school, the old dormitories becoming classrooms. All change is challenging but, as the out-going Housemistress, Mrs Elliott (1996-2002), reflected in *The Edmundian*:

Left: The Form 1 classroom in St Hugh's in 2000.

Above: The matron Mrs Kay Curran with students in a dormitory in St Hugh's in 1980.

The success of the project may be judged from the ever-increasing demand for places in St Hugh's. This year we had waiting lists for four of our year groups and almost all the others have only one or two places. This great success is largely due to a committed and willing team of staff who are prepared to "go the extra mile" for their pupils.[246]

Jacqueline Hart (2002-10) and Leonard Blom (from 2010) led the school in subsequent years. In 2011 St Hugh's was renamed St Edmund's Prep School, a change in nomenclature thought necessary to clarify the school's link with the College and its role as a prep school rather than yet another Catholic primary school. Mr Blom also made changes to the curriculum and focussed on the school's sporting tradition.

The Preparatory School has thus changed dramatically since 1874. Up until the outbreak of the Second World War, student numbers usually ranged between 20 and 40. With the opening of the Bickford building in 1939, numbers were brought up to 60 and by 1961, thanks largely to the efforts of Fr Lucas, another extension was ready, increasing numbers to 75 and ensuring a reliable supply of pupils for the College. Relations with St Edmund's went from strength to strength, as can be seen in Fr Garvey's Junior House initiative, until the decision was made to transform St Hugh's into a day school and provide education from the age of three upwards.

Top left: The St Hugh's cricket pavilion in the 1960s.

Opposite top: Old Hall was the home of Junior House between 1971 and 1993.

Above: June 1967: The St Hugh's Fathers' Cricket Match. From left: Group Captain John Ellacombe, Mr John Gillham, Dr Gordon Thick, Major Barry Canham and Major Marsh. In the 1950s and 1960s the match was an annual feature of the St Hugh's social calendar. Fathers played against students with the adults being handicapped with cut-down cricket bats.

Above left and left: A St Hugh's garden party in the 1960s.

Junior House

A Junior House was first set up as a half-way house between the preparatory and senior schools under Fr Nicholas Kelly in 1945 but was disbanded eight years later, by which time Fr Laurence Allan was acting as Housemaster. It was later revived under the leadership of Fr Michael Garvey (1960-64), Fr Daniel Higgins (1964-69) and Fr Michael Roberts (1969-71). When Junior House ('JH') was reconfigured in 1971, Fr Garvey appointed Fr Pinot as Housemaster. The Headmaster later reminisced, 'I was able to bask in the reflected glory of that choice for the next fourteen years. The Junior House was a happy house from its inception' and Fr Pinot 'ensured that he knew the parents of his charges too, and was rightly rewarded by the total confidence of parents and pupils'.[247] According to one former student, Fr Pinot was 'a man with many talents. As far as I could remember he could teach just about every subject, except, of course, Geography (a swear word as far as Fr Pinot was concerned), but the welfare of his pupils was his priority'.[248]

In the autumn of 1971 work began on adapting the central section of the Old Hall, which had most recently been used as the Infirmary, and part of the Georgian wing was rebuilt the following year to make way for a new dormitory, common room and shower block. The new buildings were blessed by the President on 26 May 1973 – and the bill was partly paid for by the (not uncontroversial) sale of the Old Hall Manuscript, containing rare English music from the fourteenth and fifteenth centuries.

Fr Pinot remained at the helm until Junior House's closure in July 1993. It was indeed a unique institution, filling the gap between the security of primary education and the bewildering world of the senior school. Indeed, for many it was their first experience of living away from home, but thanks to Fr Pinot and other staff members (not least two of its matrons, Mrs May Williams and Mrs Jane Morley) many Old Edmundians looked back to their days in Junior House as their happiest.

MANY OLD EDMUNDIANS LOOKED BACK TO THEIR DAYS IN JUNIOR HOUSE AS THEIR HAPPIEST.

Above: An oil painting of Junior House by Jim Odell, art master from 1969 until 1993. Fr Michael Pinot de Moira is depicted in the centre carrying a pile of red RE exercise books. The figure in bright green to the far left is a caricature of the then Chairman of Governors, Mr John Gillham.

Opposite top: Junior House in 1952. The House-master was Fr Laurence Allan and his assistant was Mr Hugh Strode.

Opposite bottom: Junior House in 1980. The Housemaster was Fr Michael Pinot de Moira, his assistant was Mr John Perry and the matron was Mrs May Williams.

Above: The final Junior House photograph at the time of its closure in 1993. The Housemaster was Fr Michael Pinot de Moira. The other assistant staff (from left) were Mr John Morley, Mrs June Page, Mrs Jane Morley and Mr Mike Lewis.

Below: The Junior School staged lavish productions. This is the cast of the Gilbert & Sullivan operetta HMS Pinafore in 1982.

In 2011 the Allen Hall quadrangle was transformed into a paved open space, and a life-sized bronze statue of St Edmund was unveiled.

CHAPTER XII

INTO THE THIRD MILLENNIUM
1984 – Present

At the end of August 1984 poor health and the desire for a change prompted Fr Garvey to step down as Headmaster after a total of thirty-one years of service to the College. On his retirement, he was able to travel to India for a few months to work with lepers, thus fulfilling a lifelong ambition, before serving as parish priest of Rickmansworth and then chaplain to the Carmelite nuns at Ware. Fr Garvey was replaced at St Edmund's by a married layman, Donald McEwen, previously Head of English and Housemaster at the Oratory School. Bishop Butler told the parents that 'it was soon very clear to the governors that it would not be possible to replace Fr Garvey by another priest: no suitably qualified priest was available; indeed, such is the shortage of priests in the Westminster diocese, that it seems likely that it will not be possible in the foreseeable future to spare a priest for this post'. Mr McEwen, the President continued, 'has the reputation of being dedicated to the spiritual, academic and social education of his pupils'.[249]

A married headmaster with two young daughters required a family house and plans were made to build a suitable residence, College Mead House, close to the Chestnut Drive – known colloquially as 'Swamp Cottage'. His arrival coincided with a number of other changes in the College hierarchy: Brigadier Charles Hince became Bursar and John Gillham succeeded Bishop Butler as Chairman of Governors.

There were many challenges for the new Headmaster to overcome and those who regretted the passing of the days when the senior positions within the College were held by diocesan priests. Fortunately, student numbers were increasing, in part thanks to more aggressive marketing but also thanks to improving communications and wealth in the area. Pupil registrations increased dramatically from 418 in June 1984 to 582 in September 1986. The student roll was further set to rise after the closure of Poles Convent and the decision to make the College fully co-educational from September 1986. As already noted, girls had first been admitted to the sixth form in 1974 and the following year Margaret Pole House was established in the Allen Hall buildings. In 1985 girls from the fifth form at Poles attended lessons at St Edmund's. However, the full influx of girls meant the need for appropriate accommodation and at first a bid was put in for the old convent buildings at Poles, though this proved unsuccessful and the property fell into the hands of developers who converted it into a luxury resort, hotel and country club: Hanbury Manor.

By the mid-1980s Bishop Butler's health was declining and, much to everyone's distress, his sharp mind became increasingly incapacitated. There had been rumours that he might be honoured with a cardinal's hat for his contribution to theology although the presence of two Benedictine cardinals in a single diocese seemed unlikely and his views were considered too progressive by some. He was named Assistant to the Pontifical Throne, an appointment summed up by his old Oxford College as 'an ADC to the Pope'.

Lay headmaster for St Edmund's

FR GARVEY MA, headmaster of St Edmund's College, Ware, since 1968, has very kindly sent me this photograph of Mr Donald McEwen, who will succeed him as headmaster in September 1984.

In making the announcement

the Governors of the College pointed out that the appointment of a lay headmaster is something of a new departure in the history of the oldest Catholic School in England.

Although there was a lay headmaster in the 1940's, Mr J H W King, all other headmasters have been priests.

Mr McEwen, a graduate of Oxford, aged 39, is married, with two children. At present he is housemaster and head of English at the Oratory School, Woodcote.

When he takes over from Fr Garvey he will be responsible for both senior and junior schools.

The junior school, consisting of St Hugh's Preparatory School and a Junior House, has 160 boys from 7 to 13 years of age. The senior school has 300 boys and 20 sixth form girls.

Top left: A distinguished guest at Prize Giving in 1993 was the Duke of Norfolk (centre).

Top right: Cardinal Basil Hume presenting a cheque for about £3,500 to Fr Michael Garvey on his retirement as Headmaster in 1984.

Right: John Gillham, Chairman of Governors, at Prize Giving in 1994.

Middle: The editor of The Edmundian, John Hayes (left), presenting Saint John Paul II with a copy of the publication in 1992.

Above: An article in the Catholic Herald on 18 November 1983.

He died on 20 September 1986 and the following February a Memorial Mass was held for him in the College chapel, at the end of which Dr Robert Runcie, the Archbishop of Canterbury, paid a warm tribute to his friend. A reception followed, at which it was announced that Cardinal Hume would be the new President of St Edmund's — indeed, it had been decided that the President would henceforth be the incumbent Archbishop of Westminster.

Within a short time of Mr McEwen's arrival, changes were apparent in almost every sphere of Edmundian life. Prize Giving was moved from the beginning of the October break to the end of the previous summer term. The old Allen Hall oratory, which had been used as a classroom, became the staff parlour, while new fire doors were fitted throughout the building, which 'while the school is not burning have the disadvantage of making movement from place to place an exercise for arms as well as legs, but while on the other side of the account provide endless opportunities for the exercise of politeness'.[250]

A key goal was the strengthening of the house system by allotting specific responsibilities to the individual houses and attaching more auxiliary staff. Challoner and Poynter became Houses for boarders and the remaining Houses had only day students. Inter-house competitions were inaugurated in Prose and Poetry Reading, Music and Drama. Another priority was extra-curricular activities and (from 1996) the hosting of International Summer Schools during the holidays, which raised much-needed revenue and led to school applications.

Indeed, Mr McEwen welcomed many students from Eastern Europe, China and elsewhere and developed an International Department, with its own teaching centre and specialised staff. It is thanks to this vision that events such as Chinese New Year have become such an important part of modern Edmundian life. It was also a key part of St Edmund's rise in fortunes, together with the development of the 'bus system' which transported the increasing numbers of day pupils to the College.

Many of the changes, of course, came from without – new technology; the first OFSTED inspections; the coming of GCSEs, new AS Levels and GNVQs, which were embraced 'with particular enthusiasm as broadening the Rhetoric curriculum, involving links with business and industry and enabling the less academically orientated to obtain worthwhile sixth-form qualifications'.[251] Then there was the Young Enterprise scheme, the School Bank, work shadowing and annual Careers Convention.

Given its long history, St Edmund's always has its fair share of anniversaries. A particularly notable one was marked in 1993: the Bicentenary of the College's establishment at Old Hall Green. A Bicentenary Appeal was launched to extend St Hugh's, build a new Technology Department (partly in the existing building and partly in Talbot North Quad) and erect a roof over the Allen Hall Quad to improve dining facilities. Bill Gribbin produced a useful *Bicentenary Book* and Cardinal Hume celebrated Mass on St Edmund's Day and planted, in pouring rain, a 'Bicentenary Oak' in front of the College. A further memorial was provided by the official grant of arms to the College, presented to the President by the Lord Lieutenant of Hertfordshire thanks to the services of the York Herald, Henry Paston-Bedingfeld (whose family had historic connections with St Edmund's).

Most memorably, a group of staff, students, Old Edmundians and friends of the College made a special pilgrimage to Rome and were granted the privilege of a private audience with John Paul II in the Sala Clementina on 25 October 1993, the Feast of the Forty Martyrs. Duncan Gallie recalled

We organised our seating arrangements, with students well to the fore, and waited in great anticipation for the arrival of the Holy Father. Bishops on their ad limina visitations wandered through the front of the Hall and chatted with pilgrims in the front row. "Are you from Ireland?" asked one of the bishops. "No, we're from the oldest Catholic College in England, celebrating the Faith of our Fathers with a visit to the successor of Peter. Where are you from?" "I'm the bishop of

Top left: Cardinal Basil Hume carrying the Relic of St Edmund at a Mass to celebrate the 750th anniversary of the saint's death held at Westminster Cathedral on 16 November 1990.

Top: The front of the order of service for the celebratory Mass.

Above: Cardinal Basil Hume with Charlie & Maria Smith at the planting of a tree to mark the bi-centenary of the foundation of St Edmund's College in 1993.

the Tokelau Islands, on my ad limina visit with the other bishops of Oceania" – thus the catholicity of the Church was brought home to us as we waited to greet the Holy Father.

And then suddenly a side door opened, and the Pope appeared. Greeted by our lengthy and heartfelt applause, he immediately made his way around the front and side rows of our group, shaking hands and greeting individuals. "Are you from the Philippines?" he asked Wendy and Billie Cheung. "No, from Hong Kong," answered Miss Dixon on their behalf. "Ah, Chinoise," the Pope replied. He was introduced to the Head Boy and Girl, David Logue and Joanna Drew. As he walked along the front row, he said, "Ah, young ladies too?" It became evident from the rest of the audience that he had not been briefed about the College's comparatively recent change to coeducation.

When the Pope sat down, Duncan Gallie, on behalf of the other pilgrims, came forward to deliver a short address. He firstly thanked the Pope for making the time to see us all within his very busy schedule, and then explained who we were and why we were in Rome. "The school has marked this 200th anniversary by organising this pilgrimage to Rome. We wish to reaffirm our Catholic Faith, and the enduring loyalty of the College to the Holy See." He ended, as procedure required, by asking for the Holy Father's blessing: "On behalf of the Headmaster, students and staff, together with the others gathered in this audience, I would ask you, Holy Father, to bless the work of our College, and also that of our sister seminary of Allen Hall, for both were part of the original Douay foundation, that we may continue to teach and profess the Catholic Faith as expressed by the College's motto, Avita Pro Fide. For the Faith of Our Fathers."[252]

The Holy Father then delivered his address:

Dear Friends in Christ,

I am pleased to welcome you, the staff and students of St Edmund's College, as you make a pilgrimage to Rome to mark the 200th anniversary of your school's location at Old Hall Green and its dedication to St Edmund of Canterbury.

Saint Edmund's has a long and distinguished history, of which you are rightly proud. It can trace its origin back to 1568, when Cardinal Allen founded the English College at Douay to promote the education of young Englishmen in a properly Catholic atmosphere.

Your College gave them a sound foundation in the Christian faith, as well as in the arts and sciences, while at the same time preparing some of them for the priesthood. During difficult times the school helped to keep the flame of Catholicism alive in England.

It is a happy coincidence that you are here in Rome for the feast of the Forty Martyrs of England and Wales, some of whom studied at the English College in Douay. These were brave men filled with faith and joy in the risen Lord. In spite of the hardships which awaited them at home, they were determined to return there to pastor Christ's flock. Above all they were faithful to the Holy See, suffering martyrdom for their loyalty to the Successor of Peter. Your presence here today testifies to the fruitfulness of their witness. As your motto suggests, you have preserved their heritage: Avita pro Fide.

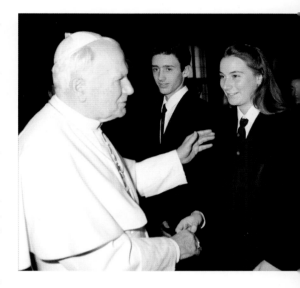

SAINT EDMUND'S HAS A LONG AND DISTINGUISHED HISTORY, OF WHICH YOU ARE RIGHTLY PROUD.

Opposite top: The Edmundian pilgrims at a private audience with Saint John Paul II in the Sala Clementina in the Apostolic Palace in the Vatican City on 25 October 1993. The room is covered in Renaissance frescoes and valuable works of art.

Opposite bottom: Duncan Gallie delivering an address to Saint John Paul II at the private audience.

Above: Saint John Paul II meeting the head boy, David Logue (1983-94), and the head girl, Joanna Drew (1987-94).

An aerial photograph of St Edmund's taken in 2013.

Above: The Greenwich Meridian runs through the College estate. In 2001 the Carey brothers erected a monument on its course. It is designed as the gnomon to a sundial.

Above right: The McEwen Wing, built in 2002, was named after Donald McEwen who was Headmaster between 1984 and 2002. This extension enabled many unsightly temporary classrooms, some dating back to the expansion of the College under Fr Michael Garvey in the 1960s, to be demolished.

Nowadays St Edmund's College is dedicated to educating young men to take their place in English society as mature, well-educated Christians. More than ever, the Catholic layman has the responsibility of bearing witness to the truth of Christ. When you return to England, as your predecessors did, proclaim that Gospel message, and "be persistent whether the time is favourable or unfavourable" (2 Tm 4:2).

The school's staff too should be inspired by the wise and holy leaders of its past and be ever ready to foster a joyful faith and sound moral values among the students in their care.

May the intercession of St Edmund of Canterbury and the Douay Martyrs deepen your faith in Christ and your love of his Church. To all the staff and students of St Edmund's College I gladly impart my Apostolic Blessing.[253]

As he left for his next appointment, the pilgrims sang *O Beate mi Edmunde*. The Bicentenary celebrations formally ended on St Edmund's Day 1994 with a Mass celebrated by the Papal Nuncio, Archbishop Luigi Barbarito, and a sermon preached by Fr David Milburn, the church historian and former Vice-President of Ushaw. The special Mass also commemorated the 400th anniversary of the death of Cardinal Allen.

Mr McEwen presided over many changes and improvements to the College buildings – including the division of dormitories into smaller units, boarding common rooms for Challoner and Poynter, new kitchen and toilet facilities, modernised Science laboratories, additional classrooms for English, the Butler Hall (replacing the covered playground), a new IT Centre and Advanced Studies Sixth Form Centre and, finally, the North Wing extension (known as the McEwen Wing). The Parents' Amenities Committee were able to sponsor two new Squash Courts, while a revitalised Edmundian Association funded various projects, including the restoration of the great Crucifix in front of the College and the chapel's Great Bell. In 1994 the Old Edmundian Cricket Society was established in order to further strengthen College ties.

In September 2002 a new Headmaster, Dr Mark Loughlin, arrived at St Edmund's with Mary-Kate and their six daughters. A skilled historian and hockey player, he brought with him a bold vision, aiming to make St Edmund's the country's leading Catholic school and encouraging the students to always aim for their 'personal best'. As *The Times* later put it, he 'seemed to find time to stand on every touchline' and 'although his administrative touch was sure, he made sure he kept contact by teaching, both English and history'.[254] He got to grips with various issues concerning discipline and staffing and changed the house system, so that Challoner and Poynter were no longer reserved exclusively for boarders. The resulting mixture of day pupils and boarders did much to integrate the College community and improve the competition between the houses.

Dr Loughlin tragically died in a road accident while on holiday in Scotland on 2 April 2004, after just five terms as Headmaster and a week after his fortieth birthday. *The Edmundian* reported that 'in the kaleidoscope of emotions that followed – disbelief, shock, numbness and an immense outpouring of sympathy for the Loughlin family – there seemed chiefly a sense of waste that the life of a loving father and dynamic leader should have been so tragically extinguished in its prime'.[255] Several Requiem Masses were organised, including one at Westminster Cathedral celebrated by the College President, Cardinal Murphy-O'Connor. In the aftermath of the tragedy, it quickly became very clear that Dr Loughlin was much loved by parents and pupils alike.

Chris Long succeeded as Headmaster, having worked as Deputy Head since 2001 under Mr McEwen and Dr Loughlin. Building on the work of his immediate predecessors, his aim was to give St Edmund's confidence in itself, for the College was sometimes being compared unfavourably with its competitors. Under his leadership, the College achieved its best ever academic results and its largest student numbers (812 at the beginning of 2012). New subjects such as Media Studies, Psychology and Italian were added to the curriculum and the senior

Top left: Dr Mark Loughlin and his family in 2002.

Above: Part of a cutting from the Catholic Herald on 9 April 2004.

Below: Chris Long succeeded Dr Loughlin as Headmaster and retired in 2012.

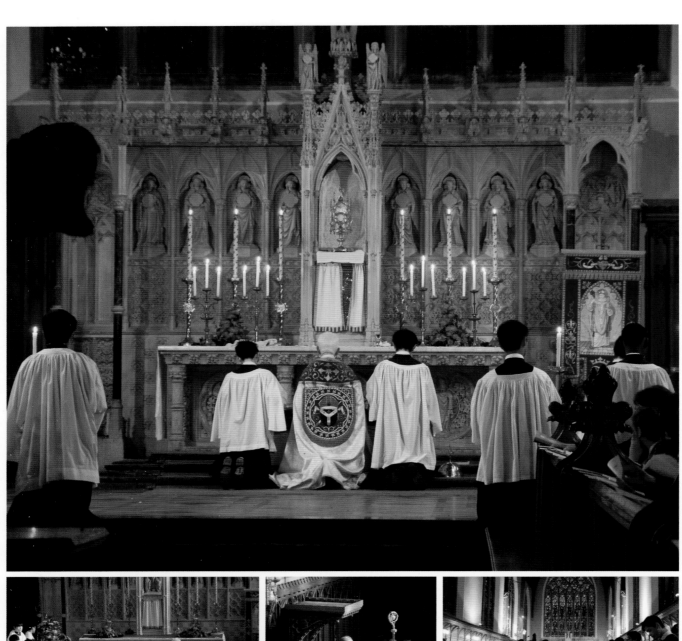

leadership team was extended to include not only the Headmaster and his deputies but the newly created Assistant Heads. Mention should be made of Mrs Janet Neal, Deputy Head until 2009, who ran the school during the ten weeks in 2007 when Mr Long was absent due to illness, and Jeremy Gillham, son of a Chairman of Governors and an occupier of that role himself, who displayed great dedication to St Edmund's.

During Mr Long's time, the College was able to deal with the backlog of maintenance, remodelling the interior to increase the number of classrooms, renewing the main staircases and Ambulacrum ceiling, demolishing the garages, creating new areas for Poynter and Challoner and saving the Old Farmhouse. He was particularly proud of the new St Edmund Quad, with its distinctive statue of the College's patron – a space which could be effectively used for special functions as well as by students. Mr Long was careful to strengthen links with the Archdiocese of Westminster and set up the Old Hall Catholic Scholarship, covering up to 100% of fees for children living in the diocese. A personal highlight of his tenure was the visit of Archbishop Vincent Nichols, the College President and Patron, to celebrate St Edmund's Sunday on 13 November 2011.

In September 2012 Paulo Durán became Headmaster. He had moved to the College with his wife Alice in 2009 and worked as Deputy Head and Registrar, during which time his daughter Inés was born. When his appointment was announced in November 2011, he stated:

I feel enormously humbled and privileged to be taking over the leadership of the College at such an exciting time: results have never been better and we have a school full of happy, confident students making the most of the many opportunities offered in and outside the classroom. Taking over from Chris Long will be no mean feat, but the College has a body of staff, students and parents that most Heads would envy and I am looking forward to the challenge of building upon his legacy as the College starts to approach its 450th anniversary.[256]

RESULTS HAVE NEVER BEEN BETTER AND WE HAVE A SCHOOL FULL OF HAPPY, CONFIDENT STUDENTS.

Opposite: Scenes from St Edmund's Sunday on 13 November 2011. The event marked the 150th anniversary of the solemn enshrinement of the Relic of St Edmund in the College. The Principal Celebrant was Archbishop Vincent Nichols, President and Patron of the College.

Above: The funeral in 2010 of Charlie Smith who had worked at St Edmund's as a groundsman from 1946 until 2007. The event brought together large numbers of the worldwide Edmundian family and demonstrated how the College Chapel is a fitting venue for solemn religious occasions.

FATHER MICHAEL PINOT DE MOIRA

Fr Michael Pinot de Moira at the annual reunion of Old Edmundians held at the Royal Over-Seas League, London, in 1998.

As this book was nearing its completion, the Edmundian community suffered the sad death of Fr Michael Pinot de Moira.

David J S Kay, President Emeritus of The Edmundian Association, observed,

"Fr Pinot was a remarkable man who spent 67 years at the College: 12 years as a student and 55 years as a priest-schoolmaster. He was still working enthusiastically at the time of his death. This is a record that is unlikely ever to be broken."

Michael Patrick Anthony Pinot de Moira was born on 12 September 1932 in Kenton, Middlesex. His early schooling was at the Salvatorian College in Harrow Wealdstone and at Finchley Catholic Grammar School. He came to St Edmund's as a 'Church Boy' in 1944, transferring to Allen Hall in 1950, and being ordained at Westminster Cathedral in on 26 May 1956. He died on 16 June 2013.

After a short spell as a curate in St John's Wood, Fr Pinot was asked by Archbishop William Godfrey to move to St Hugh's Preparatory School to fill a teaching vacancy that had arisen. Though unhappy with this move, and not qualified as a teacher, Fr Pinot soon developed his own very unique and effective teaching style. His infectious enthusiasm for whatever he was doing, whether in the classroom, on the sports fields, or just entertaining in his study, made him a central figure in the life of St Hugh's.

In 1971, he was asked to become Housemaster of the newly expanded Junior House. Fr Pinot ensured that he knew the parents of all his charges, and was rightly rewarded by the total confidence of parents and pupils. Many Old Edmundians looked back to their days in Junior House as their happiest.

When Junior House was disbanded in 1993, Fr Pinot became Priest-in-Residence at St Edmund's, and later its Chaplain. He remained at the centre of school life.

At a Mass shortly after his death, the Headmaster, Paulo Durán, told the whole school,

"There will never, ever be anyone to replace Fr Pinot and getting used to St Edmund's without him will be hard but through our sadness we need to feel gratitude for having known him, whether for one year or for forty, and keep alive not just our memories of Fr Pinot, but more importantly the unselfish, tireless love he showed to all around him."

In accordance with the wishes of his family, the Diocese and the College, Fr Pinot's Requiem Mass was celebrated at the College on 28 June 2013. There were over 1,300 mourners present. Fr Pinot was laid to rest in the crypt under the College Chapel, where he joined his former colleagues Canon Clement Parsons and Fr Michael Garvey.

Fr Pinot dedicated his life to the education and well-being of the students of St Edmund's College. His spirit and legacy will remain at the College and with those who were fortunate enough to have known him. Fr Pinot was the last priest-schoolmaster in the Douay tradition. It is therefore entirely fitting that this book is dedicated to his memory.

Avita Pro Fide

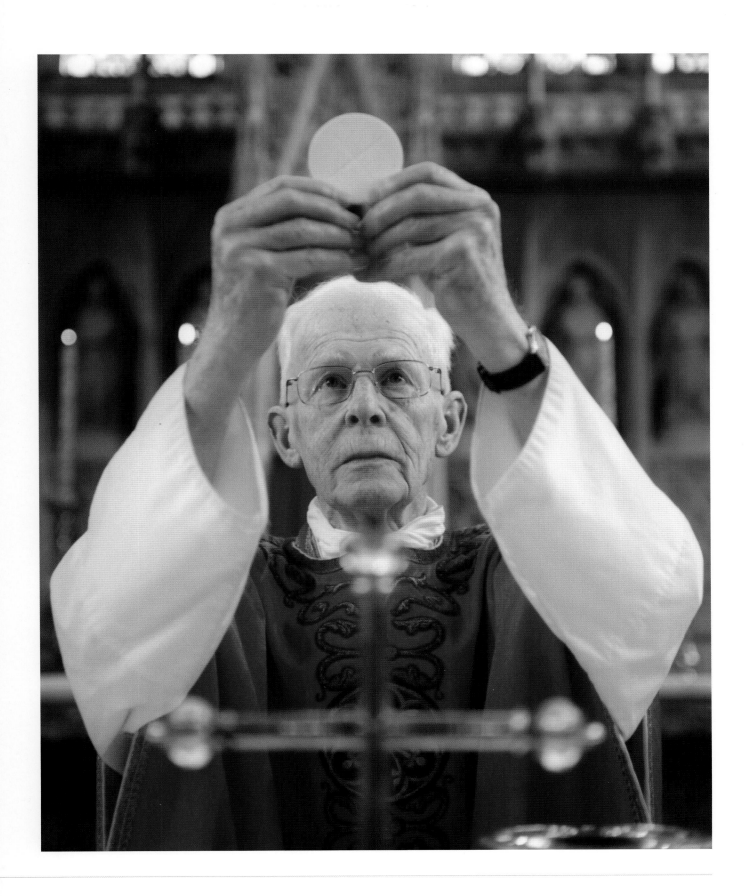

St Edmund's truly has a venerable history and, as this author lays aside his pen, it is satisfying to reflect that the College is yet to reach its final chapter. The story described in these pages will go on developing. The likes of Allen, Challoner, Douglass, Griffiths and even Ward would hardly recognise the twenty-first century school. There have indeed been many necessary changes to introduce and challenges to overcome, some more popular than others.

Bishop Cahill of Portsmouth reflected on this in a sermon that marked the opening of the Divines' Wing and Shrine Chapel in 1905, a moment of important change in the College's story. He noted that the various bishops entrusted with the care of St Edmund's had sometimes pursued very different policies:

The Church indeed is likened to a barque, a vessel, a ferry boat if you will. The master of the ship sets the course, and then places at the steering wheel the helmsman, and leaves to him all the details of the vessel. Now, if you have ever spent any time on such a boat as I have for many years, and if you have ever watched the course of the ship, you will find an almost constant and scarcely varying line of direction towards the port; but if you turn round and watch the helmsman you find him there with his hand at the wheel, constantly turning it now to port, now to starboard. He is acting not from mere whim, not to give his hands employment; but he has his eyes fixed; he is watching the waves, observing the currents, calculating the set of the tide, and counteracting by his continual movements all that would otherwise turn the vessel out of her true course. He is surmounting those difficulties and is keeping the prow of the vessel true. And so it seems to me is the action of every bishop in his diocese. The bishop is placed at the steering wheel, and to him is given discretion. He is told which way to work, and he is there watching, just exactly as the helmsman did, the course of events and is adopting his line – his policy if you will – to the circumstances of the moment.[257]

Although the needs of the times have changed, the direction of the College has remained a unified whole, centred on the education of the young in the arts and sciences and helping them become witnesses to Christ – Avita Pro Fide, 'For the Faith of Our Fathers'.

Opposite top: The leavers of the class of Rhetoric II in the summer of 2010, together with some of their teachers.

Opposite bottom: A group of contemporary Bulgarian students at a grand Edmundian reception at the Sheraton Hotel in Sofia in December 2012. Standing in the centre are (from left) Paulo Durán (Headmaster), Caroline Hugo (Director of the International Department) and David J S Kay (President Emeritus of The Edmundian Association).

Above left: A student venerates the Relic of St Edmund during Vespers on St Edmund's Sunday in 2003. Fr Michael Pinot de Moira is assisted by Canon Desmond Sheehan.

LIST OF DOUAY MARTYRS

(Place of execution shown in brackets)

1577
St Cuthbert Mayne (Launceston)

1578
Blessed John Nelson (Tyburn)
Blessed Thomas Sherwood (Tyburn)

1581
Blessed Everard Hanse (Tyburn)
St Edmund Campion (Tyburn)
St Ralph Sherwin (Tyburn)
St Alexander Briant (Tyburn)

1582
St John Payne (Chelmsford)
Blessed Thomas Ford (Tyburn)
Blessed John Shert (Tyburn)
Blessed Robert Johnson (Tyburn)
Blessed William Fylby (Tyburn)
St Luke Kirby (Tyburn)
Blessed Laurence Richardson (Tyburn)
Blessed Thomas Cottam (Tyburn)
Blessed William Lacy (York)
Blessed Richard Kirkman (York)
Blessed James Hudson Thomson (York)

1583
Blessed William Hart (York)
Blessed Richard Thirkeld (York)
Ven John Slade (Winchester)
Ven John Bodey (Andover)

1584
Blessed George Haydock (Tyburn)
Blessed James Fenn (Tyburn)
Blessed Thomas Hemerford (Tyburn)
Blessed John Nutter (Tyburn)
Blessed John Munden (Tyburn)

1585
Blessed Thomas Alfield (Tyburn)
Blessed Hugh Taylor (York)

1586
Blessed Edward Stransham (Tyburn)
Blessed Nicholas Woodfen (Tyburn)
Blessed Richard Sergeant (Tyburn)
Blessed William Thomson (Tyburn)
Blessed Robert Anderton (Isle of Wight)
Blessed William Marsden (Isle of Wight)
Blessed Francis Ingleby (York)
Blessed John Finglow (York)
Blessed John Sandys (Gloucester)
Blessed John Lowe (Tyburn)
Blessed John Adams (Tyburn)
Blessed Richard Dibdale (Tyburn)

1587
Blessed Thomas Pilchard (Dorchester)
Blessed Edmund Sykes (York)
Blessed Robert Sutton (Stafford)
Blessed Stephen Rousham (Gloucester)
Blessed John Hambley (Salisbury)
Blessed Alexander Crow (York)

1588
Blessed Nicholas Garlick (Derby)
Blessed Robert Ludlam (Derby)
Blessed Richard Sympson (Derby)
Blessed William Dean (Mile End Green)
Blessed William Gunter (Shoreditch)
Blessed Robert Morton (Lincoln's Inn Field)
Ven Hugh More (Lincoln's Inn Field)
Blessed Thomas Holford (Clerkenwell)
Blessed James Claxton (Hounslow)
Ven Thomas Felton (Hounslow)
Blessed Robert Wilcox (Canterbury)
Blessed Edward Campion (Canterbury)
Blessed Christopher Buxton (Canterbury)
Blessed Ralph Crocket (Chichester)
Blessed Edward James (Chichester)
Blessed John Robinson (Ipswich)
Blessed William Hartley (Shoreditch)

Blessed John Hewett (Mile End Green)
Blessed Robert Leigh (Tyburn)
Blessed William Way (Kingston upon Thames)
Blessed Edward Burden (York)

1589
Blessed John Amias (York)
Blessed Robert Dalby (York)
Blessed John Nichols (Oxord)
Blessed Richard Yaxley (Oxford)
Blessed Thomas Belson (Oxford)
Blessed William Spenser (York)

1590
Blessed Christopher Bales (Fleet Street)
Blessed Miles Gerard (Rochester)
Blessed Francis Dickenson (Rochester)
Blessed Edward Jones (Fleet Street)
Blessed Anthony Middleton (Clerkenwell)
Blessed Edmund Duke (Durham)
Blessed Richard Hill (Durham)
Blessed John Hogg (Durham)
Blessed Richard Holiday (Durham)

1591
Blessed Robert Thorpe (York)
Blessed Montford Scott (Fleet Street)
Blessed George Beesley (Fleet Street)
Blessed Roger Dickenson (Winchester)
St Edmund Genings (Gray's Inn Fields)
St Eustace White (Tyburn)
St Polydore Plasden (Gray's Inn Fields)

1592
Blessed William Patenson (Tyburn)
Blessed Thomas Pormont
(St Paul's Churchyard)
Blessed Joseph Lambton
(Newcastle upon Tyne)

1593
Blessed Edward Waterson
(Newcastle upon Tyne)
Blessed James Bird (Winchester)
Blessed Anthony Page (York)
Blessed William Davies (Beaumaris)

1594
Blessed William Harrington (Tyburn)
Blessed John Cornelius (Dorchester)
St John Boste (Durham)
Blessed John Ingram (Newcastle upon Tyne)
Blessed Edward Osbaldeston (York)

1595
St Robert Southwell (Tyburn)
Blessed Alexander Rawlins (York)
St Henry Walpole (York)
Blessed William Freeman (Warwick)

1597
Blessed William Andleby (York)

1598
Blessed Peter Snow (York)
Blessed Christopher Robinson (Carlisle)
Ven Richard Horner (York)

1599
Blessed Matthias Harrison (York)

1600
Blessed Christopher Wharton (York)
Blessed Thomas Sprott (Lincoln)
Blessed Robert Nutter (Lancaster)
Blessed Edward Thwing (Lancaster)
Blessed Thomas Palasor (Durham)

1601
Blessed John Pibush (St Thomas's Waterings)
Blessed Mark Barkworth (Tyburn)
Blessed Roger Filcock (Tyburn)
Blessed Thurston Hunt (Lancaster)

1602
Ven James Harrison (York)
Ven Thomas Tichborne (Tyburn)
Blessed Robert Watkinson (Tyburn)
Blessed Francis Page (Tyburn)

1603
Blessed William Richardson (Tyburn)

1604
Blessed John Sugar (Warwick)

1606
Ven Edward Oldcorne (Worcester)

1607
Blessed Robert Drury (Tyburn)

1608
Blessed Matthew Flathers (York)
Blessed George Gervase (Tyburn)

1610
Blessed Roger Cadwallador (Leominster)
Blessed George Napier (Oxford)
Ven Thomas Somers (Tyburn)

1612
Blessed Richard Newport (Tyburn)
St John Almond (Tyburn)

1616
Blessed Thomas Atkinson (York)
Blessed John Thulis (Lancaster)
Blessed Thomas Maxfield (Tyburn)
Blessed Thomas Tunstal (Norwich)

1618
Blessed William Southerne
(Newcastle upon Tyne)

1628
St Edmund Arrowsmith (Lancaster)

1641
Blessed William Ward (Tyburn)
St Ambrose Edward Barlow (Lancaster)

1642
Blessed Thomas Green (Tyburn)
St Bartholomew Alban Roe (Tyburn)
Blessed John Lockwood (York)
Blessed Edmund Catherick (York)
Ven Edward Morgan (Tyburn)
Blessed Hugh Green (Dorchester)

1643
Blessed Henry Heath (Tyburn)

1644
Blessed John Duckett (Tyburn)

1645
St Henry Morse (Tyburn)
Ven John Goodman (Newgate)

1654
St John Southworth (Tyburn)

1679
Blessed Nicholas Postgate (York)
St John Wall (Worcester)
St John Kemble (Hereford)

1680
Blessed Thomas Thwing (York)

LIST OF VICARS APOSTOLIC
OF THE LONDON DISTRICT & ARCHBISHOPS OF WESTMINSTER

VICARS APOSTOLIC OF THE LONDON DISTRICT

1688-1702	John Leyburn
1703-1734	Bonaventure Giffard
1734-1758	Benjamin Petre OSB
1758-1781	Richard Challoner
1781-1790	James Talbot
1790-1812	John Douglass
1812-1827	William Poynter
1827-1836	James Yorke Bramston
1836-1847	Thomas Griffiths
1848-1849	Thomas Walsh
1849-1850	Nicholas Wiseman

ARCHBISHOPS OF WESTMINSTER

1850-1865	Nicholas Wiseman
1865-1892	Henry Edward Manning
1892-1903	Herbert Vaughan
1903-1935	Francis Bourne
1935-1943	Arthur Hinsley
1943-1956	Bernard Griffin
1956-1963	William Godfrey
1963-1975	John Carmel Heenan
1976-1999	Basil Hume OSB
2000-2009	Cormac Murphy-O'Connor
2009-present	Vincent Nichols

List of Presidents
OF ST EDMUND'S COLLEGE

	1793-1795	John Potier (temporary President)	14	*1887-1893*	John Crook
1	*1795-1801*	Gregory Stapleton	15	*1893-1916*	Bernard Ward (initially Pro-President)
2	*1801-1813*	William Poynter	16	*1916-1918*	Edwin Burton
3	*1813-1817*	Joseph Kimbell	17	*1919-1932*	Edward Myers
4	*1817-1817*	John Bew	18	*1932-1946*	Francis Bickford
5	*1818-1834*	Thomas Griffiths	19	*1946-1952*	John Bagshawe
6	*1834-1837*	Richard Newell	20	*1952-1964*	Reginald Butcher
7	*1838-1840*	John Rolfe		*1963-1964*	Hubert Richards (Acting President)
8	*1840-1851*	Edward Cox	21	*1964-1968*	Maurice Kelleher
9	*1851-1868*	William Weathers	22	*1968-1986*	Basil Christopher Butler OSB
10	*1868-1870*	Frederick Rymer	23	*1986-1999*	George Basil Hume OSB
11	*1870-1880*	James Laird Patterson	24	*2000-2009*	Cormac Murphy-O'Connor
12	*1880-1882*	George Akers	25	*2009-present*	Vincent Nichols
13	*1882-1887*	Patrick Fenton			

List of Headmasters
OF ST EDMUND'S COLLEGE

1	*1926-1929*	Francis Healy	7	*1984-2002*	Donald McEwen
2	*1929-1936*	Albert Purdie	8	*2002-2004*	Mark Loughlin
3	*1936-1940*	Thomas Sherlock	9	*2004-2012*	Christopher Long (initially Acting Headmaster)
4	*1941-1949*	Haldane "Rex" King			
5	*1949-1968*	Denis Britt-Compton	10	*2012-present*	Paulo Durán
6	*1968-1984*	Michael Garvey			

PLAN OF ST EDMUND'S COLLEGE

The plan, which is not to scale, indicates the locations of principal buildings.

1   North wing of Old Hall (1630), renamed Willacy's (1976)

2   Old Parish Church (1818) & Gymnasium extension (1932)

3   The Hermitage (pre-1217) (purchased in 1772)

4   The Laurels (date unknown)

5   Lindisfarne (1972)

6   The Ship (site of) (pre-1793)

7   The old gasworks (date unknown), exploded (1925)

8   The old Fives courts (1928)

9   Cricket Pavilion (1894)

10 Rifle range (1980s)

11 CCF Headquarters (1980s)

12 The School in the Garden (site of) (date unknown)

13 School Block (1922)

14 Swimming Pool (1896)

15 Changing room block (1922)

16 1913 extension

17 Ward Wing (1896)

18 McEwen Wing (2002)

19 Galilee Chapel (1921)

20 Sacristy (1853)

21 Lady Chapel (1861)

22 Shrine Chapel (1905)

23 College Chapel (consecrated 1853)

24 Scholefield Chantry (1862)

25 Old Chapel (1805)

26 Main building (1799)

27 Terraces and portico (1871)

28 Crucifix (1876)

29 Old Refectory (1805) & Exhibition Room (1902)

30 The 'New Wing' (1858)

31 Allen Hall (formerly the Divines' Wing) (1904)

32 Allen Hall extension & Jakes Tower (1932)

33 Allen Hall Refectory (formerly the Divines' Refectory) (1913), now the Music School (1979)

34 Boiler house (1932)

35 Nursery (1996)

36 Old Hall House (1846-1873), St Hugh's Preparatory School (1874-2010), St Edmund's Prep (2010)

37 Bickford Wing (1938)

38 Godfrey Wing (1961)

39 Salebourne (1964)

40 Butler Hall (formerly the 'Covered Playground') (1979)

41 Garden Cottages (1972-1974)

42 Maintenance workshop (formerly the 'Handicraft Shed') (1967)

43 Old Hall Green Farm (site of) (purchased in 1826)

44 The Old Farmhouse (1693) (purchased in 1826)

45 Staff houses on Farm Lane (1960s)

46 Parish Hall (date unknown)

47 Parish Church (1911)

48 Old Hall (1630)

49 South wing of Old Hall (1630), rebuilt 1971

50 Old Brew House (site of) (date unknown)

51 Old Hall Farm (site of) (date unknown), orchard planted 1932

52 Douay Hall (1932)

53 Convent Wing (1967)

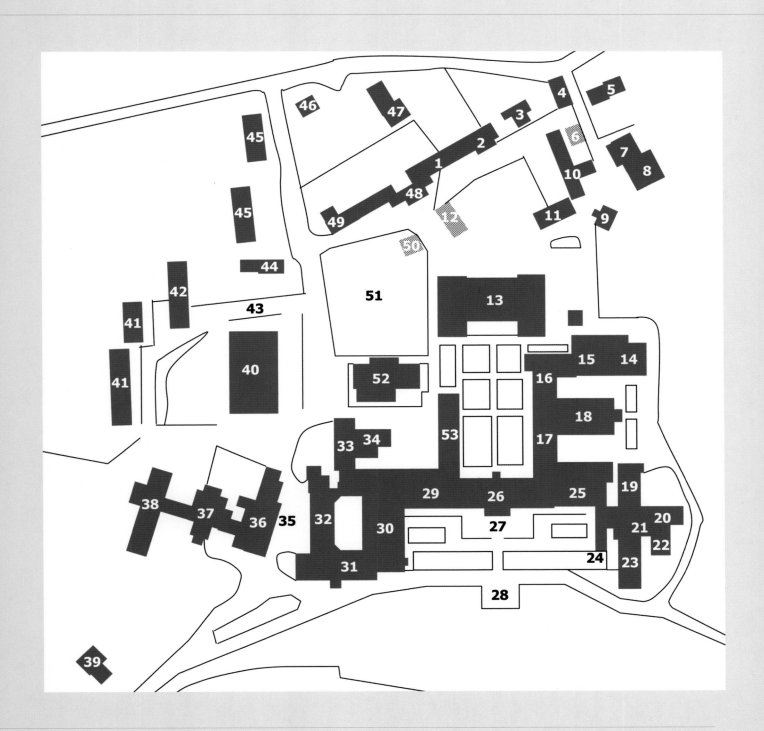

Footnotes

1 Edmundian, July 1933, p.305

2 'Douay' is the traditional Anglophone spelling, which is used in this book; the French would, of course, refer to 'Douai'

3 Beales, Education Under Penalty, p.115

4 AAW B35 Ep. Var 3/8, Paston to Mayes, 6 February 1710

5 AAW B35, Ep Var 3/53 Paston to Mayes, 22 February 1710

6 Milburn, Douay's Day, pp.48–50

7 Harris (ed), Douai College Documents 1639-1794, p.93

8 Ward, History of St Edmund's, p.70

9 Ibid., p.71

10 Ibid., p.73

11 Ibid., p. 79

12 Ibid., p.81

13 Ibid., p.95

14 Edmundian 1988-89, p.436

15 Beales, Education Under Penalty, pp.217-23

16 Ward, History of St Edmund's, pp.29-31

17 Ibid., p.4

18 Ibid., pp.39-40

19 Ibid., pp.48-49 (quoting advert in Laity's Directory 1793)

20 Ward, History of St Edmund's, p.100

21 Ibid., pp.103-03

22 Milburn, A History of Ushaw College, p.39

23 Ward, History of St Edmund's, p.131

24 Ibid., p.137

25 AAW SEC 3/20a, 3-4 (College Diary)

26 Ward, History of St Edmund's, pp.138-39

27 Ibid., p.169

28 Edmundian, July 1905, p.165

29 Edmundian, December 1903, p.12

30 Edmundian, July 1893, p.10

31 Edmundian, Dec ember 1894, p.142

32 Pevsner, The Buildings of England: Hertfordshire, p.183

33 Ward, History of St Edmund's, p175

34 Ibid., p.177

35 Ibid., p.179 (fn)

36 Ibid., pp.184-85

37 Ibid., pp.188-89

38 Edmundian, December 1903, p.12 (the student was William Bower)

39 Ward, History of St Edmund's, p.189

40 Ibid., p.193

41 Edmundian, Summer 1947, p.246

42 Edmundian, Summer 1947, p.247

43 Ward, History of St Edmund's, pp.198-99

44 Ibid., p.202

45 Laity's Directory, 1814

46 Ward, History of St Edmund's, p.205

47 Ibid., p.219

48 Edmundian, Autumn 1943, pp.9-10

49 Ward, History of St Edmund's, p.218

50 Edmundian, July 1903, pp.181-82

51 Pawley, Faith and Family, p.30

52 Ward, History of St Edmund's, p.233

53 Digby, Mores Catholici (1888), vol 1,, p.9

54 Edmundian, April 1904, p.39

55 Edmundian, December 1899, p.14

56 Ward, History of St Edmund's, p.233

57 AAW SEC 14/9/67, Memoir of William Weathers, by Dr Rymer, p.8

58 Edmundian, December 1901, p.28

59 Ward, History of St Edmund's, p.257

60 Ibid., pp.257-62

61 Hopper, 'Men of Little Showing: (3) William Weathers', p.135 (fn)

62 Edmundian, Dec ember 1893, p.43 – this is how Fr William Lloyd, a former Vice-President, described Pugin's chapel in his sermon preached for the College Centenary.

63 Ward, History of St Edmund's, p.248

64 Ward, St Edmund's College Chapel, p.37

65 Edmundian, April 1906, p.45

66 Doyle, A Brief Outline of the History of Old Hall, 1891, pp.27-28. Canon Doyle speaks of Barberi's visit in 1845 but this seems to be a mistake.

67 Norman, The English Catholic Church in the Nineteenth Century, p.131

68 Ward, History of St Edmund's, p.267

69 Hopper, 'Men of Little Showing: (3) William Weathers', p.136

70 Ward, St Edmund's College Chapel, p.45

71 Ibid., pp.50-51

72 Ward, History of St Edmund's, p.276

73 Edmundian, December 1905, p.8

74 Ward, Wilfrid Wards and the Transition, p.28

75 Snead-Cox, Life of Cardinal Vaughan, Vol. 1, p. 90

76 Ibid., p.71

77 Clifton, Quiet Administrator, p.60

78 Ibid., p.61

79 Edmundian, Dec ember 1903, p.7

80 Edmundian, Dec ember 1903, p.8

81 Edmundian, 2008, pp.202-04

82 Edmundian, July 1905, p.162

83 Snead-Cox, Life of Cardinal Vaughan, Vol. 2, pp.38-39

84 A seminary was later founded for the diocese of Southwark at Wonersh in 1891. This still exists.

85 Ward, St Edmund's College Chapel, 59

86 Burton, St Edmund's College, Old Hall (Supplement to Edmundian, Spring 1925), p.10

87 Edmundian, July 1902, p.64

88 Edmundian, April 1903, p.133

89 Ward, Wilfrid Wards and the Transition, p.39

90 Edmundian, April 1903, p.135

91 AAW SEC 2/30a, 192 (College Diary). The frescoes were based on those at Prague.

92 Ward, St Edmund's College Chapel, pp.65-66

93 Tablet, 26 July 1873, p.111

94 Edmundian, December 1899, p.9

95 Edmundian, April 1909, p.133

96 AAW SEC 14/9/67 pp11-12

97 Vance, 'Men of Little Showing: (6) Edwin Hubert Burton', p.410

98 Ibid., p415

99 Ibid., p417

100 Edmundian, July 1893, p.4

101 Edmundian, Dec ember 1916, p.96

102 Edmundian, December 1936, p.330. There were actually three arches in total, one of which was over the College gate.

103 Edmundian, Dec ember 1893, p.50

104 AAW, Box M, Recollections of Mgr Collings (1960)

105 Edmundian, April 1920, p.318

106 Barnes, Catholic Schools of England, p.125

107 Edmundian, July 1895, p.218

108 Edmundian, July 1905, p.166

109 Edmundian, April 1900, p.55

110 Edmundian, July 1901, pp.184-85

111 Edmundian, July 1896, pp.54-56

112 The historical link is still maintained by the presence of a representative Governor from St Edmund's College, Cambridge.

113 Edmundian, December 1899, p.19

114 Edmundian, April 1900, p.35

115 Edmundian, April 1900, p.54

116 Edmundian, December 1910, p.114

117 AAW SEC 2/20 (Hertfordshire Mercury, 27 May 1905)

118 AAW SEC 2/20, Cardinal Bourne's address, 25 May 1905

119 Edmundian, Dec ember 1919, p.309

120 Edmundian, July 1901, p.190

121 Edmundian, July 1893, p.9

122 Edmundian, April 1894, p.70

123 Edmundian, April 1895, p.169

124 Vance, 'Men of Little Showing: (6) Edwin Hubert Burton', pp.414-15

125 AAW, Box M, Recollections of Mgr Collings (1960)

126 Edmundian, Winter 1968, pp.84-85

127 Edmundian, July 1914, p.75

128 Ibid., p.70

129 Ibid., p.90

130 Edmundian, December 1914, p.110

131 AAW SEC 3/22, Burton's Diary 1916-18 (5 February 1917)

132 Edmundian, April-July 1917, p.131

133 Edmundian, April 1916, p.36

134 AAW SEC 3/22, Burton's Diary 1916-18 (23 March 1917)

135 AAW SEC 3/22, Burton's Diary 1916-18 (3-5 March 1917)

136 AAW SEC 3/22, Burton's Diary 1916-18 (21 October 1916)

137 Edmundian, July 1915, p.175

138 AAW SEC 3/22, Burton's Diary 1916-18 (27 November 1917)

139 AAW SEC 3/22, Burton's Diary 1916-18 (26 October 1916)

140 Edmundian, July 1919, p.278

141 AAW SEC 3/22 Burton's Diary 1916-18 (1 October 1916)

142 Edmundian, December 1917, p.189

143 AAW SEC 3/22, Burton's Diary 1916-18 (3 February 1917)

144 Edmundian, Easter 1919, p.251

145 AAW SEC 3/22, Burton's Diary 1916-18 (16 November 1916)

146 Edmundian, April 1921, p.8

147 Edmundian, July 1922, p.161

148 Foster, 'Prelates at War', p.347

149 AAW SEC 3/22, Burton's Diary 1916-18 (9 May 1917)

150 Vance, 'Men of Little Showing: (6) Edwin Hubert Burton', p.421

151 Edmundian, Christmas 1956, 111-112. The 'paddycock' consisted of a handle with a thick, foot-long tongue of leather, widening in the middle and rounded at the tip.

152 AAW Bo 1/110, Notes on SEC by John G. Vance

153 According to Rex King – see Edmundian, 1975-76, p.184

154 Foster, 'Prelates at War', p.352

155 Foster, 'Prelates at War', p.351

156 AAW Bo 1/110

157 Ibid.

158 AAW SEC 2/26, Bourne, Reorganisation of St Edmund's College

159 Edmundian, July 1922, p.151

160 AAW Hi 2/50, Letter to Pius XI to Cardinal Bourne, 8 September 1922

161 AAW Bo 1/110

162 Gribbin, Bicentenary Book, p.114

163 Edmundian, p.223

164 Edmundian, July 1933, p.307

165 AAW, Box M, Recollections of Mgr Collings (1960)

166 AAW Bo 1/110

167 Edmundian, April 1923, p.246. A collection of vestments designed by Fortescue for Letchworth were later rescued from a skip and are now safely kept in the College sacristy.

168 Edmundian, December 1919, p.298

169 Edmundian, April 1923, pp.253-54

170 Barnes, Catholic Schools of England , p.125

171 Edmundian, Christmas 1957, p.187

172 Waugh, Ronald Knox, p.180

173 Edmundian, Spring 1954, pp.167-68

174 Edmundian, Autumn 1960, p.204

Footnotes

175 Fulton Sheen, Treasure in Clay, pp.50-51

176 Edmundian, March 1930, p.270

177 Edmundian, July 1920, p.361

178 Whitney, pp.69-72

179 AAW Go 2/51, Fr Lucas to Cardinal Godfrey, 11 February 1963

180 AAW Go 2/51, Mgr Butcher to Cardinal Godfrey, 22 October 1958

181 Edmundian, 2006-07, p.148

182 Edmundian, 1975-76, p.184

183 Edmundian, 1968, p.91

184 Edmundian, Autumn 1946, p.194

185 Edmundian, 1989-90, p.92

186 Edmundian, September 1940, p.33

187 Edmundian, 1990-91, p.312

188 Edmundian, 1989-90, p.93

189 Edmundian, 1989-90, p.94

190 Edmundian, Summer 1946, pp.154-55

191 Edmundian, September 1942, p.150

192 Edmundian, 1982-83, p.342

193 AAW Gr 2/50, Mgr Bagshawe to Cardinal Griffin, 18 February 1950

194 AAW Gr 2/50, Mgr Bagshawe to Cardinal Griffin, 14 January 1949

195 AAW Gr 2/50, Cardinal Griffin to Mgr Bagshawe, 22 November 1949

196 Edmundian, 1973-74, p.4

197 Edmundian, 1975-76, p.188

198 AAW Gr 2/50, Fr Butcher to Cardinal Griffin, 15 July 1952

199 AAW Go 2/51, Mgr Butcher to Archbishop Godfrey, 22 October 1958

200 Ibid.

201 Miles, Milestones, p.66

202 AAW Gr 2/50, Mgr Butcher to Cardinal Griffin 14 March 1956

203 Edmundian, 2001-02, .p243

204 Edmundian, 1994-95, p.231

205 Edmundian, 1975-76, p.188

206 Edmundian, Spring 1965, p155

207 AAW He 1/52a, Cardinal Heenan to Abbot Hume, 12 July 1965

208 Letter to author from Fr Anton Cowan

209 Edmundian, Autumn 1965, p.183

210 AAW He 1/52a, Fr Britt Compton to Archbishop Heenan, 23 June 1964

211 Edmundian, 1985-86, p.105

212 Edmundian, 2001-02, p.15

213 Edmundian, 1985-86, p.110

214 Edmundian, 2001-02, p.237

215 Edmundian, 2001-02, p.239

216 Letter to author from Fr Brian O'Shea

217 Edmundian, 1973-74, p.7

218 AAW He 1/52c Minutes of Meeting of Bishops and Superiors, 15 November 1972

219 Edmundian, Winter 1973, p.478

220 AAW He 1/52c Minutes of Meeting, 8 May 1972

221 AAW He 1/52c Minutes of Meeting of Bishops and Superiors, 15 November 1972

222 Edmundian, 1979-80, p.105

223 Letter to author from Fr Brian O'Shea

224 AAW Box DC, Account of 'The Move'

225 Letter to author from Canon Paschal Ryan

226 Edmundian, 1994-95, p.24

227 Edmundian, 1973-74, p.5

228 Edmundian, 1978-79, p.2

229 Edmundian, Autumn 1945, p.110

230 Edmundian, Summer 1946, p.150

231 Edmundian, Summer 1947, p.237

232 Edmundian, Autumn 1945, p.108

233 Edmundian, April-July 1917, p.153

234 Edmundian, March 1915, pp.167-68

235 AAW SEC 3/22, Burton's Diary 1916-18 (5 November 1916)

236 Edmundian, April 1920, p.347

237 Edmundian, February 1924, p.41

238 AAW Go 2/51, Mgr Butcher to Archbishop Godfrey 22 October 1958

239 Edmundian, 1994-95, p.236

240 Edmundian, Autumn 1964, p.118

241 Edmundian, 1994-95, pp.237-38

242 Letter to author from Canon Paschal Ryan

243 Edmundian, Summer 1950, pp199-200

244 Edmundian, 1996-97, p.229

245 Edmundian, Winter 1972, p.447

246 Edmundian, 2001-02, p.210

247 Edmundian, 1995-96, p.13

248 Edmundian, Centenary Issue 1993, p.183

249 SEC Governing Body Folder II

250 Edmundian, 1984-85, p.1

251 Edmundian, 2001-02, p.4

252 Edmundian, 1993-94, p.131

253 Edmundian, 1993-94, p.140

254 Edmundian, 2003-04, p.188

255 Edmundian, 2003-04, p.v

256 http://www.indcatholicnews.com/news.php?viewStory=19403

257 Edmundian, July 1905, p.161

SELECT BIBLIOGRAPHY

Barnes, A. S. *The Catholic Schools of England* (1926),

Beales, A. C. F. *Education Under Penalty. English Catholic Education from the Reformation to the Fall of James II, 1547-1689* (1963)

Clifton, Michael *The Quiet Negotiator: Bishop Grant, Bishop of Southwark* (1990)

Digby, Kenelm *Mores Catholici* (1888)

Doyle, Canon *A Brief Outline of the History of Old Hall* (1891)

Foster, Stewart 'Bernard Ward: Edmundian and historian' in Sheridan Gilley (ed) *Victorian Churches and Churchmen: Essays Presented to Vincent Alan McClelland* (Catholic Record Society Monograph 7, 2005)

Foster, Stewart 'Prelates at War: Cardinal Bourne, Bishop Ward and the St Edmund's College Cadet Corps Dispute' in *Recusant History*, October 2010

Gribbin, W. T. *St Edmund's College Bicentenary Book 1793-1993* (1993)

Harris, P. R. (ed), *Douai College Documents 1639-1794*, (Catholic Record Society vol. 63, 1972)

Hopper, Frederick 'Men of Little Showing: (3) William Weathers' in *The Clergy Review*, August 1931

Kay, David J. S. *The Buildings of St Edmund's College* (2000)

Kay, David J. S. *The People of St Edmund's College* (2003)

McClelland, V. A. *English Roman Catholics and Higher Education 1830-1903* (1973)

Milburn, David *A History of Ushaw College* (1964)

Milburn, David *Douai's Day* (2010)

Miles, Frederick A. *Milestones: The Light-Hearted Memoirs of Mgr Frederick A. Miles, Prot Ap* (2007)

Nichols, Aidan *Latin Clerk: The Life, Work and Travels of Adrian Fortescue* (2011)

Norman, Edward *The English Catholic Church in the Nineteenth Century* (1984)

Pawley, Margaret *Faith and Family: The Life and Circle of Ambrose Phillipps de Lisle* (1998)

Pevsner, N. *The Buildings of England: Hertfordshire* (1953)

Pike, Joseph *St Edmund's College, Old Hall: Pencil Sketches* (1923)

Sheen, Fulton J. *Treasure in Clay* (1993)

Snead-Cox, J. G. *The Life of Cardinal Vaughan* (2 vols, 1910)

Sweeney, Garrett *St Edmund's House, Cambridge: The First Eighty Years* (1980)

Vance, J. G. 'Men of Little Showing: (6) Edwin Hubert Burton' in *The Clergy Review*, November 1931

Walsh, Michael *St Edmund's College, Cambridge 1896-1996: A Commemorative History* (1996)

Ward, Maisie *The Wilfrid Wards and the Transition* (1934)

Ward, Bernard *History of St Edmund's College, Old Hall* (1893)

Ward, Bernard *St Edmund's College Chapel. An Account, Historical and Descriptive, Written on the Occasion of the Fiftieth Anniversary of the Opening* (1903)

Whitney, John *As A Libation* (2009)

Index

List of Subscribers

1   His Eminence Cormac Murphy O'Connor
2   The Most Reverend Vincent Nichols
3   Allen Hall, Chelsea
4   The Edmundian Association
5   Association William Allen
6   Donald McEwen, Headmaster 1984-2002
7   Chris Long, Headmaster 2004-2012

8   Fr Nicholas Schofield
9   Paulo Durán
10 David J S Kay
11 Jonathan Stephens-Jones
12 Michael Stephens-Jones
13 John Hasler
14 David Hasler
15 Stephen Hasler
16 Graeme Lill
17 Michael Brewer
18 Paula Peirce
19 Joe Arnold
20 W D Wright
21 Robert P Healy
22 David J Healy
23 Christopher Holloway
24 Jonathan Grace
25 Malcolm Grace
26 Alastair Emblem
27 Mr T Roche
28 Mr J Roche
29 Ms E Roche
30 Willy Van Driessche
31 John Hayes
32 Bernard Ward 1st Bishop of Brentwood (in memoriam)
33 Austin Garvey

34 Philip Murphy
35 Peter Ward
36 Peter Klocek
37 Fra' Duncan Gallie
38 Alice Martin
39 Adrian Petty
40 Henryk Klocek
41 Terry Noë
42 Peter Lee
43 J A C Conway
44 Francis J G Jones
45 Patrick (Chad) Murphy
46 Hugh Thomas
47 Richard M Beveridge
48 Rev Fr Peter Francis Chappell
49 Alanna Easton
50 Christopher Easton
51 Alexander Easton
52 Paul McGinn
53 Helen McCallion
54 Carlos A Menezes
55 Paul Keenan
56 Peter Morgan MBE
57 Alex (deceased) & Margaret Roberts
58 Peter Lightfoot
59 M Anthony Hewson
60 Tom Hempenstall

61 Paul Hypher
62 Dr Simon Thompson
63 Mr Karl Thompson
64 Rev Richard McKay
65 Fr Brian O'Shea
66 Fr Anthony McKentey
67 Fr Guy Sawyer
68 John Wilton
69 Sheila Mary Gillham
70 John Vaughan-Shaw
71 Major (Retd) Paul Lindsay-Scott
72 Michael R Thompson
73 John Drabwell
74 Marcus Drabwell
75 Matthew James Campbell
76 Rt Rev Mgr Frederick A Miles, Prot Ap
77 Richard Gunn
78 Patrick Burgess
79 Lawrence Ross
80 Roger Weatherburn Baker
81 Kishan Patel
82 Christina Theoharous
83 George Theoharous
84 Christopher Rolfe-Bradley
85 Revd Dr Peter A Rowe
86 Harry Callagher
87 James Cockerton

88	David Dickson	114	Charlie Ponting	141	Ambassador Alberto Moyano Bonel
89	Sean McGilloway	115	The Hanley Family	142	Stuart Eves
90	Francis Peter Maher	116	The Stanley S T Wu Family	143	Alice Merino
91	Carol Lewis	117	Mike Jenner	144	Inés Merino-Durán
92	Michael Holland	118	Alexander Moore	145	Manuel & Odete Durán
93	Michael Holland	119	Antonia Lambis	146	Kathleen Merino
94	Beatrice Makulski	120	Kyri Lambis	147	Peter Brabazon
95	Fionnuala Marshall	121	The Sweeney family	148	Michael Elgood
96	Martin Savage	122	David John Blair Bett	149	Julie Lee
97	Joanne Savage	123	James Jacobs	150	Sophie Lee
98	George Sobek	124	The Kavanagh Family	151	Lucy Lee
99	Philip Collins	125	Stephen Quin	152	Maggie McCann
100	Peter Lee	126	Patrick T Ryan	153	Charlie Roberts
101	Dr Kelvin Tan	127	Kennedy D Ryan	154	Julian Kay
102	Dr Kelvin Tan	128	Michael Pargeter	155	Rupert Kay
103	Simon Malloy	129	David Norbury	156	Luis Felipe Cabana
104	Chris Milburn	130	Christopher J Groves-Kirkby	157	Ronald Gladman
105	In memory of Anthony Milburn (ex-College engineer 1974)	131	Jan Golaszewski	158	David Peel
		132	Jan Golaszewski	159	Dr & Mrs J D Nicholson
106	E F Hassett	133	Kit Slade	160	Greg Hacksley
107	Adrian Reading	134	Millie George	161	Joseph McKay
108	Susannah Routledge	135	Joseph Martin Canavan	162	Oliver Corley
109	Helen Meyer (née McEwen)	136	Peter & Brenda Sherlock		
110	Catherine McEwen	137	Christian Wolff		*Remaining names unlisted*
111	Donald McEwen	138	Alexia Boyd-Carpenter		
112	J Ivor O'Mahony KSG	139	The van de Ven Family		
113	Caroline Kinglake (née Smith)	140	Marqués de Inicio